Ken

With our very best wishes and
thanks from all your friends
in Rolls Royce plc

Sean Todd

February 1991.

Rolls-Royce
AERO ENGINES

Rolls-Royce
AERO ENGINES

Bill Gunston

Patrick Stephens Limited

British Library Cataloguing in Publication Data

Gunston, Bill, 1927–
    Rolls-Royce aero engines.
    1. Aircraft. Rolls-Royce engines, to 1989
    I. Title
    629.134′35

    ISBN 1-85260-037-3

Patrick Stephens is part of the Thorsons Publishing Group

Printed and bound in Great Britain by
Butler & Tanner, Frome, Somerset

Typeset in Century Schoolbook by Book Ens,
Saffron Walden, Essex

10 9 8 7 6 5 4 3 2

CONTENTS

GLOSSARY

Unless the reader has some interest in aircraft engines, he or she is unlikely to pick up this book. No explanation is therefore offered for such terms as bore and stroke, pressure ratio, nozzle guide vane, supercharger, cylinder block, and so forth. The following, however, may explain a few abbreviations: bpr, bypass ratio, the ratio of the mass flow of air bypassed round the core of a turbofan divided by the mass flow through the core; FS, full-supercharge gear in an engine with a two-speed gearbox in the drive to the supercharger; HP, high pressure; LP, low pressure; MS, medium-supercharge gear (see FS); NGV, nozzle guide vane; OGV, outlet guide vane; pr, pressure ratio (essentially the gas-turbine equivalent of compression ratio in a piston engine); sfc, specific fuel consumption (rate of fuel consumption for a given power output); VIVG, variable inlet guide vane(s).

ACKNOWLEDGEMENTS

A book written about the products of one company can hardly be written without that company's collaboration. In the first instance this falls upon those who wear the hat marked 'public affairs'. It is true to say that in assisting the author Dominic Leahy and Mike Farlam (Buckingham Gate), Charles Eldred-Evans (Derby) and Martin Brodie (Bristol) were only doing their job; but the way they did it calls for special thanks. Because they were picked to do such work for such a company, they are people on whom you can place absolute reliance.

Most of the many other RR people involved were doing a lot more than their regular job. Jack Titley, Chief Photographer at Derby, must at times have wanted to scream. Perhaps thirty times he wrongly thought that I had no more requests for obscure photographs from dusty archives. The other Derby man who devoted much time and effort was Mike Evans, who apart from having a demanding management job is also Chairman of the extremely active and valuable RR Heritage Trust. His knowledge of Rolls-Royce and its products is profound, and he went into especially meticulous detail to ensure that the early chapters are as accurate as we could make them. I owe him an enormous debt.

I do not know all the people who reviewed the text, but they include Alec Harvey-Bailey, who went with an impressively fine-toothed comb through the long chapter on the Merlin and Griffon; Geoff Wilde, who retired as Chief of Advanced Projects and Technology, made sure that the 'first axials' and 'jet lift' chapters did not perpetuate many well-established errors and half-truths; former Technical Director D. J. Pickerell not only checked the final chapter but added a farsighted 'view from the bridge' which the author gratefully includes in the book; and at Leavesden P. R. Stokes and Doug Valentine both made valued comments. I also talked to several engineers who, though long retired, have razor-sharp memories going back to the inter-war period and would especially like to thank Ken Fozard, who like all true engineers communicates with diagrams (which made several thorny points crystal clear). I am also deeply grateful to Alexander R. Ogston, formerly of Esso (Exxon), who helped greatly with the story of the introduction of 100-octane fuel in the Battle of Britain.

FOREWORD

By Sir Ralph Robins, Managing Director, Rolls-Royce plc.

I have known Bill Gunston for over twenty years, and have always admired his encyclopaedic knowledge and ability to write with authority about many areas of aerospace technology. In this book he has carried off a daunting task—to survey in detail the aero engines of Rolls-Royce over 75 years, as well as those of Britain's other engine companies which became part of Rolls-Royce in the 1960s.

It is a fascinating story, both of personalities and technicalities. It spans an era when, after fragile beginnings, aircraft became a dominant force in worldwide passenger transport and in warfare. The performance and economy of the aircraft which have changed the face of our world have been based on advances in aero engines. Rolls-Royce has always been at the forefront of this technical revolution.

During the period surveyed by Bill Gunston military engines have advanced from the Eagle of 1915 to the RB199 powering the Tornado aircraft on which Europe's defence largely depends today. We now look forward to even further advances with the multi-nation EJ200 engine for the agile European fighter aircraft of the 1990s.

Although the Eagle and RB199 are similar in size, the RB199 is over 100 times more powerful. The aircraft performance provided is shown by comparing the 1915 Handley Page O/100 bomber, with its two Eagle piston engines, and today's Tornado with its two RB199 turbofans. At low level the Tornado can fly at 800 knots, more than ten times faster than the O/100, and exceeds Mach 2 at altitude—nearly twenty times the speed of the 1915 bomber. The Tornado has much longer range, and, though it is a much smaller aircraft, its warload is greater than the total weight of a fully loaded O/100.

Advances in engine technology have also greatly increased the productivity and economy of airlines since the early 1950s— as well as bringing supersonic travel with Concorde. The first jet airliner, the de Havilland Comet 1, entered service in 1952. The Boeing 757 of today is similar in size, but carries six times as many passengers as the Comet 1 over increased ranges. Its two 535E4 turbofan engines together provide four times as much power as did the four Ghost turbojets of the Comet, and their fuel economy is more than twice as good.

We are, of course, continuing to develop even more economical engines for jet transports. The latest version of the RB211, currently being planned, will provide a take-off thrust of 65,000 lb, increasing with further development to over 70,000 lb along

Sir Ralph Robins.

with still better fuel economy. This steady development of successful engines has been a hallmark of Rolls-Royce over the years, as this book illustrates. The benefits to our customers worldwide have been very great—for example, by greatly increasing the payload which airliners such as the Boeing 747 can carry over long ranges.

The evolution of advanced engines requires that technology and materials work ever closer to their limits. The resulting advances pioneered by Rolls-Royce often benefit other areas of British industry in due course. Bill Gunston has shown how work at the forefront of technology has always been a way of life for Rolls-Royce. The Company's future continues to depend on its research and advanced engineering programmes—as does its major contribution to Britain's exports and defence.

INTRODUCTION

Few companies have had their history described in print as often as Rolls-Royce. This is hardly surprising, because no company is more famous. There has not, however, been a book specifically devoted to RR aero engines. To many people the name first of all conjures up an image of expensive cars, but since 1971 these have been produced by a totally unconnected firm, today called Rolls-Royce Motor Cars Ltd, which is less than one-tenth as big as the giant Rolls-Royce plc which was recently 'privatized' and attracted investors from all over the world. Some of these investors may even have thought they were buying shares in a car company.

The aero-engine business began in 1914, but the story of Royce's goes back thirty years earlier. Frederick Henry Royce was born at Alwalton, near Peterborough, in 1863, the son of a miller who spent his meagre earnings and moved from place to place seeking work. Young Henry's childhood could scarcely have been harder, and the years of overwork and malnutrition resulted in serious ill-health which dogged him for the rest of his life. He had just two years at school, but from an early age he showed enormous strength of character which was manifest in contrasting ways.

His first job was as a telegraph messenger boy, followed by a period selling newspapers for W. H. Smith. When his father died an aunt offered a little money, and Henry started as an apprentice with the Great Northern Railway, desperate to learn all about engineering. Then the money ran out and he had to leave, but he managed to get a job with the Electric Light & Power Co in London, and studied every night at the Polytechnic. When he was 21 he teamed up with another student, Ernest A. Claremont. They could put together £70 between them, and in 1884 they set up F. H. Royce & Co in Cooke Street, Manchester, making small electrical parts. An ingenious design for a sparkless commutator led to the manufacture of complete dynamos, moving on to motors and then to electric cranes. Competitors sold cheaper. Royce refused to cut a single corner, and his high-quality products continued to find a market.

Despite his frugality, in 1902 he bought a secondhand Decauville car. He soon found fault with almost every part of it, and gave up the idea of just rectifying the deficiencies. He called his small team together and, to their amazement and Claremont's chagrin, announced he was going to build a car! This was a considered decision to get in on a new market.

Back in 1877 Lord Llangattock, rich owner of vast estates in Monmouth, had been presented with a third son, the Hon

Charles Stewart Rolls. Being the third son he did not have to enter the Army or Navy, and from Eton was actually permitted to take the Mechanical Sciences Tripos at Cambridge. After taking his degree he immersed himself with whatever was the latest in what we today would call advanced technology. As a rich and handsome dilettante he indulged in almost every kind of sport, and excelled at the lot. He bought his first car back in 1894. This started a career with motors which brought him a score of famous racing trophies, as well as the World Land Speed record. One evening in 1901 he was passing through Reading when something on his car broke. He found a cycle shop, but the owner said 'I can't help, it's closing time'. But the owner's assistant, Ernest Hives, said 'Can I be of assistance, Sir?' Rolls watched with admiration as the youth made a perfect repair. He asked if he would like to come to London with him and

be his mechanic, looking after his stable of 'motors'. Young Hives got his mother's permission, and without more ado climbed up beside Rolls and joined the staff as mechanic and, on rare occasions, as chauffeur.

As almost the only member of the aristocracy who really knew about motors, Rolls was always being asked by his friends what car to buy. In 1902 he set up his own company to sell cars to the rich and famous. A year later he was joined by Claude Johnson, the first Secretary of the Royal Automobile Club. Virtually all the cars were foreign: French or Belgian, and occasionally German. Rolls longed to find a good British car. In spring 1904 his friend Henry Edmunds said 'I'm a director of a firm in Manchester called Royce's, and I'm impressed by a little car they've built. I think you ought to see it'. Rolls inwardly scorned the whole idea, because this car had only two cylinders, and he was not

The Hon Charles S. Rolls in his Mayfair office. Gentlemen often wore a frock coat, but Rolls was equally at home attired for motor racing, flying and many other interests.

interested in lowly cars with fewer than three or four cylinders. Nevertheless he did go to Manchester, and was most impressed. The Royce was about the smoothest car he had ever driven. It started when required, nothing fell off, and it seemed a product of real quality. He was lent one, took it by train to London, got Johnson out of bed in the middle of the night and got him enthusiastic too!

Arrangements were made for Rolls to take the entire output of Royce cars. More, Rolls persuaded Royce to build bigger three-, four- and six-cylinder cars, called 'Rolls-Royces'. They formed a marketing firm called Rolls-Royce Distributing Ltd, and everything went so well that in March 1906 Rolls-Royce Ltd was formed. Royce was appointed Managing Director, but his health was so critical that within a few months he was reappointed Engineer-in-Chief (though universally regarded as top man in the company). Rolls became Managing Director (Technical), the flamboyant Johnson became Managing Director (Commercial) and Claremont, who carefully watched expenditure, continued as Chairman. Everyone dovetailed perfectly, business boomed and the car swiftly gained a reputation as the world's best. In 1907–08 the firm moved into a large new works at Nightingale Road, Derby. Rolls took the firm's cars on every reliability trial and road race he could find, and won most. Young Hives, who had left C. S. Rolls & Co in order to race at Brooklands, rejoined the new firm after the move to Derby and became Chief Tester—among other things driving one of the cars continuously in top gear from London to Edinburgh.

In early 1910 Rolls resigned his executive responsibilities, retaining a seat on the Board, Johnson becoming General Managing Director and, with Claremont, effectively running the growing company. Rolls had added flying to his many sports, starting with balloons and moving on to aeroplanes,

buying a Wright Flyer from France and another from the Short Brothers. He repeatedly tried unsuccessfully to get Rolls-Royce to build aircraft. On 2 June 1910 he made the first double crossing of the English Channel, but only a month later he was killed as the result of an in-flight structural failure during a spot-landing competition at Bournemouth. Thus, Rolls had only a short connection with the company, yet today most people abbreviate the company to his name only (except around Derby, where they rightly call the firm 'Royce's'). Royce was the key figure in the company, but by 1911 he was lying at death's door. Realizing everything was at stake, Johnson took him to Le Canadel in the south of France. Henceforth, except for the war years, he spent his winters in that warmer climate, returning in summer to live with a nurse at St Margaret's Bay, Kent, moving during the war to West Wittering, Sussex. But every idea, every drawing and almost every part had to be sent from Derby for his approval, and he continued to rule with unquestioned but increasingly benevolent authority until his death in 1933.

At about the time of the move to Derby the growing firm instituted a system of shorthand for use in internal correspondence. Royce became R, and among other early people were EAC, CJ and Hs, all of whom have been mentioned. This was unambiguous, and avoided the need to mention titles, ranks or appointments, and it continues to this day. The author has, however, tried to avoid it in this book despite the fact that these references often became the universal 'name' of the person within the firm, in speech as well as in memos.

On the outbreak of World War I, on 4 August 1914, production of cars temporarily stopped, and those on the line were completed as the first of a successful series of armoured cars which saw much service over many years, especially with the RFC in the Middle East. The government told

R, pictured with Ivan Evernden at a drawing board at Camacha, the small studio in West Wittering about a quarter of a mile from 'The Old Man's' house.

Royce to start building aero engines, and orders were placed for the Renault and Royal Aircraft Factory air-cooled V-8s. Both were singularly poor designs; they offended Royce's nature, and at first he flatly refused to have anything to do with them. He did later agree to build these engines under licence, to keep the shop-floor going, but only until he could himself produce something better. The firm also mass-produced artillery shells and flechettes (steel darts for dropping from aircraft).

His order for something better came from the Admiralty, as explained in Chapter 1. From that time onwards Rolls-Royce was in the aero-engine business, though until the late 1930s it always regarded itself as primarily the builder of 'the best car in the world'. Indeed, some of the management, including Claremont and Basil Johnson (CJ's brother), considered that the aero business should have been dropped at the Armistice in November 1918—and it very nearly was. But from 1927 the company devoted as much effort to designing aero engines as it did to cars, and the aero business grew until it became a titanic war-winning effort from the late 1930s onwards.

From 1927 the firm's aircraft engines were well-cowled. Spurred by competition from Roy Fedden at Bristol, the needs of the installation were given increasing attention. In 1932 a small department was opened for this purpose at Tollerton airfield, near Nottingham, moving in 1934 to nearby Hucknall. Ever since, the company has been a world leader in selling not mere engines but complete installations. Though it always preserved an open mind, and did produce the odd air-cooled engine (such as the Exe), it never built a radial and so always appeared to favour what looked like streamlined installations. In fact, when properly installed, the air-cooled radial is every bit as good as the inline, V, H or X kind of engine, as Britain learned rather suddenly from the Fw 190 when it captured one in 1942. The subsequent history of fighter development and the world speed record bears this out. The author has no intention of taking sides, for the simple reason that there are many sides to take. For example, the Mosquito (which the author enjoyed flying) would probably not have had such a high performance with radial engines, though this is arguable. Conversely, it was a major error putting Merlins into the DC-4 airliner built by Canadair, because the high-capacity Twin Wasp and Double Wasp engines of the Douglas-built transports gave the airlines a better vehicle with less noise, fewer problems and lower costs, as emphasized in the chapter on that most famous of all engines, the Merlin.

Of course, though ancient Griffons still thunder into the sky bearing aloft Britain's early-warning radars—surely a national disgrace—Rolls-Royce's main effort has for over forty years been on gas turbines. Everything started off brilliantly. Under Stanley Hooker the Whittle type engine was more than doubled in thrust in a matter of six months in 1944, and the resulting Nene turbojet is important to this day in China and many other countries. Then work began on a supposedly more modern engine, the Avon, and it was rudely made only too evident that even a straightforward turbojet can be desperately difficult to develop.

By the 1950s the company was 'full steam ahead' once more on a broad range of gas-turbine engines. But by 1958 the Government had virtually stopped the development of military aircraft, and was beginning to hold a pistol at the aircraft firms to force them to amalgamate (which seemed a good idea at the time). In 1959 Bristol Aero-Engines and Armstrong Siddeley Motors formed Bristol Siddeley, and in November 1961 this company took over DH Engines and the engine division of Blackburn. Also in 1961, Rolls-Royce took over the Gazelle and a few other properties from D. Napier & Son. In October 1966 Bristol Siddeley was purchased, lock, stock and barrel, by Rolls-Royce. I have included chapters outlining the few engines from these other companies that have been important to Rolls-Royce.

Thus, in 1967 Rolls-Royce was a gigantic company, with 75,000 people on the payroll,

but it was still liable to get things wrong. The sudden death in that year of the great 'Lom'—Adrian Lombard, Engineering Director—was a major factor leading to a situation in which Rolls-Royce boldly took the plunge into the new field of giant high-bypass-ratio turbofans. The pressures on the balance sheet—and other potential liabilities caused by overcoming the severe technical problems ultimately led to bankruptcy. The shock to the world of business, and to the man in the British street, was cataclysmic; it was as if there had been a sudden collapse of the Church or the Monarchy.

Instantly the Government took steps to form a state-owned company, Rolls-Royce (1971) Ltd, to safeguard the nation's military airpower; but at first it specifically excluded the RB.211, the purely civil engine which had caused the downfall. To the author not least of the odd features of this episode is that, after the collapse shareholders in the original company were advised that their shares were worth nothing —'sell for whatever you can get'. The author sold his for 2.5 pence per share. By sheer chance he then happened to recoup almost exactly the same sum as he had lost in fees serving as an expert witness in helping decide the precise value of the company, its assets and its ongoing business. Also by sheer chance he found he still retained a small bonus holding, and over the subsequent years the receiver did such a good job that these were eventually sold for their full face value, 100 pence in the pound! So the people who, back in February 1971, bought RR shares for next to nothing, just for the fun of having the certificate, in due course made a colossal financial gain. But then, to the author, finance has always been a far more puzzling subject than engines.

Bill Gunston
Haslemere, Surrey
February 1989

Chapter 1

THE 200-HORSEPOWER ENGINE

Britain went to war on 4 August 1914 in a mood of patriotic fervour, convinced that it would 'all be over by Christmas'. Few people gave a thought to the fact that Britain had virtually no aircraft engine industry; there were just a handful of Green, Sunbeam and Wolseley engines made by hand. The War Office bluntly told Rolls-Royce to make existing engines under licence, and this the firm eventually did, with reluctance. Royce had always resisted the efforts of Rolls to make engines for flying machines, but with the coming of war the situation was quite different, and he immediately set about designing an aero engine.

There was only one way he could do this: aim at perfection. It was the Admiralty that offered instant encouragement. Commodore (later Admiral Sir) Murray Sueter, Commander of the Royal Naval Air Service, asked young Frederick Handley Page to build the RNAS a giant bomber—'a bloody paralyser of an aeroplane'. It was going to need two engines of about 200 hp each, and Sueter discussed the matter with the Head of the Admiralty Air Engine Section, Engineer-Commander Wilfred Briggs. Briggs had his office in a room in the Hotel Russell, and was a man of limitless vitality and energy. He saw it as part of his job to keep well informed on the technical details of all available engines, a task in which he was

greatly aided by his assistant, Lieutenant W. O. Bentley (whose car firm was later to be bought by Rolls-Royce). Bentley rightly considered that some of the best water-cooled cylinders in the world were those of the Mercedes Grand Prix cars and aero engines, which had thin sheet-steel jackets gas-welded on the outside of a forged steel cylinder barrel. One of the latest Mercedes engines happened to be in London: a wealthy British brewer had bought the racer that had won the 1914 French Grand Prix, and the car was on display in a show-room in Shaftesbury Avenue. On the first Sunday of the war, 9 August, Briggs and Bentley got the Mercedes racer out of the showroom and drove it in turns up to Derby. There it was handed over to works manager Wormald with the suggestion that the cylinders and any other parts should be used as the starting point for the 200-hp engine needed for the heavy bomber.

The Mercedes engine was first tested to 100 hp at 2,000 rpm and then dissected by Ernest Hives, who as well as being Chief Test Driver was forming a new Experimental Shop. But the man who took the decisions was 'The Old Man' down at St Margaret's Bay, 200 miles away. It was only now that the pressure was on to design a great new engine for aircraft that the inefficiency of the arrangement became manifest. Pre-

One of the first Eagles, a pre-Series 1, at the time (1915) called simply 'the Rolls-Royce 200 horse-power'. Note the flat box oil sump, and the prominent sloping pipes above the engine which returned hot cooling water to a radiator above the nacelle (probably of an F.E.2d).

viously, everyone at Derby had breathed a sigh of relief that the founder of the firm never visited them, because whenever he had put in an appearance he had been prone instantly to fire anyone whom he considered was misusing a tool or in any other way not doing his job in exactly the way Royce would have done it. (Legend has it that the disgruntled men were always immediately reinstated via the back door at Nightingale Road.) In fact Royce never came to the Derby factory again, and, while this avoided the aggravation a visit would have caused, it added to the difficulties of designing an engine. Royce spent the first week of the war considering all possible ways of designing a 200-hp aero engine, with a completely open mind. He did finally settle on water cooling, and did use a cylinder basically similar to that of the Mercedes, but there the idea of 'copying' stopped.

Indeed, he had admired this form of cylinder from Mors cars of about 1905. He was particularly careful not to infringe any Mercedes patent, and equally careful to take out patents for features new to the Rolls-Royce engine.

At an early stage Royce settled on a V-12 engine, with 60° between the left and right rows of cylinders. The twelve cylinders were all separate, the final choice of bore being 4.5 in and the stroke 6.5 in, giving a capacity (also called displacement or swept volume) of 1,238 cu in (20.32 litres). The basis of the engine was a cast-aluminium crankcase with a box-section wet sump. The twelve cylinders were each attached by being bolted through a flanged base to studs on the crankcase. Inlet and exhaust ports were forgings welded on opposite sides of the head, the two inclined valves being driven via rocker arms from overhead camshafts. There was no separate cylinder head and much of the valve gear was exposed, though the camshafts were enclosed.

Royce, with assistants A. G. Elliott and Maurice Olley, carefully considered each point in the design. They decided to place left and right cylinders exactly opposite each other, and use master connecting rods in the cylinders of one bank and slave or articulated rods in those opposite. Which side had the master rods was dictated by whether the engine was LH/RH tractor or pusher. It was vital to assemble the engine correctly, an indicating arrow showing the clockwise (viewed from the front) crank-shaft rotation being fixed to one pair of rods. Great care was taken to preserve dimensional accuracy and rigidity—just as is done in today's three-shaft jet engines—and this explained the deep so-called cellular construction of the crankcase and the choice of an epicyclic propeller reduction gear. In fact, at the start the War Office considered an engine as powerful as 200 hp would need to drive two propellers, one driven from each end, and one of the first engines was actually made with a drive at both ends. In the event it proved entirely possible in the final versions of the engine to transmit almost double this power to a single propeller. The choice of a complex epicyclic gear over plain spur gears was another instance of avoiding distortion of the casings. Most unusually, the choice fell on the crankshaft driving the outer ring or annulus gear, whose inner teeth meshed with those of three small pinions running round a fixed central sun gear. The three small pinions, spaced at 120°, were con-nected to a three-armed spider on the rear end of the propeller shaft. The sunwheel was held by an Oldham coupling which allowed the three elements of the gearbox to remain in perfect alignment (see p 21).

Of course, the first engine was run on a testbed, but in aircraft installations there were three sources of air pressure to feed the fuel, which was almost always an 80/20 mix of aviation petrol and benzole, from the tank(s). First, the pilot or a crew-member would pump up the tank with a hand-pump until the correct gauge reading was reached, which was typically 4 lb/sq in: a relief valve blew off if pressure became excessive. After the engine was started, its own engine-driven air pump pressurized the tank, and in flight a windmill-driven pump also came into action. The first engines had two Claudel-Hobson carburet-tors between the middle of the cylinder blocks, each feeding the six cylinders on its own side. Before starting, the engine was primed by a cockpit pump which sprayed a little neat fuel into the inlet manifolds. The pilot needed much experience in order to judge how much priming would be needed for a hot or cold engine on any particular day.

For reliability, the engine was designed with dual ignition, with a separate high-tension supply to each of two sparking plugs in each cylinder. But when war broke out most magnetos came from Germany, and until British firms got into production there was a severe shortage. Many of the first engines had to make do with two six-cylinder magnetos, but the main run of the big Rolls-Royce engine had two twelve-cylinder or, later, four six-cylinder magnetos. Starting so big an engine was difficult, and it could not be done by swinging the propeller because in reverse the geared drive acted as a step-up gear. Accordingly the engine was turned over by a low-geared handcrank (two, one on each side, in later engines). At the low cranking speed the magneto gave a weak spark, so a hand-turned booster magneto was fitted, at first driven by the starter handle and later cranked by the pilot. The main magnetos were at the rear, driven by bevel shafts which also drove the centrifugal water pump, air compressor, main oil pump and tachometer, and also provided connections for the starter handle(s) which were automatically thrown out of engagement when the engine started. The water cooling piping was complicated by the fact that each cylinder had its own welded jacket. With so many pipes, joints and welds it is small wonder that—even without any knocking (detonation) in the cylinders—water leaks were frequent. There were various proprietary additives to the water which lessened leakages, and legend has it that a particularly effective remedy was Campbell's or Symington's pea soup, always carried by the chauffeurs of early water-cooled cars. The most direct method of stopping leaks was chewing gum, and it was certainly a common practice for the pilot and navigator to have a mouthful ready for immediate use.

Inevitably the 200-hp engine was a massive piece of machinery, but Royce strove to make it as light as possible. Johnson acted as the vital link at Derby, receiving drawings from the designers in Kent, getting parts made and sent back for Royce's inspection. With several important parts Royce had prototypes made of wood, so that he and his small team could easily shave off material to reduce weight without losing strength. The crankshaft went back and forth three times before being made in metal. Despite this the whole design and construction of the first engine took less than six months, and Hives started it on the Derby test bench in late February 1915. It had a gear ratio of 0.64, and was expected to run at 1,600 rpm and give the required 200 hp. The weight was about 820 lb, exclusive of the steel mounting feet (14 lb), exhaust boxes (16.5 lb), propeller hub (16 lb), water (31 lb), oil (10 lb) and hand starting gear and booster magneto (30 lb). Very soon it was running at 1,600 rpm and giving 225 hp on the Froude dynamometer, which everyone considered very satisfactory. But the sound engineering of the new engine enabled its power to be increased in a way that was to become characteristic of Rolls-Royce aero engines. There was at this time virtually

no established procedure for 'development' of an engine. If it ran reasonably well that in itself was regarded as an achievement, and the main effort was usually devoted to curing faults and trying to achieve some kind of useful and reliable life between the frequent inspections and overhauls. Only in the case of the handful of car engines used for racing was there much attempt to wring out more power, and these had a short life anyway. Royce intended his 200-hp engine to have a long life, and to set a new high standard in reliability.

Today it is taken for granted that the first run of a new engine, no matter how successful, or the first flight of a new aircraft, is not the end of development but the beginning. In 1915 hardly anyone appreciated this. When Royce heard the good news from Hives that the aero engine was already giving 25 hp more than prediction he could easily have considered that the job of the design team at St Margaret's Bay was finished, and that all that now needed to be done was to get the engine into production at Derby. Royce never adopted this complacent attitude for a moment. Instead he drove his small team to ever greater efforts in an endeavour to increase power, reduce weight, reduce specific fuel consumption and improve reliability.

Accordingly, from the very start of testing he continued his stream of written instructions to Wormald or Johnson, but instead of being concerned with design and manufacture the memos now concentrated on the new art of engine development. On 22 March 1915, for example, he wrote 'Re 200 hp Aero Engine—short-duration tests, etc. We presume that you are continuing the test at high compression and increased speed, first finding out how fast you can run for one or two-hour spells with the lubrication as in the 20 hour test, and then whether the big-end will bear an increase of speed with (1) Castrol, (2) cooler oil, or (3) higher pressure'. In other words, from the outset

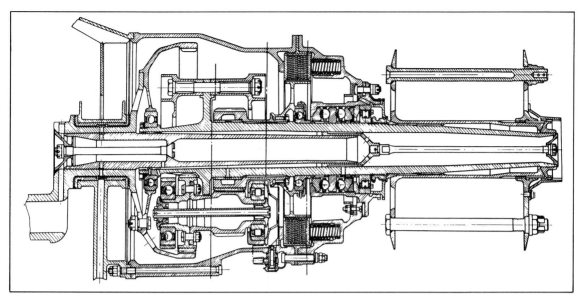

Detail from an original drawing from St Margaret's Bay showing the epicyclic reduction gear. Anyone used to reading such drawings will see that the crankshaft drove the outer annulus gear. Three meshing pinions transmitted the drive to the massive central shaft on which the propeller hub was mounted.

Royce insisted on the new engine being tested under conditions of gradually increasing severity, until something failed or broke. The failed part would then be strengthened or in some other way re-designed to bear the harsher conditions, when testing would continue. After the establishment of a major increase in power, the running conditions would be eased, and a long-endurance test undertaken in order to clear the engine for service at a new higher level of power, as in the modern Type Test or Certification Testing.

At Derby the pile of drawings and instructions from St Margaret's Bay soon built up into an impressive pile of paper, and in December 1915 these were committed to print and bound into a volume with a limited edition of 100 copies, entitled 'The First Aero Engines made by Rolls-Royce'. The preface stated 'In the opinion of the Board of Directors, the Memoranda and letters written by Mr F. H. Royce, the Engineer-in-Chief, in connection with the design, testing and manufacture of these engines are so admirable as evidence of extreme care, foresight and analytical thought, that the Directors decided to have them printed and bound in order that copies may be available for study and as an example to all grades of Rolls-Royce Engineers, present and future'. The book was headed 'CONFIDENTIAL, not to be shown to anyone without the authority of the Directors'. It is easy today to regard Royce's instructions as obvious, but they were far from obvious in 1915. Certainly, the foundation of engine design and development principles that he established with the 200-hp engine soon became normal practice everywhere.

Under Chief Tester Hives the progress of the engine was nothing short of brilliant. The 'Old Man's' instructions were followed meticulously, and nothing was left to chance. Speed was increased almost immediately to 1,800 rpm, and by August 1915 to 2,000 rpm, the maximum brake horsepower then reaching 300. After prolonged testing it was decided to clear the engine for production at a rating of 255 hp at 1,800 rpm, with 1,900 permitted for short periods. By this time the engine was being referred to not as 'the 200 hp engine' but by the RNAS and aircraft industry as 'the 250 Rolls-Royce'. An early modification was to change to a dry sump, with a deep vee-shape for extraction of the oil.

Royce considered himself under-utilised, now that the firstborn was ready for series manufacture. Though he continued to bombard Derby with all sorts of comments and exhortations, he told Johnson he considered there was a market for smaller aircraft engines, for lesser aircraft than 'bloody paralysers', and he straight away got down to planning a smaller V-12 followed by a six-inline. It was soon evident that some kind of unambiguous designation for the different engines was needed, and Johnson hit on the happy idea of naming them after birds of prey. The initial big engine he named the Eagle. The paper projects he named the Falcon, for the V-12, and Hawk, for the six-cylinder. These smaller engines are the subject of the next chapter.

Commander Briggs and Lieutenant Bentley naturally were delighted at the progress of the Rolls-Royce engine. At his Cricklewood (north London) factory Mr F. Handley Page had been preparing to fit 150-hp Sunbeam engines into his prototype O/100 bomber, but in October 1915 he received official details of the Rolls-Royce, and instructions to redesign the big bomber to take this much more powerful engine. The engines were mounted in armoured nacelles midway between the lower and upper wings (which were arranged to fold to the rear). Behind each engine was an armoured fuel tank. The completed O/100 was rolled out of the factory late at night on 17 December 1915, and then pulled by a team of RNAS seamen all the way up the Edgware Road to Hendon aerodrome. The

wings were folded, of course, but even so numerous trees had to be trimmed or cut down along the route. By daylight on the 18th the giant was being readied for flight, and it took off on a faultless first flight at 1.51 p.m. on that day (a Saturday). This was the first flight of a Rolls-Royce aero engine.

Like Rolls-Royce, 'HP' kept improving his bomber, and only forty O/100s were delivered to the RNAS, beginning in September 1916. For these Rolls-Royce delivered 100 Eagle I engines. Both the aircraft and engine were totally new and unknown to the enemy, so it is rather unfortunate that the third Handley Page to be flown to its squadron in France, on 1 January 1917, was put down twelve miles inside enemy territory. Another early recipient of the '250 Rolls-Royce' was the FE.2d, an upgraded version of a useful multirole night bomber/reconnaissance/fighter two-seater with a single pusher engine. Originally built with a 120-hp Beardmore engine, it had a pathetic performance, and the 160-hp version of the Beardmore proved unreliable. It was utterly transformed by the power and reliability of the Rolls-Royce engine, which was fitted as the 255-hp Rolls-Royce Mk I, later renamed Eagle I, in May 1916. For example, despite a considerable increase in weight, the time to climb to 10,000 ft was cut from 51.8 min with the 120-Beardmore to just 18.3 min! Here again, the new engine was neatly presented to the Germans, the very first FE.2d to go to France landing at Lille on 30 June 1916! The enemy tested the V-12 engine carefully and formed a high opinion of it, yet curiously the German production engines remained six-inlines until well after the war.

With the Eagle II of 1916 four carburettors were used, two amidships as before and two at the rear, and this arrangement continued through the next five marks of engine, though there was continual tinkering with the inlet manifolds. Throughout these vital war years the team of Hives and his mechanics, directed by Royce and his little drawing office staff, succeeded far beyond their wildest expectations in wringing more and more power out of the Eagle. This was done without changing the normal rpm from 1,800; it depended entirely on increasing the bmep (brake mean effective pressure) in the cylinders. The pistons, changed to aluminium at the suggestion of Lieutenant Bentley, were fitted with progressively better sets of rings to reduce gas leakage under the more arduous conditions, and the 'breathing' of the engine was several times improved, though each cylinder continued to have two valves only. Apart from changes to the carburettors, magnetos, reduction-gear ratio (which changed with the Mk VI from 0.64 to 0.60) and engine overall dimensions (which affected the ease with which one mark could replace another) the actual design of the engine remained remarkably unchanged.

One of the biggest markets for the Eagle continued to be the great Handley Page heavy bombers, the O/100 belatedly giving way in late 1917 to the O/400 which, the heavy night bomber by this time being

vindicated, was at last ordered in large numbers. Well before this, in late 1916, an Eagle was fitted to one of the outstanding Airco DH.4 day bombers, and this amazingly fast bomber flew with the Eagle III, VI, VII and VIII. Another important application was the Felixstowe (Porte) series of large flying boats, the F.2 and F.3, as well as the Fairey Campania float seaplanes.

By September 1917 the Eagle VIII had appeared, and this represented the pinnacle of Eagle power at 350 hp at normal rpm, with up to 375 hp available at the five-minute speed of 2,000 rpm. The chief difference in the Mk VIII was the use of a totally revised inlet system with a pair of carburettors—by now called 'Rolls-Royce', though still really Claudel-Hobsons—at each end of the engine, each serving the nearest three cylinders via a branched manifold. A fair number were made of each of the previous marks (104 Mk I, 36 II, 110 III, 150 IV, 100 V, 300 VI and 200 VII), but the Mk VIII ran to 3,302 copies, which at a price of £1,622.50 each was business on a massive scale. Indeed, many more could have been used, had the Derby works been able to supply them. The

With the Mk VIII of 1917 Rolls-Royce reached a level of power almost double that for which the original engine had been designed. The Eagle VIII had two carburettors at the front (visible here, feeding the inlet manifolds to the first three cylinders in each bank) and another pair at the rear.

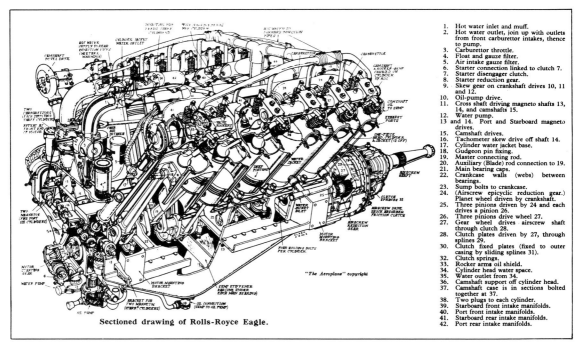

1. Hot water inlet and muff.
2. Hot water outlet, join up with outlets from front carburettor intakes, thence to pump.
3. Carburettor throttle.
4. Float and gauze filter.
5. Air intake gauze filter.
6. Starter connection linked to clutch 7.
7. Starter disengager clutch.
8. Starter reduction gear.
9. Skew gear on crankshaft drives 10, 11 and 12.
10. Oil-pump drive.
11. Cross shaft driving magneto shafts 13, 14, and camshafts 15.
12. Water pump.
13 and 14. Port and Starboard magneto drives.
15. Camshaft drives.
16. Tachometer skew drive off shaft 14.
17. Cylinder water jacket base.
18. Gudgeon pin fixing.
19. Master connecting rod.
20. Auxiliary (Blade) rod connection to 19.
21. Main bearing caps.
22. Crankcase walls (webs) between bearings.
23. Sump bolts to crankcase.
24. (Airscrew epicyclic reduction gear.) Planet wheel driven by crankshaft.
25. Three pinions driven by 24 and each drives a pinion 26.
26. Three pinions drive wheel 27.
27. Gear wheel drives airscrew shaft through clutch 28.
28. Clutch plates driven by 27, through splines 29.
30. Clutch fixed plates (fixed to outer casing by sliding splines 31).
32. Clutch springs.
33. Rocker arms oil shield.
34. Cylinder head water space.
35. Water outlet from 34.
36. Camshaft support off cylinder head.
37. Camshaft case is in sections bolted together at 37.
38. Two plugs to each cylinder.
39. Starboard front intake manifolds.
40. Port front intake manifolds.
41. Starboard rear intake manifolds.
42. Port rear intake manifolds.

Sectioned drawing of Rolls-Royce Eagle.

A cutaway drawing, by J.H. Clark of The Aeroplane, *of an Eagle VIII. Apart from the cylinder construction, all Rolls-Royce production engines were broadly similar to the end of World War 2. This drawing shows the inner propeller shaft (called here 'airscrew shaft') without the multi-bolted propeller hub which fitted around it.*

Fairey Campania, for example, had to switch to the Sunbeam Maori II engine, of only 250 hp, and many other aircraft were also produced with inferior engines. By far the most serious was the DH.9, which replaced the superb DH.4 in production in late 1917. The RFC commander in France, Major-General Trenchard, was seriously perturbed and wrote 'I should have thought that no-one would imagine we should be able to carry out long-distance bombing raids by day next year with machines inferior in performance to those we use for this purpose at present'. It was partly to alleviate the situation that just one firm, Brazil, Straker, & Co, was allowed by Royce and Johnson to make parts for the Eagle. The same Bristol-based company also made complete Falcon and Hawk engines—the only one to do so—because Royce trusted

its technical director, young Roy Fedden, who later was to form the Engine Department of the Bristol Aeroplane Company.

At the height of Eagle development, in 1917, St Margaret's Bay began receiving shells from German guns across the Channel. Bombs fell from aircraft, guns around Dover fired across the bows of unidentified ships, and such was the fear of a 'Hun' invasion that Elliott was arrested as he walked home from his drawing board late one night. A move seemed desirable, and Johnson found Elmstead, a pleasant house at West Wittering, then a virtually unknown village on the West Sussex coast. There was only a minor hiccup in work, and later additional designers were set to work mainly on cars in a small artist's studio, called Camacha, in the village. Royce's little team remained here until his death in 1933.

Altogether the Eagle reflected the qualities of the Rolls-Royce cars. A big, rather complicated and superbly designed and manufactured engine, it was appreciably more powerful and more reliable than its simpler rivals, but needed a lot of careful attention. More than any other engine of the entire war, it made constant progress. Each new mark offered greater power, reliability or some other major advance, and the fact that over four hectic years its power was to increase by nearly 90 per cent was to prove not untypical of what Rolls-Royce was later to accomplish with both piston and turbine engines.

One of the most famous writers of later years was to be former RFC Captain Norman Macmillan. In *Shell Aviation News* he wrote 'I flew the Series VI and VIII Eagles, the first in the DH.4 and the Mk VIII in Fairey IIIC floatplanes, the F.5 flying boat and the Vickers Vimy bomber. They rumbled very happily in flight, but a clatter came from the valve rockers and the valves. I found oil was apt to leak from the overhead camshaft casing. Rolls-Royce attributed this to unsuitable cowling causing a depression in the neighbourhood of the valve rockers which tended to draw oil out of the casings. I remember reaching Madrid in a DH.4 with an oil-smothered engine; it must have suffered from a severe depression. I was glad when I had crossed the Guadarrama Mountains and could throttle down to glide towards Madrid and so reduce the quantity of oil that riffled over my opaque windscreen. When I reached Madrid my oil tank was almost empty.

'A risk with this oil leakage was that of seepage down the ignition leads into the distributors. This was serious with the Eagle, because if it caused misfiring, torsional vibration might increase the stresses in the crankshaft, gearing and propeller shaft to many times the full-power loads. Metal fatigue might result and start a fracture, which could cause a subsequent breakage, quite possibly while in flight. The makers stipulated that Eagle engines were never to be run with only three, six or nine cylinders firing, or even with one or more cylinders missing fire. But what was the pilot to do when there was nowhere suitable to land if misfiring began? The makers also objected (for similar reasons) to switching on and off when running at full throttle. If there was any oil leakage from the camshaft casing it was essential at each stop to clean the plug leads and to examine, and if necessary clean, the distributors.

'In temperate or cold climates it was impossible to start a flight quickly with an Eagle engine. It had to be run slowly for at least ten minutes before opening the throttle to full power. This was necessary to warm both water and oil in the circulating systems. Time taken to warm up varied with the temperature, density and quantity of oil in circulation and the ambient temperature, so no definite time could be laid down; each pilot had to use his discretion in every case. For visual aids he had water-temperature and oil-pressure gauges; correct readings were 75° to 80°C at sea level and 40 lb/sq in normal (never below 25 lb/sq in). He controlled water temperature by manually operated radiator shutters.

'The pilot had three engine controls—throttle lever, mixture regulator lever and ignition lever (and dual switches). The regulator varied the mixture from strong through normal to weak. On later series engines the closing of the throttle lever automatically pulled the regulator lever back to strong; with this exception, the pilot controlled the mixture for varying conditions.

'To start the engine the pilot first shut the throttle, overrode the mixture control to strong, and set ignition midway (23°–25° before TDC, about which plus or minus 10° were full advance and full retard). Next he gave fifteen to twenty full strokes of the primer pump and turned all main fuel cocks and ignition switches to "On".

'At a signal from the pilot, the mechanic(s) now turned the starting handle(s), simultaneously pulling the engaging lever by ring and cable through the cowling until the mechanism clutched in. The pilot opened the throttle to one-quarter as the engine began to turn, then with one hand pumped the primer slowly (over-priming now choked the engine) and twirled the booster-mag handle with the other hand until, perhaps after a few isolated explosions, the engine ran steadily. When the engine over-ran them, the starting handles were automatically thrown out by their clutch. The pilot throttled down and turned the primer cock to "Off".

'In the absence of turning handles the propeller could be turned with the ignition switched off for the initial priming, but it was never swung for the actual starting; this had then to be done with the engine stationary. The mechanics' muscular strength and the pilot's dexterity were the royal roads to quick starting. If the engine were warm, or in hot climates, priming was reduced or perhaps avoided. Experience was the best mentor. A well-tuned Eagle started readily, and I once started an Eagle VIII in a Fairey IIIC plunging wildly in a 50 mph gale at sea, myself at one of the handles.'

Though there had been plenty of troubles at the start of development back in 1915, notably on big ends, camshaft drives, water pumps and detonation on anything but the best 80/20 fuel mixture, by late 1916, when production began to get into its stride, the Eagle was one of the most reliable engines in the sky. Most other engines averaged thirty hours or less between complete overhauls, but the standard figure for the Eagle was 100. At the same time, this was achieved only with the aid of frequent detailed inspection and attention. For example, *every day* an engine in active service had to be carefully inspected, all nuts, bolts and pipe unions checked for tightness, magnetos and contact breakers dried and

cleaned along with all HT wires and plug connections, and all 24 valve guides oiled and, if sticking, freed with paraffin. After ten and thirty hours there were successively more comprehensive overhauls, and at the 100-hour point the engine had to be returned for overhaul at Derby—Rolls-Royce were insistent upon this. The increasing burden of overhauls and manufacture of spares was partly responsible for the company progressively falling behind with deliveries, but the main reason was that the Government had not the slightest understanding of industry, was unwilling to finance the capital outlay required to increase production, and changed its mind 'at the drop of a hat'. Rolls-Royce were naturally cautious. In 1918 the Ministry of Munitions tried to make up the deficiency by widespread licence-manufacture, but Johnson took an extreme stand on this issue, saying it would 'yield nothing but mountains of scrap. I would tear up the drawings and go to prison rather than agree to it'. In fact, he did permit Brazil Straker to make Eagle parts.

In October 1917 the Air Board paid $11 million for 1,500 sets of Eagle parts to be supplied before the end of 1918 from the USA, but none of these were accepted and they formed 'the American dump' at Nightingale Road.

Rolls-Royce deliveries started at £950, with unit price gradually escalating to a peak of £1,622.50 for the Mk VIII. Discounting spares, this meant an income of some £7 million, no mean sum in those days. The official figure for all Eagles by 11 November 1918 is 4,080, many of which were assembled from Brazil Straker parts. Six Eagle VIIIs achieved fame by making some of the greatest flights in history, in each case in a Vickers Vimy. Engines 5244 and 5246 powered the unmarked (no British civil markings had been thought of) aircraft which left St John's, Newfoundland, on 14 June 1919, and made a non-stop overnight

Vickers Vimy bombers in production at the Linslade (Bedfordshire) factory of Morgan & Co in April 1918. The man who understood the Eagle VIIIs was 'the Rolls-Royce expert' (trilby hat, extreme right).

flight to Derrygimla, near Clifden, Ireland. Engines 5466 and 5716 powered *G-EAOU* ('God 'elp all of us') which on 12 November 1919 left Hounslow, west London, and flew in stages to Darwin (and later to Adelaide), Australia. When they reached Darwin the engines had been in the air for 135 hours without overhaul. Two other Mk VIIIs powered the *Silver Queen G-UABA* which on 4 February 1920 left Brooklands and eventually crashed at Wadi Halfa. Transferred to another Vimy, *Silver Queen II*, the same engines struggled on, only to be wrecked at Bulawayo (the two pilots transferred to a DH.9 and eventually reached Cape Town).

It is often overlooked that up to six Eagles formed the powerplant of each of the large rigid airships (No.23 to R.31) built in Britain at the end of the war. An unusual feature of their installation was that the entire power car, or engine gondola, was pivoted so that each engine could give vectored thrust—horizontally or vertically.

Another part of the Eagle story often overlooked is that it did not end with the Mk VIII. The Eagle was one of the most important engines of post-war British commercial airliners, and for this purpose a special new version, the Eagle IX, was developed. It retained four six-cylinder magnetos at the rear, but its carburettors could hardly have been more differently arranged. Instead of there being four carburettors there were only two, which facilitated tuning. Moreover they were mounted as low down as possible on each side of the engine amidships. Here they could be fed from the tankage of most aircraft by gravity alone, without the need for pressurizing the

A post-war Eagle IX, as fitted to civil airliners in fair numbers until 1928 (see production table in next chapter). It introduced a totally different arrangement of the carburettors and induction pipes.

tanks. The head of fuel needed was only 8in (203mm) above the centreline of the crankshaft. Each carburettor had twin inlet pipes and a redesigned float chamber and feed. It is remarkable that Rolls-Royce sold 373 Mk IX engines, some of them in Handley Page airliners, because it was possible to buy a new Mk VIII from the Aircraft Disposals Co (Airdisco) for about one-quarter of the price. A production table appears in the next chapter. The Eagle total was 4,675 engines.

Last of the Eagles to be built was the Mk XV, in which the propeller reduction gear incorporated an additional gearwheel with a controllable friction clutch which governed rotation of the peripheral ring gear. This converted the geared drive into a two-speed type, which at little cost gave an appreciable improvement in aircraft performance which, in the days of fixed-pitch propellers, was greatly welcomed.

Military Eagle VIIIs continued in service with the RAF until 1926, and in some other countries until at least 1930. Commercial Eagles appear all to have been withdrawn by 1931. The so-called Eagle XVI is described in Chapter 3.

Chapter 2

HAWK, FALCON AND CONDOR

In the first chapter it was explained how Rolls-Royce 'jumped in at the deep end' in the world of aviation, producing an engine for the very top end of the spectrum of combat aircraft. It was apparent almost from the outset that in this segment of the market you can never have too much power. The company showed, by its painstaking attention to detail and its procedure of increasing bmep at low rpm and then holding the same cylinder pressures up to full operating speed, that it is possible to wring more and more power from an engine of a given size. Generally similar principles have been applicable to aero engines ever since, right up to tomorrow's gas turbines, and no company has equalled the record of Rolls-Royce in doubling and even tripling the power available from the same basic design.

At the same time, there is a market for engines of lower power, where reliability is more important than output. From the start of the war on 4 August 1914 this was evident to Royce, and it was partly his extremely poor opinion of the RAF and Renault air-cooled V-8s which his company was asked to make that led him to consider designing an engine in the same power class. He had no doubt that he could fairly quickly produce an engine for training aircraft that, through better reliability, would

save the lives of hundreds of pupil pilots. There is evidence, though, that Royce tended to leave the low-power engine to his assistants Elliott and Olley, and they got round to producing the drawings in the summer of 1915.

Predictably, the smaller engine, which Johnson later named the Hawk, was basically half of the original V-12, though with slightly smaller cylinders and a direct drive to the propeller. The bore and stroke were 4 in and 6 in respectively, giving a capacity of 452.4 cu in (7.4 litres). As before, all six cylinders were separate, with welded-on water jackets, and held down by studs on the rigid aluminium dry-sump crankcase. There were two inclined valves per cylinder, driven by rockers from an overhead camshaft turned by a bevel gear from a vertical shaft at the rear, which also drove the various pumps and other ancillaries. Most Hawks had a single six-cylinder magneto and a complementary coil serving the two plugs in each cylinder, and twin carburettors on the left-hand side.

Unlike the Eagle, the Hawk could be started by swinging the propeller, after first priming the engine with the usual cockpit-mounted hand priming pump. In the few twin-engine installations this pump could squirt fuel into the induction manifold of either engine, by means of a changeover

Left *The Hawk was almost half an Eagle, on a smaller scale and conservatively rated for reliability rather than output. Production was handled by Brazil Straker at Fishponds, Bristol.*

Right *This Hawk has been beautifully restored by Rolls-Royce apprentices. Note the magneto and twin carburettors.*

cock. All forms of the 'priming device' were the subject of Rolls-Royce patents. Starting was usually no problem, with proper priming and use of the hand-driven booster magneto.

The six-cylinder engine was designed for reliability above all else, so its operating conditions were not severe. The design figure was 75 hp at 1,370 rpm, and this was achieved on the test bench at Derby on the first run, which was before the end of 1915, at about the time the Eagle first flew. Though there was no intense pressure to do so, the test crew under Hives inevitably set about getting greater powers, and in this case they soon cleared the engine to run a little faster. By February 1916 the Hawk was giving 91 hp at 1,500 rpm, and by the war's end the Hawk was giving 105 hp at the same speed, having been cleared to 94 hp a month earlier (October 1918). Nevertheless, the Hawk was already officially regarded as a 75 hp engine, and almost all of them were actually run at that power. Under these conditions the fuel consumption (aviation petrol, or an 80/20 mixture with benzole)

was 6.5 gal/h, the oil consumption being 0.5 gal/h.

Because of its modest rating and applications, initially regarded as for training aircraft, the Hawk was actually approved by Johnson and the co-directors for manufacture under licence, the firm being Brazil Straker of Bristol under its dynamic technical director Roy Fedden. In permitting him to make the Hawk, Claremont acted in a strictly legal capacity, and not only tied Fedden and Mr Brazil into a very tight agreement but even got them to agree not to design a competing water-cooled in-line or V-type engine for at least ten years. After the war Brazil Straker's assets were dispersed, and Fedden started the Engine Department of the Bristol Aeroplane Co, as outlined in Chapter 15. His initial product, the Jupiter air-cooled radial, eventually achieved such wide acceptance that he had no wish to depart from this kind of engine, but he regarded himself as still bound by the Rolls-Royce agreement even though he was now with a totally different firm. What

is ironic is that towards the end of the war, when he was designing the Jupiter, Fedden was strongly advised by Royce not to hitch his wagon to the star of the air-cooled radial. He did not tell Royce that he was prohibited from the alternative configuration by Rolls-Royce itself! Just to round off this particular facet of the story, in 1927 Fedden's Jupiter was far more important in the RAF than all the RR engines combined. Royce generously called Fedden over to see him at the RAF Pageant at Hendon and said 'I never thought you'd make a go of the Jupiter. I am delighted to see that I was so wrong'.

In fact, orders for the Hawk were small, and Rolls-Royce made only the prototypes. Thereafter Brazil Straker produced the main run of about 200, and rather unexpectedly most of these were for blimps (non-rigid airships) of the Royal Naval Air Service. Nearly all of these installations were pushers, and on the extremely rare occasions when the engine stopped (one famous occasion was when the ship hit the ground and the propeller could not rotate) it was difficult to climb to the aft end of the gondola and swing the propeller to get the engine going again. Accordingly, most Hawks had a geared-down starting handle on the rear of the engine, in other words the forward-facing end readily accessible to the crew in the gondola, with which cranking the engine in flight was simplicity itself. Cranking was seldom needed, however, because the Hawk in the S.S.Z. (Sea Scout Zero) blimps soon achieved a reputation for reliability second to none. The first S.S.Z. was built at Capel and ready in June 1916. The RNAS received 66, as well as two S.S. Twins each powered by two Hawks. Twenty hour patrols were quite routine, and in August 1918 one S.S.Z. completed an anti-U-boat patrol which lasted 50 h 55 min. Altogether, of 55,700 hours flown by British airships of all kinds in World War I, just over 36,000 were flown on Hawk power.

Apart from the blimps the Hawk was used mainly in Maurice Farman Longhorn trainers made by the Phoenix company. A handful were used in B.E.2Es and in such one-offs as the Avro 504F and Sage Type 3.

The Hawk had virtually no post-war usage, unlike the Eagle. But in terms of longevity in RAF service both engines were outclassed by the third Rolls-Royce aero engine, which was also the first to be designed at Derby. Precisely why it was designed is not clear. There was no airframe specifically waiting or earmarked for it, and it appears to have been a mere hunch on Royce's part—perhaps that it would be a good idea to build a smaller Eagle for fighters, to give Hispano-Suiza some competition. It was aimed at 190 hp and was initially called the I.190. It was to prove the perfect partner for a two-seat fighter which was being designed at Bristol by Capt Frank Barnwell, and this aircraft was to remain in service with the RAF until 1932!

Royce was not a man to give away responsibility to others, yet he allowed the '190-hp fighter engine' to be designed at Derby, by the embryonic design team there under R. W. Harvey-Bailey, a long-time servant of the company on cars (and father of Alec, who was to be a famed RR man for 42 years and whose 'retirement' in 1981 was in name only). 'By' in company shorthand, he set about design of the I.190 in late 1915, just as the Hawk was being drawn at St Margaret's Bay. This time the operation could hardly have been more efficient. Once Royce had approved the basic drawings By was able to work closely with the experimental shop at Nightingale Road, and the first engine was on test around February or March 1916 after amazingly fast progress. It was a V-12 basically similar to the Eagle but scaled down to a bore of 4 in and stroke of 5.75 in, giving a capacity of 867 cu in (14.2 litres). It is interesting to note that, though the new engine was designed for almost the same power as the original '200-hp engine' its capacity was just less than 70 per cent as great, showing the

significant advance in specific power achieved in the first year or so of engine development.

In general design the I.190 was very like an Eagle. The cylinders were almost identical, though smaller, with high-compression aluminium pistons, welded-on sheet water jackets and two inclined valves driven via an overhead camshaft turned by a bevel shaft at the rear of each row of cylinders. The crankcase was of the same cellular aluminium dry-sump type as in the other engines, and on the front was an epicyclic reduction gear almost identical to that of the Eagle, but smaller. Virtually all engines of this type had two twelve-cylinder Watford or Dixie magnetos at the rear. Early engines had two Claudel Hobson carburettors, with barrel throttle valves, and these could be either at the front of the engine or at the rear. The usual hand-turning gear, priming pump and booster magneto were fitted for starting.

When the first I.190 was on test in early 1916 Johnson gave it the proud name of Falcon. Between September 1916 and June 1917 a total of 250 Falcon Is were delivered. It is difficult to determine the date of the first flight, or in what aircraft. The three possible contenders, all in September 1916, are the first prototype Bristol F.2A Fighter, the Fairey F.2 and a Short 184 seaplane (No *8104*). The seaplane, often said to have had an Eagle engine, could have flown as early as late August 1916, in which case it was the first Falcon-powered aircraft. There were many other applications, including the three big 'escort fighters' built to the same specification, the Armstrong Whitworth F.K.12 (again often said to have been Eagle-powered), Sopwith LRTTr tractor triplane and Vickers FB.11. Other types included the Martinsyde F.1, F.3 and F.4; RE.6 and 7; Avro 523 and 529; Blackburn Kangaroo, SP and GP seaplanes and Sprat; Parnall Perch; and Vickers FB.14D and Vendace (post-war design). Confusion arose over the use of engine mark numbers without names; the FB.14D, for example, was said to have had an Eagle like several others in the above list, but actually had a Falcon.

Of all applications, that named first above was by far the most important. Captain Barnwell originally planned his reconnaissance Fighter, the R.2A, around the 120-hp Beardmore. It was obvious that this was nothing like sufficiently powerful, and before building a prototype he totally redesigned his Fighter into the F.2A to be powered by either the new Rolls-Royce engine or the 150-hp Hispano-Suiza. The first aircraft, *A3303*, was built between July and September 1916, possibly making the first flight of a Falcon on 9 September. The engine was beautifully cowled, though driving a bluff four-blade right-hand propeller. The radiators for the cooling water were arranged on each side of the fuselage just behind the engine, and the test pilot—Capt Hooper, RFC, the CO of the Filton Aircraft Acceptance Park, who was engaged on a freelance basis—complained that they interfered badly with pilot view, especially on landing. *A3303* was quickly rebuilt with a radiator on the nose, of almost circular form but of course with the geared propeller near the bottom. This was a great improvement, and delivery of production F.2As began on 20 December 1916, the fifty aircraft being followed by increasing numbers of an improved model, the F.2B. Virtually all the 3,576 Bristol Fighters built at Bristol had left-hand two-blade propellers. Over 1,000 'Brisfits' were made under licence, but with other engines because Rolls-Royce could not meet the demand, not even when helped out by several hundred complete Falcons made by Brazil Straker at Fishponds, just 'down the road' from the British & Colonial (Bristol) factory at Filton.

To say that the F.2B was the greatest two-seat fighter of the First World War is an understatement. Once it had been learned—very much the hard way—not to fly straight and level but to fly the aircraft like a single-seater, the F.2B carried all before it. For sheer strength, all round tractability, the ability to dive faster than any other aircraft, and the ability to get home with severe combat damage, the Brisfit, or 'Biff', was in a class of its own. The back-seat observer, who could easily talk to the pilot, often had twin guns and scored roughly as many victories during the course of the war as did the pilots with their fixed gun. F.2Bs were built with many engines, including types from Britain, France and the USA, but the standard engine was the Falcon. With this fitted its reliability became a byword. The contemporary *Ballad of the Bristol Fighter* contains such verses as:

> 'But few of them know the secret
>   Of making my heart rejoice,
> Like a well-rigged Bristol Fighter
>   With a two-six-five Rolls-Royce.
>
> Is there a sweeter music,
>   Or a more contented sound,
> Than the purring clop of her broad
>   curved prop
>   As it gently ticks around?'

There is a lot more besides, but this extract show the esteem in which this fine machine was held. Even in the tough field conditions of the Western Front the Falcon regularly ran its 100 hours between overhauls, typically three times as long as rival engines. This is especially noteworthy when it is recalled that virtually none of the rivals had as many cylinders, and the standard German counterparts were six-in-lines, which got their power through having much bigger cylinders. When the I.190 was first designed twelve might have seemed a lot of cylinders for 190 horsepower, but true to form the Falcon soon showed its propensity for development, and in the above verses it is called a '265'. The Falcon II, which had car-

Above *Apart from being smaller, the Falcon was very similar to the contemporary Eagles, and had a very similar epicyclic reduction gear. All later Falcons had four carburettors.*

Below *Rear view of a Falcon III, showing the oil and water pumps at the bottom, the magnetos on each side, the carburettors on the back, and the circular casings over the camshaft bevel drives.*

burettors enlarged from 34 to 36mm, and was rated at 220 hp, was put through its officially observed tests in an F.2B in September/October 1917, a total of 250 being delivered between June and November 1917. Even earlier, in May 1917, an F.2B had flown with the first Falcon III of 275 hp, with four 38-mm carburettors. The position at Derby was more complex because Falcons had risen in power in numerous stages. While holding speed at 1,800 rpm the power rose to 205 hp in late April 1916, 228 hp in May, 247 hp in February 1917 and 262 hp in April 1917. On being cleared to 2,000 rpm the power increased to 278 hp in November 1917 and 285 hp in July 1918. A typical engine weight was 650 lb for a Falcon I, later marks being 10 lb heavier, and fuel consumption rose with power from an initial 16.6 to an eventual 18.75 gal/h. Total production of the Falcon was 2,185 by Rolls-Royce and 1,500 by Brazil Straker at Bristol.

Certainly 285 hp was beyond anything possible by the German six-in-lines of similar capacity, and it amply justified the choice of twelve small cylinders. The combination of numerous parts and high running speed (for the day) might have seemed a sure recipe for unreliability, yet the Falcon was unmatched in this respect by any other fighter engine of its era. Suffice to say the Falcon III continued in production until March 1927, the total being 1,685. The Bristol F.2B carried on in front-line service in such harsh environments as the North-West Frontier until 1932, where engine reliability meant life or death.

While the Falcon was to a large extent a scaled-down Eagle, the fourth wartime engine was even bigger than the Eagle. Named by Johnson as the Condor, it was planned to be the most powerful aircraft engine in the world, to suit the propulsion requirements of several giant landplanes and flying boats which were being designed from 1916 onwards. The most important application was to power the Handley Page V/1500, the big bomber planned to carry an appreciable bombload to Berlin, so that over shorter distances it could carry as many as thirty bombs of 250 lb each. In order to be powered by just two engines these had to be of 550 to 600 horsepower each, and in October 1917 Royce began studying how best to attain such a figure. He gave careful consideration to an engine of W or 'broad arrow' form with three rows each of six cylinders of Eagle size. He also considered, but quickly rejected, an engine with two rows each of eight cylinders. His final choice, towards the end of the year, was simply another V-12 but of considerably greater capacity. He settled on a bore of 5.5 in and a stroke of no less than 7.5 in, giving a capacity of 2,138 cu in (35 litres). Such a cylinder size was quite typical of the big German six-in-lines, but Royce wanted his engine to run at higher speeds than the 1,400-odd rpm of the Teutonic engines.

Several design changes were introduced with the Condor, which in many other respects resembled the latest Eagles. To improve breathing of the big cylinders twin inlet and twin exhaust valves were fitted, though each row of cylinders continued to have a single overhead camshaft driving via exposed rockers. The crankcase was split into upper and lower sections bolted together all round, and the latter had a horizontal sump with the water pump beneath the centre of the engine. The camshafts were driven by the usual bevel shafts up the rear of each row of cylinders. There were several arrangements of carburettors, depending on Mark, some being mounted low down on each side of the engine with a modified float chamber and barrel-type throttle in the single induction pipe which passed through the slightly larger gap between cylinders 3 and 4 on each side in line with the crankshaft centre bearing, thus feeding the induction manifolds between the cylinder blocks. There were two twelve cylinder magnetos driven by the usual transverse shaft at the rear, and instead of manual crank handles an electric starter was usually fitted. This last was not so much to save toil by the ground crew as to take account of the expected installations, often 20 or more feet above the ground with no place for cranking crews to stand. Another new feature was a drive for a dynamo.

The first Condor was on test in August 1918, but this was too late for the V/1500 which went into production with four Eagles in tandem pairs. An even bigger aircraft, John Porte's Felixstowe Fury (better known at the time as the Super Baby), a vast triplane flying boat, had been designed for three tractor Condors but flew with five Eagle VIIs, two tractor and three pusher. The Armistice of November 1918 brought a general termination of contracts and easing of pressure on the development of defence equipment, and the infant airlines were far too cost-conscious to think about engines as large as the Condor. Despite this, the Condor did find numerous applications in

As its applications material-ized mainly in the 1920s one tends to overlook the fact that the massive Condor was a wartime design. This is a Mk IA, with four-valve cylinders, 12-cylinder magnetos and provision for an electric starter and dynamo.

prototypes, the original Mk IA engine power-ing the Avro Aldershot and Ava, the first of the monster Fairey N.4 flying boats *Atalanta*, and the Short Cromarty flying boat. The Aldershot, first of a series of large single-engined machines, was the only one to have an engine cowling.

Far from being 'over by Christmas 1914' the Great War, as it was then called, had lasted over four years and had completely transformed both the world of aviation and the Rolls-Royce company. At its end no aero-engine firm stood higher than Rolls-Royce, but there were major problems. A minor one was that Royce and his design cell were at West Wittering, the factory and test beds were under Wormald and Hives in Derby, and the sales staff under Managing Director Johnson were in Conduit Street, in London's West End. Much more seriously, most of the directors had always regarded aero engines as a sideline, reluctantly carried on in the national interest to help win the war. With the return of peace they wished to devote the company's energies—which had been vastly enhanced by the wartime aero efforts—back into its proper business. This was certainly the view of Chairman Claremont, Managing Director

Claude Johnson and (especially) his brother Basil, and to some degree of the Old Man himself, Royce.

Reluctantly, the newly formed Service Department, under Eric Platford—once Royce's apprentice at Cooke Street, who had become Chief Tester (Production) and in fact went to Newfoundland to prepare engines for the various would-be trans-atlantic aviators—was permitted to spend modest sums supporting the many engines in service with the RAF, airlines and foreign governments. Design effort on aero engines essentially ceased, there being no funding and no spare design capacity.

The aero engines greatly assisted the design of improved car engines to replace the rather outdated Silver Ghost, but once the backlog of car orders had been filled orders tailed off. Royce began once more to think about aviation, but with no clear objective. At the still young Air Ministry Lieutenant-Colonel L.F.R. Fell, a man later to serve with distinction in Rolls-Royce, had been appointed the first Assistant Director of Technical Development (Engines). He urged the company to modernize the Condor, and increase its power from 550/600 hp to 650 hp to suit

The Condor IV was a direct-drive engine. Though the lightest Condor, it still weighed almost 2 lb/hp. It powered the Hornbill fighter and, with small changes, other prototypes.

various Air Ministry specifications, notably for a new single-engined torpedo bomber. In 1921 the Chief Designer of Napier, A. J. Rowledge, had fallen out with that company, and he was recruited by Rolls-Royce as Royce's Chief Assistant, stationed at Derby. This gave Royce the capacity to 'think aero' again. Rowledge's first brief was to modernize the Condor. The planned Condor II was scrapped, and under Rowledge a largely new Condor III was planned.

The engine's appearance was transformed, and it was made much lighter. A major change was to switch to fork-and-blade connecting rods. On each crankpin the connecting rod from one cylinder was forked, while that from the opposite cylinder terminated in a big-end slim enough to drive the crankpin directly, being located between the twin big-ends of its partner and bearing not on the crankpin itself but on the forked rod's outer shell. This was in many ways preferable to the master-and-link arrangement, though initially it was difficult to retain a good oil film on the narrow

big-ends. Another major change was to use a spur reduction gear, which made the engine shorter, improved cowling geometry and helped in single-engined applications by raising the propeller shaft, giving more clearance above the ground or floats for a giant propeller, typically of 16 ft diameter. Considerable complication was resorted to, with various internally toothed gears and intermediate splined shafts, to ensure that no transverse loads were transmitted from the gears into the crankshaft. The rear wheelcase was redesigned, with provision for an electric or Bristol-type gas starter. The single carburettor mounted at the rear was of a new pattern with a completely different altitude control valve. All the other ancillaries were grouped under the rear of the crankcase, there being three oil pumps, the water pump and, for the first time, an engine-driven petrol pump.

Whereas the Condor IA had weighed some 1,600 lb, the Mk IIIA weighed about 1,320 lb, though hardly any two engines were exactly alike because they tended all to have different applications, most rated at

650 or 705 hp at 1,900 rpm. The only production application was 200 engines for the Hawker Horsley, winner over three other types for the torpedo bomber order for the RAF. Other applications included the second Fairey N.4 *Titania*, the Avro Andover, Fairey Fremantle seaplane, HP Handcross, Saunders-Roe Valkyrie, Short Singapore I (used by Alan Cobham for his overland flight to South Africa, though it was a flying boat), Vickers Vixen and Vanguard (on 6 July 1928 the latter airliner broke the world's load-carrying record), Westland Yeovil, and the Beardmore Inflexible which on some counts was the largest aircraft of its day. Sydney Camm's Hawker Hornbill, fastest fighter of 1925, had a 698-hp direct-drive Condor IV, which weighed only 1,240 lb. In Germany Rohrbach used Condors in the Rocco flying boat.

None of these applications accounted for more than a handful of engines, but in 1928 design began on the Condor IIIB, which had a stronger crankcase housing a crankshaft of increased diameter carried in longer main bearings. This was the final service version, used in the four Blackburn Iris III flying boats and as a retrofit in some Horsleys. Major production was ruled out

by a decree of 'Boom' Trenchard, as related at the start of the next chapter. A further important application, however, was the wholly successful British rigid airship *R.100*, whose six Condor IIIBs drove it at the unrivalled speed of 81 mph.

Thus, with modest production (see table), the aero work ticked over, mainly on account of the old Eagle and massive Condor, through the 1920s. Two technically interesting Condor developments were built but not flown. Around 1926 a Condor was run with an exhaust-driven turbosupercharger, which (it is alleged) gave the remarkable boost pressure of 13.5 lb/sq in at the full-throttle height of 2,000 ft. At about the same time the Condor VIII was developed for the 'engine room' of a giant flying boat planned at Supermarine by Reginald Mitchell, with shaft drives to the propellers, but this was not constructed. One experimental Condor which did fly was the Mk V compression-ignition (diesel), weighing 1,500 lb and rated at 500 hp. Developed mainly at Farnborough's Royal Aircraft Establishment, it was flown there after four years of work in 1932 in a Horsley. Ironically, a Horsley with a regular Condor succeeded on 21 May 1927 in setting a world long-

Last of the production Condors was the IIIB, with a crankshaft of increased diameter carried in longer main bearings in a stronger crankcase. In 1929 this 675/690-hp engine powered the Iris flying boats.

The Condor V was an experimental engine with a turbosupercharger developed by Rowledge assisted by Ellor at the RAE. To accommodate the turbo between the cylinder banks it had two small-diameter stages (7.5 and 8.25in). Rig tests at the RAE showed that at 26,000 rpm the pressure in the two induction pipes along the top could be maintained at 13.5 lb/sq in (almost sea-level value) at 20,000 ft. Note the two auxiliary water radiators.

distance record. Two hours later Lindbergh landed in Paris and just beat the Horsley's figure!

Production in the 1920s

	Eagle	Falcon	Condor	Buzzard	Kestrel	R
1919	VIII,960	III,348	Exptl,1			
1920	VIII,98	III,177	I,45			
			I,27			
1921	VIII,111	III,11	II,34			
	VIII,10					
1922	IX,49	-	-			
1923	IX,65	III,1	III,6			
1924	IX,116	III,1	III,29			
			III,83			
			IV,4			
1925	IX,97	III,4	V,1			
			III,69			
1926	IX,29	-	IV,9			
			III,9			
1927	IX,12	III,4	IVA,9		26	
1928	IX,5	-	-	1	37	
1929	-		IIIB,20	7	22	
1930			-	6	107	1

Chapter 3

KESTREL, GOSHAWK AND PEREGRINE

During 1925 Air Chief Marshal 'Boom' Trenchard, after discussion with the Air Ministry, decreed that all future engines for RAF front-line aircraft should be capable of being made under licence by firms in the car industry. Obviously this made sense, if production in time of crisis was ever to be suddenly increased. The Air Ministry sent out Colonel Fell's assistant, Major G. P. Bulman, to check up on what the various aero-engine firms had to say about this requirement. Nobody disagreed except Rolls-Royce. Claude Johnson had just died, but brother Basil saw Bulman and managed to persuade him that, in conformity with company tradition, nobody else could build Rolls-Royce engines. When he saw the report, Trenchard scrawled across it 'No more Condors'. The company was officially advised to this effect (though, as the table on a previous page shows, Condors continued to be ordered in small numbers).

At this, Royce began to see a warning red light. The surfeit of wartime engines had been either used up or rendered obsolete, and the RAF and airlines were very much back in business buying new engines. All the business was going to the Armstrong Siddeley Jaguar, Napier Lion and, above all, the Bristol Jupiter. Rolls-Royce had essentially opted out of the aero business, because it had virtually stopped develop-

ment; but, with its cars selling at the rate of 35 a week, the company was profitable and stable with some 4,000—almost all very long-serving—on the payroll. Had Rolls still been on the board there is no doubt the company would never have slackened its aero effort. As it was, it was left to Hives at Derby—who, though a vital cog in the machine, was still merely the head of the Experimental Department—to keep pushing wherever he could for new aero work to be started.

To be fair, Royce had never ceased thinking about a new aero engine, but there is no record of anything being drawn. West Wittering has a fine sandy beach, and legend has it that Royce used to draw possible engines in the sand with his stick, studying and arguing about them but then leaving them to be washed away by the next tide. He had come to think that the best configuration should be an X-16, with four banks each of four cylinders spaced at 90°. Even so, it is possible that nothing would have been made had not competition come from an unexpected quarter.

In 1924 planemaker C. R. (later Sir Richard) Fairey went to the United States and was impressed by the Curtiss D-12 engine which had won the 1923 Schneider Trophy race (it won the next, in 1925, also). In many respects this V-12 engine was ahead of all current practice, not least in its almost perfectly streamlined installation. Fairey bought a D-12 and a licence to build it in Britain as the Fairey Felix. On returning to his Hayes factory he at once organized the design of a fast day bomber with the American engine, and this emerged as the Fairey Fox. When Trenchard saw it fly in October 1925 he asked Fairey how it was that he could supply the RAF with a bomber (the Fawn) which could just exceed 100 mph, and then build the Fox which was half as fast again, and could in fact outrun every fighter in the RAF? Fairey naturally replied that, while the Fawn was built to an Air Ministry specification, the Fox was not thus restricted (the same thing was to happen repeatedly in the future). Trenchard could hardly avoid ordering a squadron of Foxes; No 12 got them instead of their clumsy Fawns, and became the envy of the RAF.

At the same time, the Air Ministry bluntly informed Fairey it had no intention of supporting an additional British aero-engine company. Colonel Fell formally invited the existing firms to build an engine superior to the Curtiss D-12, and he brought particular pressure to bear on Rolls-Royce which he was eager to see return to its former position as a leading supplier of high-power engines. Whilst at Napier, Rowledge had been involved in the design of an X-16 engine of no less than 1,000 hp, but this engine, the Cub, was merely a pedestrian monster which appeared to owe a lot to the Eagle. Rowledge's own Lion was a much more advanced engine, and he was eager to surpass it with a new engine for Royce in the monobloc X-16 layout which he favoured.

This was called the E16, or Eagle XVI, even though—apart from the cylinder bore of 4.5 in and the maker's name—it had little in common with other Eagles. Stroke was reduced from 6.5 in to only 4.75 in, bringing down piston speed to less than that in the V-12 Eagles even at the design rpm of 2,500. The Eagle XVI was a very clean engine, made chiefly of aluminium, with four cast blocks each of four cylinders, with dry liners and quadruple overhead valves, set at 90° to each other. Royce's innate

Only one example was ever run of the Eagle XVI. Marking a total break with established RR practice, it exemplified Rowledge's belief in cylinder blocks cast as one piece of aluminium. It also introduced a supercharger. This picture shows the front end.

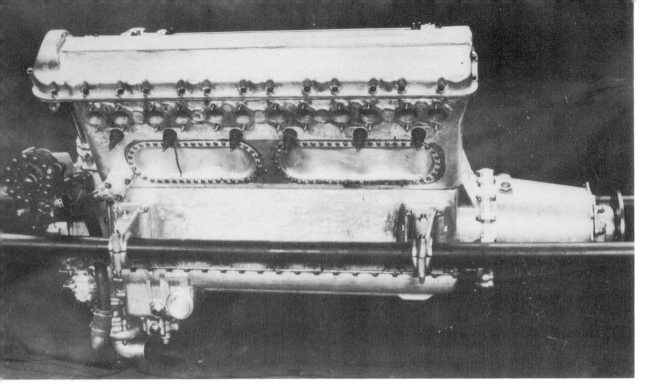

Even though it still lacks its ignition harness and some piping, the prototype F can be seen to have been a clean and, by comparison with the Eagle XVI, very simple engine. It was designed and built quickly. Without the spur from Fairey it would probably have been years later.

engineering sense made him avoid star master rods, and instead use side-by-side fork/blade rods. At one end was an epicyclic reduction gear, and at the other a double-sided gear-driven supercharger. The company had no experience with superchargers, so this was contracted out to Jimmy Ellor at Farnborough, who quite soon had the double-sided impeller (blower) on test, the company's representative being A. A. Rubbra, a brilliant graduate who had just joined.

Even before the XVI was completed, Royce instructed Rowledge to spend no more money on it, but instead to design an equally advanced engine in V-12 configuration. This was partly because Royce hated change unless it was deemed essential, but mainly because Trenchard told Royce he wanted the new engine to be retrofitted into No 12 Squadron's Foxes. With the X-16 engine this would have been difficult, and Rubbra pointed out that the engine would pose major problems in any installation.

Rowledge accordingly started afresh with a completely new V-12, but again it received an existing name: F, for Falcon. Meanwhile the prototype Eagle XVI went on test at Derby in March 1926, without its supercharger, and quickly reached 500 hp. Five more examples of this engine were planned but none was completed, and a 1,000-hp version, the E20 (Eagle XX), remained on paper.

The first F engine went on test in about December 1926 as the F.10. Compared with the XVI it was a compact direct-drive engine which promised simplicity and lower cost. The basis was a light but rigid cast aluminium crankcase made in one piece with two cantilevered mounting trunnions on each side, and with a flat sump bolted all round underneath. On top, set at 60°, were the two blocks each of six cylinders. Each block was a single casting in aluminium, with all the necessary water passages, inlet and exhaust systems and holes for long through-bolts to secure the block to the

An early production Kestrel, at the time called an F, with reduction gear but natural aspiration. Air entered via two inclined pipes above the engine looking like ship funnels (only the right-hand duct can be seen here).

crankcase. Each cylinder had a wet (ie, with the water in contact all round) liner of thin carbon steel, bore and stroke being 5 in and 5.5 in respectively, giving a capacity of 1,296 cu in or 21.24 litres. The two inlet and two exhaust valves per cylinder were of the new austenitic steel, containing about 14% each of nickel and chromium and 2% tungsten. Valve heads were seated on renewable rings of similar material screwed into the aluminium, and stem guides were cast iron. A soft aluminium ring sealed the joint between the block and the head of the steel liner, and the watertight joint at the bottom of the liner was a rubber ring fitted into a groove in the liner and squeezed inside the block skirt. Where the hold-down bolts passed through the cooling water they were encased in aluminium tubes, swaged to the block at both ends. Overhead camshafts were used, driven from the rear end, with a separate rocker for each valve.

At the rear was a vertical shaft driving three gear-type oil pumps and the centrifugal water pump, the return water pipes lying along the inner sides of the cylinder heads. There were two twelve-cylinder magnetos, and between the blocks at the mid point

were two RR duplex carburettors with all four barrel throttles ganged together to open and close in unison. Altitude mixture control was automatic. Starting was by hand turning via a multi-plate clutch and worm gear. The clutch slipped if torque became excessive, and saved the gears from damage in the event of a backfire.

The original F.X (F.10) weighed 760 lb, and was rated at 490 hp at 2,350 rpm, with fuel consumption of 30 gal/h. It passed its Type Test in June 1927. By this time it had been decided to offer the engine with a range of gear ratios and different degrees of supercharging. A gear-driven supercharger was still something new to Rolls-Royce. Colonel Fell persuaded the greatest British supercharger engineer, Jimmy Ellor, to leave Farnborough and go to Derby instead of the USA (which had been in his mind). Perhaps the most unexpected and crucial element, the centrifugal clutch, had been the work of Major F. M. Green and Sam Heron working at the Siddeley-Deasy company on what became the A. S. Jaguar engine, and they had patented it. The pinion at the rear of the crankshaft was geared up to the supercharger impeller via three or four planet gears, inside each of which was a friction drive by means of slippers held by light springs against the inner faces of the gear rims, rather like the drum brakes on a car. The faster the engine ran, the greater the pressure of the slippers, the drive torque actually increasing in proportion to the square of the rotational speed. This is just what was needed, because the torque required also increased with the square of the speed of the supercharger, so there was always about the same margin above that causing slip. The rather complex arrangement was needed to eliminate overloading due to sudden changes in crankshaft speed fighting the high inertia of the spinning impeller, while in turn the latter damped out torsional oscillations in the auxiliary drive shafts including the supercharger itself.

Virtually all production engines had a geared drive, with a spur gear very similar to that of the Condor III. Engines with mark number XI had a gear ratio of 0.632, and the Mk XII a ratio of 0.552; later the XIV was added with a ratio of 0.475. Suffix 'A' indicated a compression ratio of 6, and suffix 'B' a compression ratio of 7. F.XIA No 1 was taken off the bed and fitted into Fairey Fox *J9026* and made the engine's first flight on 29 August 1927, thus becoming the first Fox IA. In fact the definitive engine for the Fox was the XIIA, and this engine was first flown by Fairey's Chief Test Pilot, Norman Macmillan, in a DH.9A in September 1928. Slight delay was caused by two inflight engine failures, on one of which Macmillan had Rolls-Royce's Willoughby (Bill) Lappin, Hives' personal assistant and trouble-shooter, in the rear cockpit. Big-ends were the problem, and it was finally discovered that the bolts were being over-tightened. This led to universal use of pre-set torque spanners in all future assembly. Soon No 12 Sqn had its Foxes re-engined.

A far more important application was the Hawker Hart, built in more variations and in greater numbers than any other British aircraft between the wars. The Fox at last awoke the Air Ministry to the improving performance of aircraft, and the Hart competed against such types as the Avro Antelope and Fox II to meet Specification 12/26 for a day bomber to fly at some 160 mph, to be powered by the new Rolls-Royce F. Hawker Chief Test Pilot P.W.S. 'George' Bulman (no relation to the Civil Servant Major George Bulman) made the Hart's first flight on an unrecorded date in June 1928, powered by the F.XIB engine. It quickly ousted its rivals and began a brilliant career of service and diversified development. Moreover, Hawker's Sydney Camm scored another smash hit with his Hornet single-seat fighter, built to Hawker's own ideas following the appearance of the Hart (which had instantly rendered obsolete the current Air Ministry fighter specification of F.20/27). With serial *J9682*, the one-off Hornet was powered by an F.XIA engine, soon replaced by one of the first supercharged models, the F.XIS. Reaching 205 mph at full-throttle height of 13,000 ft the Hornet led to the Fury, a fighter almost as successful as the Hart. As far as Britain was concerned, the new F engine had made possible, first, a world-beating light bomber and, secondly, a fighter able to shoot it down.

In 1930 the new engine was officially named the Kestrel, and a completely new series of mark numbers was introduced. Marks I, II and III respectively had gear ratios of 0.632, 0.552 and 0.475; suffix letters A, B, MS and S respectively denoted compression ratio 6, compression ratio 7, medium supercharge and full supercharge. The A and B engines continued to have the carburettors between the cylinder blocks, while the supercharged engines had them repositioned upstream of the supercharger at the extreme lower rear of the engine. This moved the air inlet to the underside of the cowling, and it was realized that useful additional air could be rammed in by turning the inlet duct to face forwards, where it received the full force of the propeller slipstream. Rather remarkably, because it is such a basic idea, Rolls-Royce was able to patent the concept of an inlet diffuser in which the progressive increase in cross-section converts velocity into pressure.

After 1930 Kestrel variations and applications proliferated, and it was increasingly obvious that the company was in the aero-engine business not only permanently but also profitably. Later versions of the engine introduced a two-tone colour scheme that was to be seen on over 100,000 engines, the crankcase being polished aluminium and the cylinder blocks painted black. All the early Kestrels had a normal crankshaft speed of 2,250 rpm and typically weighed 820 lb, or 900 lb with supercharger. Typical ratings included 490 hp at sea level for a Mk IA, 480 hp up to 3,000 ft for a B-series, 525 hp at sea level and 500 hp at 3,000 ft for an MS and 480 hp at 11,400 ft for an FS.

Next came the Mks IV, V and VI, all fully supercharged and with respective reduction gear ratios of 0.632, 0.553 and 0.477, rated at 600 hp at 11,000 ft at the increased speed of 2,500 rpm. The Kestrel VII, VIII and IX were all medium supercharged, with the same gear ratios, and were rated at 630 hp at 3,000 ft. The X, XI and XII were unsupercharged, with compression ratio of 7, again with the same gear ratios, and were rated at 575 hp at sea level. In the IV, V and VI the supercharger was geared up to 8.8 times the crankshaft speed, but by 1934 Rolls-Royce had introduced a 9.4 gearing and restressed the Kestrel to deliver appreciably greater power, showing the first fruits of its experience with the R in winning the Schneider Trophy. This led to the final development stage of the engine in the Mks XIV, XV and XVI, all fully supercharged and with the same choice of gear ratios as in the IV, V and VI. Weighing 975 lb, these engines had a normal rating of 690 hp at

11,000 ft at 2,600 rpm, but in emergency were cleared to 3,000 rpm—the same as the design speed on the PV.12 which became the Merlin—at which the maximum power was 745 hp at 14,500 ft. The Mk XVI was installed in the Hawker Furies exported to Yugoslavia, which could reach 242 mph, some 20 mph faster than the RAF's Fury II which had the Kestrel VI.

The ultimate version of the Kestrel was the Mk XXX, specially modified and derated for the Miles Master I trainer. This engine was rated at 535 hp at 12,500 ft, and virtually all were produced by converting engines of earlier marks retired from squadron service in the old Hawker bi-planes. Most of the latter had unsupercharged engines, even the Harts of 39 Squadron which regularly patrolled the North-West Frontier at 18,000 ft. According to one pilot 'At this height the engine gave so little power it used almost no fuel, and a Hart would fly forever'. Certainly the Kestrel maintained the RR tradition of reliability. Many saw active service in World War 2, including Belgian Firefly II fighters and Fox III bombers, Hawker Hardies of RAF 237 Squadron in Abyssinia and the Audax trainers of 4 SFTS at Habbaniyah in the action against Raschid Ali in 1941.

Kestrel production just exceeded that of any of the World War 1 Rolls-Royce engines, the 4,750th and last being delivered in 1938. These engines were used in some eighty types of aircraft. My old boss, Squadron Leader H. F. King MBE, Editor of *Flight*, gave the following as the British military applications: Avro Antelope, Blackburn Nautilus and Sydney, Fairey IIIF, Fox I, II, III and IV, Firefly II and III, Fleetwing, Hendon II and S.9/30, Gloster C.6/28 and Gnatsnapper III, Handley Page Heyford, Hawker Hart, Hornet, Demon, Fury, Osprey, Nimrod, Audax, High-Speed Fury, Hardy, Hartbees (Hartebeeste) and Hind, Miles Master I and IA, Parnall Pipit, Phillips & Powis Trainer, Saunders-Roe

As the British aircraft industry had nothing remotely comparable to offer, Rolls-Royce bought a German He 70 as a streamlined aircraft in which to test engines. It proved ideal for the purpose. It was always powered by an engine of the Kestrel/Peregrine family.

A.10, Short Singapore II and III and Gurnard, Supermarine Scapa, Vickers 141, B.19/27 and 163, and Westland Wizard, the last-named being one of the rare mono-planes. There was just one civil application, in the Junkers Ju 86C-1 airliners of South African Airways, but these were soon converted to have P&W Hornet radials.

By 1934 it was obvious to the small band of Rolls-Royce test pilots that they needed a modern aircraft in which to test engines. Virtually every British installation was a fabric-covered biplane with so many struts and wires that tinkering with details of the engine installation made little difference to the speed. It was Cyril Lovesey, the first young graduate engineer to be taken on by Hives (in 1923), who suggested that the company should buy the latest and cleanest monoplane available, and the choice wisely fell on a Heinkel He 70. The company shipped a Kestrel to Heinkel's works at Rostock, and were told it would take two months to instal it in the He 70 airframe, which normally had a BMW VI. In those two months that Kestrel was used to make the maiden flights of two of the most important German warplanes of World War 2, the Junkers Ju 87 'Stuka' (in late March 1935) and the Messerschmitt Bf 109 (in May)! But Rolls-Royce found the He 70 a most valuable

acquisition, and with British civil registration *ADZF* it flew until the start of World War 2 with many different engine installations. Right at the start it opened the eyes of Rolls-Royce—and probably the British Air Ministry—by reaching 260 mph on the power of a Kestrel with six people on board, some 30 mph faster than the single-seat Fury fighter with a similar engine. Sadly, this aircraft was broken up in 1946.

It is not generally known that, once it was obvious that aero engines were going to be big business, Rolls-Royce began long-term research and built not only various single-cylinder rigs but also complete experimental engines. One such was a Kestrel with sleeve valves, basing the design of the sleeves and drive cranks on those laboriously being perfected by Fedden at Bristol. This engine ran satisfactorily, but was never flown. Another experimental Kestrel was a compression-ignition version, again with sleeve valves, running on heavy fuel oil and aimed at the long-range aircraft market. This did not fly either, but installed in a big racing car, *Flying Spray*, it set a new world diesel record at 159 mph. Previously the same car, then called *Speed of the Wind*, had set world records for everything from 1 to 48 hours, as well as the 500 to 10,000-km records, powered by a regular spark-ignition

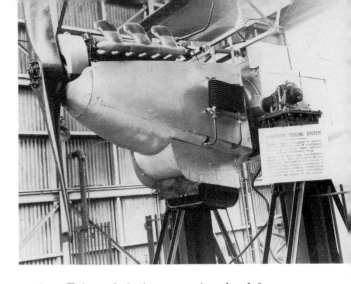

This test stand was used by Ellor to develop a composite cooling system. Steam and water from the Kestrel cylinder blocks was piped to an engine-driven separator from where the steam was passed to a dragless condenser in the mock-up wing above. Condensed water returned to the engine via an ejector. This led to the evaporatively-cooled Goshawk.

Kestrel. This engine is in the basement of the National Motor Museum at Beaulieu.

There were, however, developments of the Kestrel that found applications in aircraft, and these were, in chronological order, the Goshawk and Peregrine. The former was a Kestrel modified for steam cooling, also known as evaporative cooling. Soon after he joined the firm, in 1927, Ellor began working on alternatives to plain water cooling. One drawback to water is that the difference in temperature between the water in the radiator and the surrounding air can never be very much, and can never even approach the temperature difference between the air and a finned air-cooled cylinder head. Thus, the radiator for a water cooling circuit has to be extremely bulky and have high drag. In addition, the sheer weight of water needed can be formidable. Ellor reasoned that it might be possible to do much better if the water were to be allowed to boil. The radiator would then be replaced by a condenser, and turning the steam back into water would release 540 calories per gram, giving a theoretical heat-exchange rate many times greater than the mere cooling of water. The bulky radiator could be replaced either by a much smaller radiator or, preferably, by condensers which could be the actual skin of the aircraft and have no extra drag at all.

Before 1927 was out, Ellor was running a test rig at Derby which used an early F engine. As the first customer for the new engine, Fairey Aviation were involved from the start, and that company bought back from the Air Ministry a production Fox IA, *J9027*, which was quickly fitted with large condensers installed around the top and bottom surfaces of the upper centre section, the engine remaining one of the first F-series. The Air Ministry then decided to help fund the research, and paid for steam-cooling experiments with the original prototype Fox, which by this time had received the official serial of *J9515*.

By late 1930 sufficient experience had been gained for steam cooling to be considered the most likely next development in engines, as the main alternative to Fedden's air-cooled radials. When the Air Ministry drew up its classic F.7/30 specification for the next-generation fighter it stated that designers would be encouraged to use the Rolls-Royce Goshawk, which at the time was still known within Rolls-Royce only as the P.V.G. (Private-Venture Type G). The engine differed from the Kestrel only in details, and as far as possible the water coolant was circulated in the liquid state inside the engine by being kept under pressure, flashing into steam only on passing through a restrictor valve as it left the engine. Far more significant were the differences in the radiator installation, a Kestrel needing a conventional radiator and the Goshawk needing none, requiring instead flush condensers which were usually built into the wings.

Last of the Kestrels, the Mk XXX was the engine of the Master I trainer. Nearly all were rebuilds of earlier engines.

Beautifully finished in black, this early Goshawk has a side-entry supercharger. Many parts were unchanged from the Kestrel.

Though only 20 Goshawks were built they came in numerous versions (Mks 1, II, III, VI and VIII), all of them supercharged. This was a typical example, in this case with an up-draught carburettor.

The company's first sleeve-valve engine was this experimental supercharged Kestrel, run on the bench in about 1937. The cylinder blocks were totally new, with sparking plugs in the top of each cylinder. Large covers along each side gave access to the sleeve drives. The only previous high-power sleeve-valve engines, designed at Bristol, were air-cooled radials.

After 1932 Goshawk variations began to proliferate. The Goshawk I, II and III had reduction-gear ratios of 0.632, 0.553 and 0.477 (as in the Kestrels), and were all fully supercharged engines with a rating of 600 hp at 2,600 rpm at 12,000 ft and 650 hp at 5,000 ft. The weight was typically 975 lb, the same as for the Kestrel XVI. Goshawks VI, VII and VIII had the same gear ratios, but were medium-supercharged and rated at 660 hp at 2,600 rpm at 6,000 ft. Various types of Goshawk, not necessarily the officially preferred Mk III, were fitted to five F.7/30 contenders, by Blackburn, Bristol, Hawker, Supermarine and Westland. Goshawks were also fitted to the Gloster S.15/33 (TSR.38) torpedo bomber, the two-seat Westland-Hill Pterodactyl V tail-less fighter and the big Short R.24/31 'Knuckleduster' flying boat. A great deal of valuable experimental work was also done in the Hawker High-Speed Fury, *K3586*. Originally built on company charge, *K3586* was funded by the Air Ministry from just before its first flight in May 1933. Originally flown with a Kestrel and a tapered upper

wing with V-type interplane struts, it was later re-engined with a Goshawk III rated at 695 hp, cooled by condensers covering the entire leading edge of a new untapered upper wing, with N-type interplane struts. The condensers extended to 28% chord on the underside and to 50% on the wing's upper surface. Unlike the first Goshawk steam condensers, they exactly fitted the wing's aerofoil profile.

It was the prolonged flying of the fast and highly aerobatic High-Speed Fury and Hawker F.7/30 (known as the P.V.3) that finally 'cooked the goose' of the Goshawk, and only twenty engines were built. In all the surface condensing installations there had been problems with steam leakage and similar faults, which were doubtless rectifiable. The installed weight was found to be not very different from that of a water cooling system. In combat the condensers were clearly much larger targets than the traditional radiator, and this problem seemed fundamental. Not least, the system tended to work badly or not at all in inverted flight, the steam and water tending

Above *The shapely Hawker High-Speed Fury was originally flown with a Kestrel and a tapered upper wing with V interplane struts. It is seen here after being fitted with a Goshawk cooled by flush-fitting condensers along the leading edge of an untapered upper wing with N struts.*

Below *Though it had cylinders of the same size, the Peregrine differed from the Kestrel in most of its parts, and incorporated the results of a decade of experience.*

The most striking feature of the Peregrine was its downdraught carburettor. Its application, the Whirlwind, called for a full range of accessories, unlike most Kestrel-powered aircraft.

to swap places, and by 1935 it was finally obvious that evaporative cooling was a non-starter in the then-current state of the art. Specification F.7/30 was finally abandoned, and the RAF picked the conventional Gladiator biplane as a stop-gap while Hawker and Supermarine prepared entirely new monoplanes, far in advance of any official specification, to be powered by the new Rolls-Royce P.V.12 engine. Mention should, however, be made of the B.41 Goshawks, rated at 700 hp, which used an experimental ethylene glycol/water cooling system maintained under pressure, with a conventional (but small) radiator. This was to prove the key to the cooling systems used in World War 2.

There was one final development of the Kestrel, named the Peregrine. This was simply a completely modernized Kestrel designed in 1937. Many of its features were based on the Merlin, which by then was coming 'out of the wood', but a particularly unusual feature was the use of a down-draught carburettor, mounted above an improved supercharger. This left room round the lower part of the engine for hydraulic and air pumps, higher-capacity generators and other new auxiliaries required by the new breed of fighter. There was only the one mark of Peregrine, rated on 87-octane fuel at 860 hp at 2,850 rpm at 13,500 ft. On 100-octane it was cleared to 885 hp at 3,000 rpm at 15,000 ft, and it used high-pressure, high-temperature glycol/water cooling.

Peregrines powered the Westland Whirlwind, first flown in October 1938, and the Gloster F.9/37, both being twin-engined fighters with an excellent performance. In the event just two squadrons (137 and 263) were equipped with the Whirlwind, operating mainly in the ground attack role for a fairly brief period. This was no reflection on the Peregrine, which, after a shaky start, performed well in its role mainly at low level. The installations in the striking-looking Whirlwind were especially neat, and the radiators were arranged inside the centre section with ram inlets along the leading edge as in the later Mosquito. De Havilland and others were later to show that a properly installed liquid-cooling radiator could be made to give net forward thrust, acting as a low-temperature ramjet.

Chapter 4

BUZZARD AND R

The year 1927 was something of a turning point in the history of the company. Prior to that time Rolls-Royce's aero work had been so run down that it was on the point of disappearing altogether. Had there been investment analysts around in those days they would have based the company's prospects totally on its cars. After 1927 subtle changes steered the company very firmly back towards aero engines. The first new engine, the Kestrel, was the outcome of several years of planning. But in 1927 the company was persuaded to plan a bigger engine, with contrasting applications in mind.

The moving spirit behind this was none other than Colonel L.F.R. Fell, Assistant Director of Technical Development (Engines) at the Air Ministry. In the mid-1920s the company, largely under the far-sighted influence of Hives, had begun recruiting handpicked engineers to work chiefly on aero engines. First came Cyril Lovesey, followed by A. A. Rubbra, Ray Dorey and, after 1927, many more. It was mainly through the influence of Hives that in 1927 Fell himself was persuaded to join the firm, to head a previously non-existent aero sales and marketing staff. Based at the original West End car showroom in Conduit Street, Fell soon became the company's ambassador on the aero side, forming a vital

and experienced link with the Air Ministry and with various airlines and foreign governments.

One of his objectives was to see Britain win the Schneider Trophy three times in a row, which would mean for keeps. He saw with great clarity that this would be impossible unless someone could design a new engine, and he could see no company in a position to do this except Rolls-Royce. The only existing engines with a chance were the Napier Lion and Rolls-Royce Condor, and the latter was too old and unwieldy to form a good basis for a racing engine. Napier's management continued to be so shortsighted that they judged the Lion would just go on for ever. Even their chief experimental engineer, H. C. Tryon, was convinced the Lion could be kept ahead of the opposition, and the win of the Lion-engined S.5 in the 1927 contest strongly reinforced this view. Fell was one of the few who could see that this was not so. Future wins were likely to need the power of a wholly new, bigger and much more powerful engine than the Lion, which at around 1,400 hp in racing trim was stretched to the limit in 1927.

By the start of 1928 Fell had convinced Royce of the need for a new and highly rated engine for the 1929 Schneider Trophy race. There was never much doubt about the layout: not only did the company have far more experience with liquid-cooled 'V' engines, but such an arrangement fitted most nearly into the frontal area dictated by the smallest possible conventional cockpit. Royce and Rowledge spent some time studying the prospects for a 45° V-16, before deciding to design a new 60° V-12. The decision was taken in principle to go ahead, in the teeth of opposition from Managing Director Basil Johnson. The latter considered not only that Rolls-Royce was a car company, but he also vehemently opposed any involvement with racing, which he considered not a fit subject for gentlemen, and one that courted possible failure that would damage the company's image. This was the real turning-point of 1927, and it marked the company's acceptance of the fact that, alongside horseless carriages for the nobility, it would employ a growing team of brilliant engineers who would toil to put more power into the skies. This turning-point was in due course not only to bring Britain the Schneider Trophy but also, a decade later and somewhat more important, to prevent total military defeat and subjugation of Great Britain at the hands of the Nazis. Basil Johnson could not, of course, foresee any of this. After heated discussions he resigned in 1928, his place as MD being taken by A. F. (later Sir Arthur) Sidgreaves. Now everyone was pulling in the same direction.

Royce was eager to get ahead with the R, the racing engine, but so far he had no customer. In 1928 the Air Ministry was not prepared to fund such an engine, and one of the Schneider contenders, Gloster Aircraft, decided to stick with the Lion in their new monoplane Gloster VI. This left just the Supermarine company, builders of the winning S.5 of 1927. Their Chief Designer, Reginald Mitchell, was eager to see an alternative to the Lion appear, but was not prepared to recommend that his directors should pay to have one developed. In

November 1928 the Supermarine Aviation Works was taken over by Vickers (Aviation), and while this put the works on a much sounder footing, it also meant the adoption of a very keen commercial outlook. For a 1929 Supermarine Schneider contender to be built, someone would have to put up the money; certainly the Vickers board had no interest in funding an engine.

It says much for the reconstituted board of Rolls-Royce Ltd that in early 1928 they decided, as an essential foundation for the planned R engine, to go ahead with a V-12 of the same capacity and incorporating features expected to be needed in the R but aimed at ordinary aircraft. The Air Ministry put up a small sum to help pay for development, and encouraged the firm to expect some military orders, in particular to power the contenders for the M.1/30 torpedo-bomber specification. In early March 1928 Royce sanctioned the go-ahead on the new engine, which was at first called the H and later named the Buzzard.

Royce permitted the design to be handled at Derby, though as usual under his close personal control of design details. Partly because of the vastly increased strength of the design staff—compared with the early 1920s the design team at Derby numbered ten instead of two—the H was drawn with what seemed amazing rapidity, and construction of the prototype engine went ahead under Hives day and night. Already 'Hs' was putting into practice his favourite sayings, later to become famous, of 'There's no fun like work', and—when the pressure was really on—'Work until it hurts!' The result was that the H was completed in three months, and sailed through its first Type Test without failure. The next day, 13 June 1928, Royce sent almost the only message of praise anyone could remember. His telegram read 'WORMALD, BAILEY, ROYCAR DERBY. EXTREMELY PLEASED WITH EXCELLENT WORK DONE INTRODUCING LARGER AERO ENGINE SO QUICKLY

THANKS TO YOUR EFFORTS AND THOSE ASSISTING. ROYCE.' Noticeably, while he addressed this to R. W. Harvey-Bailey, he did not include Rowledge.

The H, or Buzzard, closely resembled a Kestrel scaled up to a bore of 6 in and stroke of 6.6 in, giving a capacity of 2,239 cu in or 36 litres. As it was planned from the start to be the basis for a racing engine it was made particularly robust. The most important new feature was that, in addition to the usual 24 long through-bolts (four per cylinder) holding each cylinder block to the crankcase, the cylinder blocks were extended in the form of a strong vertical web down each side of each cylinder, adding to rigidity. At its lower end each web terminated in left and right flanges called a saddle, held down to the crankcase by two extra studs. This greatly added to the engine's strength and was expected to make possible a future bmep far beyond anything to be attempted with the original Buzzard. In addition, all other mechanical parts were made so that in the R it would be possible to increase their strength readily where this might become necessary.

The Buzzard I, II and III were all medium-supercharged engines, with a modest supercharger impeller able to be used to the full to boost take-off power, the engines differing in having reduction-gear ratios of 0.632, 0.553 and 0.477 respectively, as in the Kestrel. Normal power rating was 825 hp at 2,000 rpm at sea level; maximum power was either 925 or 955 hp at 2,300 rpm at sea level, and dry weight varied from 1,460 to 1,540 lb.

The engine was tested in a Horsley, and later in three re-engined Blackburn Iris flying boats. Production Buzzards were fitted to the four Blackburn Perths, the largest biplane flying boats ever used by the RAF, based on the re-engined Irises. Prototype installations were made in an even bigger flying boat, the Short S.14 Sarafand built to specification R.6/28, which had six Buzzard

IIIs in tandem pairs. Other engines powered the three M.1/30 contenders, built by Blackburn, Handley Page and Vickers, but this specification was cancelled. Buzzards were also retrofitted into the Short Singapore I and used in the Short K.F.I, but no production ensued. According to historian Schlaifer 'Less than fifty production engines were sold altogether, 32 of them to the Japanese', but the actual figure appears to have been 100 (see table), most going to Japan to power large biplane fighters and bombers. One went to Canada to replace the BMW engine in a Ju 52 which for many years was flown by Rod Grattan, a former Rolls-Royce premium apprentice.

Despatches of new Buzzards

1928	H-MS	1
1929	H-10MS	7
1930	H-10MS	1
	H-12MS	5
1931	Buzzard IIMS	7
	Buzzard IIIMS	15
1932	Buzzard II	13
	Buzzard IIMS	17
	Buzzard IIIMS	6
1933	Buzzard II	3
	Buzzard IIMS	19
	Buzzard IIIMS	1
1934	Buzzard IIMS	5

This was a rather poor reward, because the Buzzard was a fine engine. In some aircraft, such as the Short Singapore III, tandem pairs of Kestrels were used instead of single Buzzards. The engine never had any appeal to the small airline market. Perhaps the most ironic thing about the Buzzard is that the winner of the 1929 Schneider Trophy, Flying Officer H.R.D. Waghorn, was killed two years later in one of the Buzzard-engined Horsley test-beds.

Throughout 1928 the planned R hung fire, but suddenly in November the Air Ministry announced that Britain was to

It is just possible to read on the nameplate of this Buzzard 'IIMS . . . . No 97', indicating that it was one of the final batch of five engines of 1934.

take part in the 1929 Schneider Trophy race, with Air Ministry backing for the RAF High-Speed Flight, the actual competitors. Maj G.P. Bulman, Deputy Director R&D (Engines), asked Royce whether the R could be produced in time, and received a positive assurance that it could and would. Immediately, Royce summoned Hives, Rowledge, Lovesey and Ellor to visit him at West Wittering. By this time his own team had grown to comprise Elliott, Charlie Jenner, Bill Hardy, Ivan Evernden, Bernard Day and 'junior' Don Eyre. All were on parade to greet the team-leaders from Derby, and a grand council of war was held on the lawn at Elmstead and on West Wittering's sandy beach. They had with them engineering drawings of the Buzzard and project drawings of the R, but Royce again got out his stick and drew in the sand. The first drawing was of the streamlined nose of Mitchell's planned S.6 seaplane, to see how best a V-12 could it into it. One part, the reduction gear, fell into place very neatly because the redesigned gear to handle double the Buzzard's power naturally had

longer gear-teeth, and this pulled out the external shape of the gearbox to suit the cowling lines. Gear ratio was 0.6. It was also clear that the valve covers at the top of each cylinder block would not only project far out from the fuselage cowling line but would themselves need to be profiled for minimum drag. In the event the front portion of each block was tapered in both height and width, by Rubbra.

Ellor was clearly going to play a key role in the R because, under Rowledge and Lovesey, he was going to plan the giant supercharger which was to be by far the most important new feature and the key to the R's power. Royce traced in the sand the arrangement of a totally new double-sided impeller, to handle the greatest possible airflow within the given frontal area (a year or two later young Flying Officer Frank Whittle was to choose the same kind of compressor for his planned turbojet, for the same reason). Rowledge had drawn a double-sided supercharger for the stillborn Eagle XVI, but this had never been tested. Now the pressure was on in earnest.

A Buzzard IIIMS, showing the carburettor inlet facing to the right. This forms an interesting comparison with the photograph on a later page of the first Griffon, an engine in many respects almost identical.

Morover, the Kestrel had shown the advantage of using a ram type of air inlet, and for the R a gigantic ram inlet duct was located between the cylinder blocks, where it would get the benefit of every bit of aircraft forward speed and propeller slipstream. At the rear of the blocks the mighty duct curved downwards around the rear of the engine to connect underneath with the carburettor, which was integrally cast with the casing of the impressive supercharger. The mixture then flowed through front and rear branches to the front and rear of the impeller. Then, by now compressed to a higher pressure than ever before in any aero engine, it left the supercharger via a single pipe which split into left and right manifolds feeding the inner sides of the cylinder blocks. This left the outer faces of the blocks clear for the open exhausts.

The blocks themselves were altered in many important details. The cylinders, pistons and rings were all modified to breathe more easily, transmit higher powers and run at high bmep without detonation. One detail was that the sparking plugs were installed at an oblique angle. The connecting rods, of the fork and blade type, were strengthened, as was the crankshaft. The crankcase was largely redesigned to transmit much greater loads. Anything not subject to high stress, such as various auxiliary castings and covers, was made in lightweight magnesium alloy, and most of the auxiliaries were rearranged to fit inside the tight cowling lines with minimum drag. It was decided to choose 100 per cent benzole as the fuel, and pure castor oil as the lubricant.

It took December 1928 and much of January to design the R and begin testing vital components, including the first single-cylinder rig. Full go-ahead for manufacture of eight engines was not received until February; then Hives and Lovesey drove the team at Derby as they had never been driven before, and the first R was started up on the test bench at Derby a mere three months later on 14 May 1929. Testing was in the capable hands of Vic Halliwell, assisted by Ray Dorey. On the very first run the first R, which weighed 1,530 lb, recorded a power of 1,545 hp at 2,750 rpm.

This was an excellent start, but Royce held off sending a congratulatory telegram lest anyone should think the job was done. From Hives downwards everyone at Derby knew this was only the beginning, and Royce had proposed to the Air Ministry that the design objective should be a one-hour non-stop run at 1,800 hp—well beyond anything possible with the Lion. All went reasonably well at the start, the problems mostly being quickly rectifiable. Gradually the power and running endurance increased, but as 1,800 hp was neared the engine began to show clear signs of distress. Two of the forked connecting rods fractured, and a panic redesign followed to increase the strength of this component and also improve both the big-end and main bearings. More intractable was burning of the almost white-hot exhaust valves, and sooting up of plugs which occasionally caused violent misfires and prevented the engine from being opened up to high power at all.

In August the objective of 1,800 hp for one hour was at last achieved, but it was a fluke. Nobody had confidence in repeating it, and most runs ran into trouble after about twenty minutes. With just a month to go, F. R. Banks, of the Associated Ethyl Co, was consulted. He was unable to do all he would have liked in four short weeks, but by diluting the benzole with a light-cut Romanian leaded petrol he was able to make a big improvement, the mix being 78 per cent benzole and 22 per cent petrol, with 2.5 cc per gallon of TEL (tetra-ethyl lead) added to inhibit knocking. This gave a power of 1,900 hp at 2,900 rpm, with clean running which could be maintained for an hour with some confidence.

According to Alec Harvey-Bailey, 'It was only by watching the exhaust flames and knowing the sound of the engine that testers could prevent expensive failures by shutting down on the instant that some change was noted, and before it showed on the instruments. The noise was christened "the Derby Hum", and such were the pressures of work that when an emergency arose cinemas would flash a notice on their screens asking any experimental employees to report for work, while local pubs would be checked to get people back on the job. It is interesting to note how the people of Derby, knowing what was at stake, accepted with relatively little complaint the day and night testing of these racing engines with open exhausts'.

In fact, the noise exceeded anything previously imagined. Not only was there the deafening R running at full throttle, but in front there was a Kestrel driving a blower to create a 400-mph ram effect at the inlet, a second Kestrel blowing air through giant pipes to cool the sump, and a third Kestrel out in the yard driving a propeller to blow away fumes. All four engines ran at full power on open exhaust! This was the first of countless special rigs subsequently built by Rolls-Royce to test engines under simulated operational conditions.

As the key to the R's performance, the mighty supercharger was expected to prove a major challenge, but in fact it gave little trouble. Ellor planned it to be right at the limit of what was considered attainable in 1929, and actually achieved a pressure ratio of 1.80 with an efficiency of just over 61%. Later, after much further development, a pressure ratio of 1.92 was reached, at 62% efficiency. (In parentheses, this underscores the almost unbelievable design target of Frank Whittle, who comes into the story at Chapter 7, who aimed at a pressure ratio of 4 and efficiency of 75 or more per cent in his first turbojet.) Suffice to say the pumping ability of the supercharger of the R was approximately double that of any other aero-engine supercharger of its day, and the R was the first engine to run at a high supercharged boost pressure at sea level. This imposed a severe strain on every part.

Even the sparking plugs, which were

always Lodge type X170, were tested more severely in the actual engine than in any special test rig the makers could devise. It became standard practice to run all plugs in the engine on the Derby bed, and then send them back to Lodge, fit them with new outer bodies and then deliver them to the race HQ at RAF Calshot, on the corner of Spithead and Southampton Water. Even the BTH or Watford magnetos had to be specially stressed and, because of the vibration, every nut and bolt had to be retained by lock-wire or a split-pin. Many structural parts of the engine were 'lifed' as a result of experience, and were scrapped at this life even if they appeared flawless; this was found to avoid a lot of problems. It was generally reckoned that getting ready for a single Schneider race was the equivalent of five years of 'normal' engine development, but the comparison is vague because the pace was quickening all the time on all engines.

On the testbed the R drove a large Froude dynamometer to measure brake horsepower. The installed engine drove a Fairey-Reed metal propeller with two blades set at an extremely coarse pitch angle, and a run with the propeller was always made before an engine was delivered. This propeller naturally resulted in a very long take-off run for the aircraft, during which the violent torque reaction caused the left float to try to dig deep into the water, making the machine curve to the left. To alleviate the torque Mitchell put all the fuel in the right-hand float. Oil was carried in the fin and circulated to the engine via the banks of steel pipes along the sides of the fuselage which served as the oil radiators. Like all the later Schneider aircraft, the S.6 was a tricky machine demanding great pilot skill and constant attention.

Supermarine built two S.6 seaplanes for the 1929 race, *N247* and *248*. Rolls-Royce delivered four flight examples of the R engine. The company also built a special lorry to carry engines between Derby and the Supermarine works at Southampton or the High-Speed Flight at Calshot. Based on

Though derived from the Buzzard, the Rolls-Royce R for the 1929 Schneider Trophy race was a very different engine! It was shaped to fit the nose of the S.6 seaplane, which in turn was designed by Mitchell to fit tightly round the engine.

a Phantom II car chassis, this truck was soon dubbed 'Phantom of the night' by the media, because it was seldom seen at anything less than 75 mph, even with a massive R engine on board. It became the objective of almost every police constable along the route, who personally made it their intention to prosecute the driver for speeding, but the Phantom was never caught! No other motorist was ever known to stay the pace for long, not with testers of the calibre of Charlie Lee at the wheel.

The first S.6 was completed in July 1929, and quickly showed in practice that it was much faster than either the S.5 or the Macchi and Fiat seaplanes of the Italian team. The actual race was run on 7 September 1929. Flying Officer R.L.R. Atcherley clipped a corner and was disqualified, but Flying Officer H.R.D. Waghorn completed the race successfully— indeed, having lost count, he flew one lap too many and ran out of fuel. All was well, and he won easily at 328.63 mph. Only then was he told of the panic of the night before. During routine inspection of the R, newly installed for the race in *N247*, some aluminium was found on one of the plugs. The piston in that cylinder was obviously scored and 'picking up' and would never last the race. The rules prohibited an engine change, but it was permissible to change a part, with the engine remaining installed. It seemed just possible to change the offending piston, though it meant removing the cylinder block. A large number of Rolls-Royce employees had come to watch the race. Hives and Lovesey dashed around Southampton, winkling out the skilled fitters from hotels and pubs all over the city. Taken to Calshot in groups, they formed a kind of shock-troops team, which toiled non-stop through the night. Next morning at 8.00 Lovesey started up the R and it ran sweetly. Waghorn's son still has the failed piston.

Later Atcherley made amends by setting World Records in *N248* at 332 mph for the 50 km circuit and 331 mph for 100 km. On 12 September Squadron Leader A. H. Orlebar AFC raised the World Speed Record in *N247* to 357.7 mph. Soon afterwards

Externally the 1931 R engine did not differ greatly from the first R built two years previously, but hardly any parts were common. The intensity of effort put into the 1931 engine has perhaps never been surpassed by any development team.

Royce was awarded a baronetcy, though it was recognized that this reflected a lifetime's work and not just 1929.

With two consecutive wins it was clear that to Great Britain it all depended on the third race, in 1931. But Britain had elected a Labour government which, despite much pressure, resolutely announced that it would not fund a British entry at a time of global depression; the money, it said, could be put to much more important purposes. There the matter might have rested had not outspoken Lady Houston put up £100,000 of her own money, saying 'Every true Briton would rather sell his last shirt than admit that England could not afford to defend herself before all comers'. Once again there was no time to do a complete job, so while Mitchell designed the S.6B Rolls-Royce strove to wring much more power from the already highly rated R.

Beyond question, the effort put in by Rolls-Royce for the 1931 race surpassed the entire effort of design and development of the original R in 1929. There was no time to develop a new engine, but though it looked little changed externally the 1931 R was almost a new engine inside. Every stressed part was redesigned and stiffened or strengthened. The ram air inlet was enlarged, a new carburettor fitted, and a revised supercharger run at much higher speed, gained partly by increasing the step-up gear ratio and partly by running the whole engine at 3,200 rpm instead of 2,900. Boost pressure rose from a peak of 13.5 lb/sq in in 1929 to 17.5 lb in 1931. The crankshaft was redesigned for greater strength and with integral balance weights, and the crankcase was greatly strengthened (the load on the central main bearing due solely to centrifugal and inertia forces exceeded nine long tons, 20,160 lb). The connecting rods were completely redesigned, and instead of fork-and-blade were made of the same articulated type as in the World War 1 engines in order to get a full lubricated bearing surface on each rod. The exhaust valves were cooled by sodium in the hollow stems, and there was endless trouble with

Full ram effect was used to feed air down the huge upper duct of the R engine, and thence to the front and rear of the enormous double-sided supercharger. (At about the same time a certain Flying Officer Whittle was designing independently a compressor to handle ten times the airflow with more than double the pressure ratio and with efficiency raised from 62 to 79 per cent!)

valve springs. The first of twelve new engines came out in March 1931 at a weight of 1,630 lb, with the target being a one-hour run at 2,300 hp. Nothing like such performance had ever been attempted; it was the first time any engine made by man had exceeded 1 hp for each cubic inch of capacity.

One of the 1929 R engines had been used in Sir Henry Segrave's speedboat *Miss England II*, and this unfortunately crashed, killing Segrave and Rolls-Royce's Vic Halliwell. Testing of the R accordingly passed to the energetic Ray Dorey, and before long all twelve of the 1931 engines had been built, and often four were running in Derby at once! According to the magazine *Flight*, 'The oil consumption rose to terrific figures, partly owing to great quantities lost through the breathers. On one 25-min run the oil consumption was at the rate of 112 gallons an hour; the test house was a sight after it! By weeks of work on combinations of scraper rings and crankcase breathers, by modification of the scavenging system, and by the final adoption of a deeper sump which filled all the available space in the machine, the consumption was reduced to about 14 gallons an hour for the final race engines. It also effected a considerable reduction in the oil temperature rise through the engine; oil entered at about 80°C and came out at about 140°C. The oil remained pure castor'.

For many weeks, all kinds of trouble would strike within about twenty minutes. Even at Supermarine, where the two slightly bigger S.6B seaplanes (*S1595* and *1596*) were fast taking shape, there was terrible difficulty with the water and oil-cooling radiators. The former covered the wings and upper surfaces of the lengthened floats, while the oil radiators, of a much more effective design, filled the sides of the stressed-skin fuselage. Water leaked from all over the system, and later in 1931 test flying was to show the need for even greater cooling surface, and 'patches' were added.

Rapidly the final race day of 13 September 1931 approached, but on 13 August the redesigned R had still not demonstrated its one-hour run, though plenty had exceeded the half-hour. A few days before the August Bank Holiday a one-hour run was attempted; after 34 minutes the crankshaft broke. It was found that this shaft had exceeded its design life, so a new shaft was put into another engine and a second attempt made. This engine recorded 2,360 hp for 58 minutes; then it too broke its crankshaft! Rowledge decided the only solution was to leave more metal by boring out smaller holes through the journals and crankpins. Bob Coverley, head of the special R building department, drove that night to English Steel Corporation in Sheffield and saw the manager. The latter got a forging team together and, by working non-stop right through the holiday period, Rolls-Royce got new crankshaft forgings, the first being rushed to Derby for machining on the last day of the holiday. Within a week an R had run an hour at full throttle, logging 2,350 hp.

Thus, with days to spare, a reliable R was ready at a power sufficient to demolish the opposition. It was an anti-climax that the rival teams were delayed, and on 13 September the coveted trophy was won outright by Flight Lieutenant J. N. Boothman who had a walkover win at 340.08 mph. The original S.6s, modified with more fuel and extra cooling surfaces, were available as S.6As but were not needed. The other S.6B, *1596*, was to be used for a speed record attempt on what Hives called 'the mark that matters': 400 mph. But on 16 September Flight Lieutenant G. H. Stainforth was landing after testing a propeller when his heel caught in the rudder bar, and *1596* slewed wildly and sank (later being salvaged).

The race had been won on 70 per cent benzole, 20 per cent straight-run California petrol and 10 per cent methanol, with 3.3 cc per gallon of TEL, giving an octane number

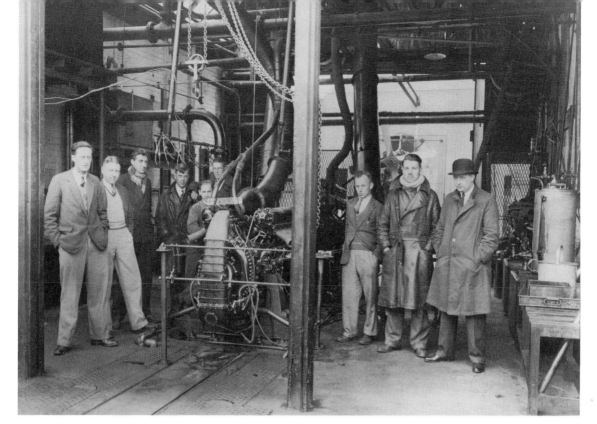

A famous picture of the 1931 R on the testbed, with (from left) Stewart Tresilian (supercharger), Bob Young (tech assistant), Stan Orme (tester), Frank Nicholls (tester), Bill Thacker (lad on the job), Charlie Conway (ram-effect Kestrel), George Parkin (performance), Ray Dorey (test manager), and Rod Banks (Associated Ethyl Co).

of around 92. Hives asked Rod Banks if he would brew a special cocktail for the 'sprint' engine to attack the speed record. This record attempt was done in the teeth of opposition from the Air Ministry, which demanded that the High-Speed Flight should clear out of Calshot and hand the base back to the regular flying-boat squadron. Banks and Dorey mixed a high-alcohol fuel and increased the blower ratio to give around 2,800 hp, but, after only a minute or two, cylinder hold-down bolts began to fail! The final sprint fuel was 60 per cent methanol, 30 per cent benzole and 10 per cent acetone, plus 5.0 cc per gallon of TEL. It was then found that the correct carburettor jet size demanded a fuel flow beyond the capacity of the fuel pump. That night the man who cut the gears was located at home, brought to work and set up machines to cut fresh high-ratio gears.

The fuel tests were thus completed in 48 hours, but a vast amount of work was still needed on *S1595*, the serviceable S.6B, because the strange fuel was an excellent solvent of paints and sealing compounds. All kinds of clever dodges were resorted to to get the sprint engine started, run up, and then into the air without coughing or sooting up. At last on 29 September Stainforth set the mark of 407.5 mph, with liquid fuel pouring from the exhausts every time he throttled back!

The 1931 R engines saw much use in other duties. Sir Malcolm Campbell used them in his *Bluebird* land-speed-record car of 1935 and in his *Bluebird* water-speed-record boat. Sir George Eyston used a pair in his giant LSR car *Thunderbolt*. In each case the record was raised repeatedly.

Chapter 5

MERLIN AND GRIFFON

It is a matter of some significance that, whereas in 1925 Air Marshal Trenchard and the Air Ministry had exhorted Rolls-Royce to build a new engine for the RAF's combat aircraft, in the 1930s the Air Staff and Air Ministry took no action in this regard. It was left to Sir Henry Royce, Hives and others to express unease at the situation. By 1932 the Kestrel was beginning to look too small, and fundamentally dated. Though it was an excellent engine, selling like the proverbial hot cakes, Rolls-Royce recognized that future warplanes would need more power than the Kestrel could give. A new engine, taking into account all the many lessons learned during the development of the R, could start off at not less than 750 hp and later be developed to give 1,000 hp, but running on normal service fuels and with good reliability over a long service life.

It was to be a matter of the most profound importance that, lacking interest from the customer, the sick and ageing Royce decided around October 1932 that the company should go ahead on its own initiative with a new engine for service use, bigger than the Kestrel but smaller than the Buzzard, and incorporating as much R technology as possible. It was called the P.V.12 (from Private Venture 12-cylinder). From the start it was agreed that the engine should be a 60° V-12, broadly similar to the company's existing engines, with minimum frontal area, a supercharger and geared drive. Cylinder bore and stroke were selected at 5.4 in and 6.0 in respectively, giving a capacity of 1,649 cu in (27 litres).

There is some doubt about whether a conventional upright design was selected in parallel with an unconventional inverted one, but there is no doubt that a full-scale mock-up was made of the latter. Elliott and Rowledge agreed that the inverted layout offered numerous advantages and, so far as they could tell, no drawbacks. Royce followed their arguments and eventually agreed. In a single-engined fighter an inverted engine offered better pilot view, both in the air and on the ground, as well as putting the plugs, valve gear and other maintenance-intensive items within reach of a man standing on the ground. There were also technical advantages, but when Rolls-Royce sought the opinion of the aircraft manufacturers the latter were generally hostile—perhaps because they were technically illiterate where engines were concerned, and unable to assess the pros and cons. They regarded the inverted engine as 'upside down'. There is no doubt that a German delegation saw the mock-up of the inverted engine, and the story later gained credence that this influenced the design of the DB 600 and Jumo 210 and their successors which powered the

Luftwaffe. Elliott later said it was all a ploy to mislead the Germans!

Whether this is the case or not, the fact remains that by the late 1930s the inverted V-12 was universally regarded as a Germanic style of engine. Had this not been the case, the author believes there is a chance that later Merlins, and unquestionably the larger Griffon, might have adopted this configuration. As it was, any notion of 'copying the Germans' soon ruled out such a possibility.

The P.V.12 therefore went ahead at the beginning of 1933 as a conventional upright engine, and drawings poured from the office at West Wittering, with some parts designed at Derby under the now ailing Rowledge. Apart from its larger size the new engine differed from the Kestrel chiefly in that the crankcase and cylinder blocks were all one enormous casting, with separate left and right cylinder-head blocks bolted on. Other changes were the use of a double-helical reduction gear and a compromise 'composite' cooling system using both water and steam and thus incorporating a radiator and a condenser. Almost all the drawings had been issued to the shops by April, and with them came Elliott, who decided his rightful location was now Derby, as Chief Engineer. Royce was sinking fast, and he died on 22 April 1933, the day the last P.V.12 drawing was completed. It was the end of the initial chapter of the Rolls-Royce story. His design cell, which had already shrunk, was closed forthwith and all staff moved to Derby.

The company funded two P.V.12 prototype engines, and the first made its first run on 15 October 1933. At this point the company agreed to accept the Air Ministry's offer to finance development, as a result of which the engine received the name Merlin, perpetuating the choice of the names of birds of prey (many later users of the engine thought it was named after the mythical wizard). From the very start there

was trouble, which multiplied and threatened even the existence of this particular design. Part of the trouble was inability to make sufficiently accurate double-helical gears, and the answer was to switch to simple straight-tooth spur gears. More intractable was persistent failure of the cylinder water jackets. Various strengthening features were resorted to, but the giant castings kept cracking, and there was increasing pressure to go for separate castings for the upper crankcase and cylinder blocks, especially as any major mechanical failure resulted in scrapping a large casting that took a lot of time and money to replace.

The two P.V.12 prototypes had separate pancake heads, each with four parallel valves. Years earlier, before 1927, Elliott had designed a new car engine with a so-called ramp head, or penthouse head, with two flat roofs of unequal width and angle, and with the two inlet valves on the inner side of the head inclined at an angle of about 45°. The objective with the car engine had been rapid turbulent mixing and shortened flame travel. It had worked well, and it worked well during testing of single Merlin-size cylinders. The Merlin B, with ramp head, was authorized in July 1934, and in the same month the original P.V.12 at last succeeded in passing a Type Test. This engine weighed 1,177 lb, and had an international (30-minute climb) rating of 790 hp at 12,000 ft at 2,500 rpm. Take-off power was 625 hp at 2,500 rpm. Meanwhile, the other P.V.12, with identical features and the same rated boost pressure of 2 lb/sq in, was installed in test Hawker Hart *K3036*, with plain stub exhausts, a rear radiator under the cockpits, and driving a four-blade wooden propeller. This aircraft made the engine's first flight on 21 February 1935. Ronnie Harker considered it the fastest-climbing aircraft in Britain, and beaten for speed only by the special High-Speed Fury *K3586*.

Design of the Merlin B was completed in

The earliest known photograph of a Merlin, showing the eleventh Merlin C installed in the Hawker F.36/34 High-Speed Monoplane in spring 1935 (still with a Vickers gun beside the cockpit). The author is indebted to Francis K. Mason and Chris Ashworth for this rare picture.

October 1934, and two B engines were ready for test in February 1935. It was found that they delivered 950 hp under conditions equivalent to 11,000 ft altitude. After fifty hours' running the decision was taken to make the crankcase and cylinder blocks as three separate castings, the cylinder blocks having separate ramp-type heads bolted on. The first two Merlin Cs with these features were on test in April 1935. By this time the Merlin had been chosen for several important new aircraft. Hawker and Supermarine had abandoned plans for Goshawk-engined monoplane fighters and designed totally new and very much better aircraft powered by the Merlin.

They were not asked to do this by the Government. Indeed, the author delights in a letter sent to the Air Ministry by Sir Robert McClean, Vickers' aviation director: 'After unfruitful discussions with the Air Ministry, my opposite number in Rolls-Royce, the late A. F. Sidgreaves and I, decided that the two companies together should themselves finance the building of such an aircraft. The Air Ministry was informed of this decision, and were told that in no circumstances would any technical member of the Air Ministry be consulted or allowed to interfere with the designer.' Thus, the immortal Spitfire was born.

The eleventh Merlin C powered the Hawker F.36/34 High-Speed Monoplane, prototype of the Hurricane, on its first flight on 6 November 1935. The engine gave persistent trouble and was replaced successively by Merlin C No 15, No 17 and then No 19. Carburation was poor, and mechanical failures included pistons and supercharger bearings. The Supermarine 300 fighter, prototype of the Spitfire, flew on 5 March 1936. Its Merlin C was beautifully cowled, but, as in the Hawker aircraft, drove only a Watts fixed-pitch wooden propeller. An unusual feature was that the coolant radiator was under the right wing, the smaller oil cooler being under the left wing. It has been said that Mitchell was forced to put the radiator there because of earlier plans to use steam condensers, but his successor, Joe Smith, told the author this was nonsense. It was a good low-drag position, and Mitchell deliberately put the heavy radiator under the right wing to help offset torque,

The earliest photograph of a Merlin possessed by Rolls-Royce shows a production Mk I destined for a Fairey Battle. This had the ramp-type cylinder head.

in the same way he had put fuel only in the right floats of the Schneider racers.

It had been hoped that the Merlin C would lead straight to a production engine, but as bench and flight testing continued it became increasingly evident that the engine was still in serious difficulty. The results of single-cylinder testing clearly did not read across to the complete engine, and the troubles became ever more varied. The ramp heads cracked, in both manufacture and running, and the predicted performance was not attained in practice. Local detonation caused severe erosion, and distortion led to exhaust-valve failures. In May 1935 a C attempted the civil fifty-hour type test, but failed. Meanwhile even the original P.V.12 in the Hart gave serious difficulty with the composite cooling system, and after eight hours of flying the whole scheme was abandoned and replaced by use of pure ethylene glycol coolant with no boiling. A high-temperature glycol system had been pioneered by the US Army from 1923. Indeed, Rolls-Royce tried to use it on the 1929 S.6 seaplane, but the hot glycol leaked past rivets in the wing-surface radiators.

Small differences led to the Merlin E and F, and in December 1935 an E at last passed the civil type test with a rating of 955 hp at 2,600 rpm at 11,000 ft, with maximum power of 1,045 hp at the full design speed of 3,000 rpm at 12,000 ft. Another E was submitted to the military 100-hour test in March 1936 but failed. Things were rapidly reaching crisis proportions, because not only the Hurricane but also the Fairey Battle bomber were being held up. The first flight of the prototype Battle was delayed until 10 March 1936, when *K4303* at last flew on the power of the 25th Merlin F, the latest standard, driving a Fairey-Reed fixed-pitch metal propeller. At about the same time Hucknall's test Horsley, *S1436*, began flying with a Merlin E driving an imported Hamilton Standard three-blade variable-pitch propeller of the kind for which de Havilland had obtained a British licence. This 'bracket-type' propeller used oil pressure to rotate the blades into fine pitch against the pull of bobweights which forever tried to return them to coarse. Early examples had just two settings, but by 1936 a CSU (constant-speed unit) was available.

Many aircraft were used in flight development of the P.V.12 and Merlin. Two were Horsleys, the other aircraft being S1436 which did not have an enclosed cockpit for the observer. Here J8611 has a Merlin I driving a Hamilton metal propeller.

It was clear that, from having led the world in V-P propellers in 1922, Britain was now desperately behind other countries. In 1936 Rolls-Royce linked with Bristol to form the Rotol company, between Cheltenham and Gloucester. The initial hub, with internal cylinder, did not suit the low frontal area of the Merlin. For the Merlin a new hub was designed by A. A. Rubbra, who registered the patents. His hydraulic hub, with two-way 35° pitch change applied by means of an external cylinder in front of the blade roots, was a classically simple design which was later made in tens of thousands. The first Rotol propeller was made in the Derby Experimental Department and tested on a Merlin in the original hangar on Sinfin Moor—today the site of the company's vast headquarters.

There were other big changes in the mid-1930s. From 1934 the Flight Test Department at Hucknall grew rapidly, and took on an extra test pilot each alternate year under Chief Test Pilot Captain R. T. Shepherd. Their work diversified, but for another decade the Merlin dominated all else. In 1935 Colonel T. B. Barrington returned to the firm as Chief Designer. In 1936, following the death of Wormald, Hives was appointed General Manager, with a seat on the board. This was an appointment of immense significance. Hs had acquired towering stature, in many ways like Churchill, and he was the perfect leader to drive the great company through the stern test of the war that he could see coming. One of the first things he did was to separate the chassis and aero work, and plan for a vast expansion in future aero production. The stately and courteous Elliott was appointed Chief Engineer of the new Aero Engine Division.

As an emergency solution Hs decided to replace the separate ramp head with a Kestrel-type one-piece block scaled up to Merlin size. Traditional flat heads were to be used with all valves parallel. Drawings for this version, the Merlin G, were issued in May 1936. It was realized in advance that the space between the cylinders was too small to permit reliable sealing between the liner and head. Meanwhile, such was the pressure to begin deliveries that the Air Ministry agreed to buy the imperfect Merlin F (ramp head) as the Merlin I, and from July 1936 a total of 180 were delivered for the Battle Mk I. The official Type Test rules were relaxed to permit the replacement of valves, but despite this the Merlin I could not get through the test until November 1936, at a rating of 975 hp at 2,600 rpm at 12,500 ft. In contrast, the G sailed through a Type Test a month earlier, in October 1936, and this followed the Merlin I on the production line as the Merlin II, the first being delivered in August 1937.

Hawker Aircraft had received its first, massive (600 aircraft), order for the Hurricane I in June 1936. The company was advised of termination of the Merlin I, and accordingly had to effect complete redesign of the engine mountings, cowlings, controls and coolant header tank. Thus the first production Hurricane, with Merlin II, did not fly until 12 October 1937, but from then on output was high. As in the Battle, the first Hurricanes had plain slit exhausts, but by mid-1938 these had been replaced by triple ejector exhausts giving considerable (about 150 lb) useful thrust.

It is appropriate at this point briefly to describe the Merlin I and II. Both weighed about 1,335 lb. Take-off power was 890 hp at 2,850 rpm, international rating 950/990 hp at 2,600 rpm at 12,250 ft, and maximum (combat) power on 87-octane fuel, 1,030 hp at 3,000 rpm at 16,250 ft. The main elements comprised the sump, the upper crankcase (incorporating the rear half of the reduction-gear housing, unlike the previous engines), the reduction-gear front cover, the one-piece cylinder blocks, the supercharger front casing, and the supercharger

rear casing incorporating the carburettors and inlet duct. The hollow crankshaft was carried in seven lead-bronze bearings, with 0.477 spur gear at the front and the wheelcase for the ancillaries and supercharger drive at the rear. Con-rods were of a slim fork-and-blade pattern. Two scavenge pumps drained the front and rear of the crankcase, and the pistons and floating steel gudgeon pins, with phosphor-bronze bushes, were lubricated by splash, a baffle preventing excess oiling. All valves had twin concentric springs, and the exhaust valves were sodium-cooled, ran in phosphor-bronze guides and seated on high-Si/Cr steel rings, coated with Stellite, screwed into the light-alloy heads. The Rolls-Royce/SU carburettor was of the updraught type with twin choke tubes, each choke having a separate diffuser at right-angles to the airstream. The semi-automatic mixture control was acted on by boost pressure, air-intake pressure and the cockpit lever, while the automatic boost control maintained a constant (selectable) induction-pipe pressure without the pilot having to look at the boost pressure and adjust the throttle.

In January 1934 work had begun on a two-speed supercharger for the Kestrel, so that take-off and climb could be carried out in a low gear, absorbing comparatively little power, switching to the high gear at around 15,000 ft. In January 1935 design began on a two-speed Merlin supercharger, but the compact gearbox ran into severe trouble. Rolls-Royce decided to take a licence for the French Farman two-speed drive, despite the very serious drawback that this added to the length of the engine and the fact that it then made two-speed Merlins installationally non-interchangeable. The first two-speed engine was the Merlin X, fitted to the Whitley IVA and V and Wellington II bombers, and later the Halifax I. Production of the Mk X began in December 1938, combat ratings on 87-octane being 1,145 hp at 3,000 rpm at 5,250 ft and 1,010 hp at

17,750 ft; normal maximum ratings were 1,125 hp in MS gear at low level and 980 hp in FS gear at 16,750 ft. The two-speed engine weighed 1,430 lb.

By the outbreak of war about 4,800 Merlins had been delivered, almost all of the Mks II and X varieties. However, production began in August 1938 of the Mk IV engine which introduced a superior cooling system which quickly became standard. Pure glycol was inflammable, and always tended to creep through supposedly leakproof joints. From 1936 Rolls-Royce had experimented with pure water maintained under 18 lb/sq in pressure, with 30% glycol added purely as an anti-freeze. The mixture was non-inflammable, did not creep through joints, and maintained cylinder temperatures at least 21°C (70°F) lower for any given coolant temperature, with very beneficial effects on engine life. The pressurized system operated at up to 135°C (275°F), and used a radiator no larger than before, so drag and weight were unaffected.

All the early fighter Merlins were started by hand-turning gear on both sides. The Mk X and other bomber engines introduced electric starters, and the Mk VIII, for the Royal Navy Fulmar fighter, was the first of many Merlins to have a Coffman starter energized by one or more cordite cartridges.

By 1937 the Merlin was at last coming 'out of the wood'. A production Merlin II completed 100 hours' flying in Horsley *J8611* in 6.5 days, the pilots being Shepherd, Harker and Harvey Heyworth. This augured well, and in August 1937 intensive development began on a racing Merlin which transcended anything achieved by the R! It was planned for the Speed Spitfire, the 48th Spitfire I which, greatly modified and given prototype registration *N.17*, was planned to attack the World Landplane Speed Record. The Merlin II (it could not have been a III as often reported) was fitted with specially strengthened pistons, gudgeon pins and

con-rods—all of which were later embodied in production engines—and run at 3,200 rpm at 27 lb/sq in boost (84.9 in manifold pressure) on a fuel comprising 60% benzole, 20% straight-run California petrol and 20% methanol, plus 4 cc per gallon of TEL. The corresponding horsepower was no less than 2,160, representing a weight/power ratio of only 0.621 lb/bhp, a figure seldom if ever equalled by any other piston aero engine before or since. The Speed Spitfire never attacked the record, but the development of its engine, ending in May 1938, demonstrated what was already clearly evident: that, despite all its development problems, the Merlin was the toughest engine Rolls-Royce had ever made, and better able to stand up to long periods at full throttle than any previous engine. The most important single accomplishment during this racing programme was a fifteen-hour endurance run at 1,800 hp, at 3,200 rpm at 22 lb boost. This, it was considered, demonstrated beyond doubt that the Merlin would be able to meet all the demands that would be made on it for a long time to come.

One result of the racing effort was to gain experience at very high supercharger tip speeds, around 1,500 ft/sec, but the efficiency was extremely poor. Typical figures for efficiency for a pre-war Merlin supercharger were 66% at a pressure ratio of 1.9, falling to 64% at 2.2 and little over 50% at 2.9. Ellor's original Kestrel figures were about the same, and the overall picture was stagnant. In 1938 water injection as a method of preventing detonation at higher boost pressures was studied, but this was abandoned in 1940 and not used again until Packard V-1650-11 Merlins used water at the very end of the war. Thus, the only route to realizing the Merlin's vast potential and getting more power from it appeared in 1938 to lie in using fuel which would tolerate boost pressures higher than 6 lb/sq in without detonation—in other words, fuel of a higher octane rating. High-octane fuels were pioneered in the United States, though the crucial breakthrough of the alkylation process is credited to Dr S. F. Birch of Anglo-Iranian's laboratory at Sunbury on Thames, in 1935.

In 1934 the US Army Air Corps had issued the first experimental specification, X-3575, for 100-octane fuel, octane number being measured by an unsupercharged variable-compression knock test engine. The operating conditions had been established by the Cooperative Fuel Research (CFR) Committee in the USA so as to correlate as closely as possible to an air-cooled aviation engine operating at cruise power in lean (weak) mixture. The British Air Ministry, having decided in 1937 to support the development of aircraft engines to use 100-octane fuel, began importing small supplies of American 100-octane in 1938, mainly for testing by Rolls-Royce in the Merlin, by the Bristol Aeroplane Company in a single-cylinder Pegasus test engine, and by the Royal Aircraft Establishment at Farnborough in single-cylinder test engines. There is little doubt in the author's mind that this would never have happened had not F. R. Banks, of Ethyl, given a memorable RAeS/Institute of Petroleum paper on 8 January 1937 in which he urged that the RAF should be provided with engines able to use 100-octane 'even if the supply of such fuel were limited, because the use of high-duty equipment might prove decisive in the air in the early stages of a war'. How prophetic can you get?

A valuable discovery was made when it was found that different samples of the American 100-octane varied widely in anti-knock performance at rich mixture and supercharged high boost pressure, corresponding to take-off or combat power, whereas at weak mixture, corresponding to cruise conditions, they were all essentially equal in anti-knock performance. An intensive research programme by Esso, both in the UK and USA, established that what

was termed the 'rich-mixture response' of the supercharged British engines depended very largely on the aromatic content of the 100-octane fuel. British engines had been developed on petrol that almost invariably contained 20% or more of aromatic hydrocarbons (benzene, xylene and/or toluene) whereas the US Army Air Corps had restricted aromatic content to less than 2%, due to the adverse effect of aromatics on the type of seals and flexible tubing then in use in their aircraft. As noted earlier, the standard fuel used by the RAF in the 1920s was '80–20', a blend of 80% light gravity petrol and 20% benzene and xylene. The DTD.224 77-octane fuel specification introduced in 1930 by the Air Ministry usually contained at least 20% aromatics. The DTD.230 specification for 87-octane fuel, permitting the use of tetra-ethyl lead, likewise usually contained aromatics. Prior to World War 2, Shell was a major supplier whose aviation fuel was usually refined from a richly aromatic Asiatic crude oil.

The vital importance of 100-octane was by 1939 fully appreciated by Rolls-Royce and Bristol, and a provisional Air Ministry specification, naturally at first known as BAM.100, was drawn up to cover 100-octane fuel with the essential rich-mixture response. At the time, the supercharge rich knock rating could be checked only by a special test procedure in a single-cylinder Bristol Pegasus. Tests of 100-octane were also conducted by Rolls-Royce at Derby, both in a single-cylinder Merlin and in a full-scale Merlin, where certain highly skilled operators were able successfully to detect detonation audibly. A classic remark said to have been made by Cyril Lovesey was that 'old Trevor Jones' right ear is much more reliable for picking up detonation than a Midgely bouncing pin'. It was not until 1942 that a supercharged single-cylinder test engine, the CFR-3C using the F-4 method, was developed in the United States for reliably measuring the supercharge rich-mixture performance of 100-octane. BAM.100 became British specification DEngRD. 2485, Grade 100/130.

The first full cargo of BAM.100 was shipped in June 1939 from the Esso refinery at Aruba in the tanker *Beaconhill*. Part of this cargo was set aside as a reference fuel; all subsequent shipments from any supplier were required to match (or exceed) the *Beaconhill* 100-octane in both weak-mixture octane number and supercharge rich-mixture performance number. It seems remarkable both that the British government made no effort to produce such fuel in Britain and that the vital imports remained unknown to German intelligence.

The Air Ministry began stockpiling 100-octane while the RAF continued to use 87-octane. In 1939 and 1940 nearly all supplies were imported from the Esso refineries at Baytown, Texas; Baton Rouge, Louisiana; Aruba in the Caribbean; the Shell refineries at Houston, Texas; Curaçao in the Caribbean; and from the Trinidad Leaseholds refinery in Trinidad. Of the shipments to the UK made in 1939 and 1940, and thus used in the Battle of Britain, approximately 67% was supplied from the Esso refineries, 30% from the Shell refineries and 3% from Trinidad Leaseholds (some years later taken over by Texaco). In one of the 1940 convoys one out of six tankers carrying aviation fuel was torpedoed by German submarines and sunk with severe crew losses.

Following Britain's declaration of war on 3 September 1939, the US Congress invoked the Neutrality Act which was intended to prohibit the export of strategic materials (which included aviation fuel) to belligerent nations (which included Britain). As a result, for a period of nearly three months, Esso and Shell could make shipments only from their Aruba and Curaçao refineries which were then in neutral territory. Fortunately, representations made to President Roosevelt resulted in a resumption of shipments from US refineries, subject to payment being made in US dollars and shipments made in non-US vessels. When Britain ran short of dollars in early 1941, President Roosevelt introduced Lend-Lease, which relieved the dollar payment requirement.

In March 1940, RAF Fighter Command converted all Spitfires and Hurricanes from 87 octane to 100 octane. Instead of being limited to a maximum of 6 lb/sq in boost, pilots could 'go through the gate' to full throttle and 12 lb boost, thus increasing the power of the Merlin II or III from approximately 1,000 hp to 1,310. This 30% power increase made a significant improvement to take-off, rate of climb and maximum speed up to about 9,000 ft, above which boost had to fall away. The new fuel really came into its own on the central-entry blower Merlin XX and 45, which could maintain 12 lb up to fighting altitudes around 20,000 ft. Even so, the difference 100-octane made to the Battle of Britain Merlins was very important, in a closely fought campaign. Lord Tedder listed it post-war as one of the three deciding factors.

Strict security was imposed by the Air Ministry at the outbreak of war on all matters relating to the performance of the Rolls-Royce Merlin and Bristol radials on 100-octane. RAF pilots were not advised about the switch from 87 to 100-octane in March 1940, and were informed only that they could safely operate at 12 lb boost when necessary. The Germans had evaluated the performance of the Spitfire and Hurricane based on 87-octane fuel and did not discover until September 1940 that the RAF fighters were using a superior green-coloured fuel.

The importance of 100/130 fuel was underlined by other factors. The Luftwaffe's standard single-seat fighter, the Bf 109E, was much lighter than either the Hurricane or Spitfire, and it was powered by an engine of 25 per cent greater capacity

(2,069 cu in compared with the Merlin's 1,649). As there was not much difference in weight between the two engines, it was imperative for Rolls-Royce to develop the Merlin both to tolerate higher manifold pressure for more power at low altitudes and, especially, superior supercharging for greater power at high altitudes. It is a truly amazing fact that Rolls-Royce succeeded on both counts, and kept the Merlin consistently ahead of the larger DB 601 and later DB 605 right to the end of the war. Another factor emphasizing the need for 100/130 fuel was that, until the start of the Battle of Britain, large numbers of Hurricanes and Spitfires still had the Merlin II driving crude two-blade wooden fixed-pitch propellers, whereas every Bf 109E had the constant-speed VDM. Perhaps the one thing the Merlin installation had going for it was the realization in 1936 that useful

thrust could be obtained from suitably designed exhaust pipes. Quite early in the production of the Spitfire and Hurricane the previous plain stubs were replaced by curved ejector exhausts facing to the rear, each taking the exhaust from two cylinders. These exhaust stacks were developed in the spring of 1937 using the company's He 70, and, when perfected, added about 15 mph to a fighter's speed at full power—the equivalent of 150 extra horsepower. It was partly because of their useful thrust that Rolls-Royce were loath to consider fitting the Merlin with a turbosupercharger.

In early 1939 the standard Hurricane/ Spitfire Merlin II began to be replaced in production by the Mk III with a standard shaft suitable for a variable-pitch propeller, and fitted with a constant-speed unit. In September 1939 Spitfires built at Castle Bromwich began receiving the Merlin XII,

A Merlin III, the vital engine that equipped almost every Hurricane and Spitfire in the Battle of Britain. At the front can be seen the propeller constant-speed unit, introduced with this engine.

The Merlin 32 was a low-level engine for carrier-based aircraft such as the Barracuda, rated at 1,640 hp at 2,000 ft and fitted with a Coffman cartridge starter.

turning the aircraft into Mk IIs. This engine had a higher supercharger gear ratio, giving 1,175 hp at 12.5 lb boost, pressure water cooling and a Coffman L.4 cartridge starter. Thus, the crucial Battle of Britain was fought by RAF fighters powered by the Merlin II, III and XII, plus a few Mk XXs, described later.

RAF pilots must have experienced negative-g many times before the summer of 1940. This threw all the fuel in the carburettor float chamber to the top, starving the engine and causing it to splutter or even cut out. It was not appreciated that in combat this could be serious. Negative-g had no effect on the direct-injection DB 601, and the Bf 109s seemed to make a habit of pushing over into steep dives at full power (when they were faster than the British fighters, in any case). Attempting to follow, the British aircraft would splutter and misfire, the propeller would go into fine pitch, slowing the dive further, and when the engine picked up again it would overspeed violently. Pilots tried rolling into the dive, but this also lost ground.

The first person to come up with a cure was the capable Miss Tilly Shilling at Farnborough. Her idea was elegantly simple:

to add a diaphragm with a small calibrated hole across the float chambers. This kept the fuel in place, the small hole passing just enough fuel for full power at sea level. 'Miss Shilling's orifice' was installed throughout Fighter Command by March 1941. For the longer term, improved carburettors were designed, as described later.

The He 70 was used to perfect many aspects of the Merlin installation. One of the most important concerned the coolant radiator and oil cooler. How liquid radiators should be designed had been explained in a classic 1935 paper by F. W. Meredith, from Farnborough, who had also drawn attention to the advantages of ejector exhausts. He pointed out that the radiator should be ducted in a streamlined casing which internally should be a diffuser, slowing the incoming air and increasing its pressure through the radiator matrix. The hot air could then be ejected through a smaller exit nozzle or slit, reaching a high velocity and imparting useful (ramjet type) thrust to the aircraft. Later Spitfires, Mosquitoes and other aircraft achieved either zero cooling drag or positive forward thrust from their radiators. Other development had a beneficial effect on the detail design of the radiator matrix, so that between 1937 and 1940 the weight of a Merlin radiator and coolant was cut by half.

In the longer term an even more important development was a much deeper look at superchargers, begun in late 1937. For the first time the staff at Derby attempted detailed study of the airflow through the Merlin supercharger, in an endeavour to make a better supercharger on a basis of previously unknown knowledge. Back in 1934 the P.V.12 supercharger, designed by Ellor, had been the best in the world; but it had been designed somewhat empirically, almost on a basis of ignorance. In January 1938, thanks to the vision of Hives, the company hired a brilliant young mathematician and aerodynamicist, Dr Stanley Hooker. In his life-story *Not Much of an Engineer* (written by this author) it is related how he was left to his own devices when he first came to Derby. He wandered into an office and found a set of test results on the Merlin supercharger. Having mugged up the theory he was amazed to find the design of the impeller rotor and the diffuser to be ill-matched. In trepidation he wrote a report outlining how the supercharger should be redesigned to improve its efficiency from about 64 per cent to over 70 per cent, despite an increase in pressure ratio from 2.3 to 3.1.

Hooker backed up this tremendous improvement in the supercharger by an equal improvement in the air inlet. The Merlin had been made as short as possible to match the fore/aft balance of the Hurricane and Spitfire, and the air entered through a duct which, thought Hooker, had an unnatural squashed shape, especially at the elbow to the supercharger. Working from basic aerodynamic principles he designed a new inlet of consistently maximum cross-section, which curved smoothly up the back of the engine to enter at the eye (centre) of the supercharger. Inevitably, this made the engine longer: by chance

Hooker found the original length could be restored by turning the previously overhung SU carburettor back to front. There still had to be a constriction in the carburettor choke tube, but even this could be slightly enlarged. Altogether the new inlet system completely transformed the 'breathing' of the Merlin, so that without change to the engine itself it could give significantly greater power up to higher altitudes. In fact, to match the greater output, Lovesey and Rubbra did judiciously strengthen many parts of the new engines, while to meet the proliferating number of different installations the accessories grew in number and arrangement.

Hooker's new supercharger came on production in July 1940 in the Merlin XX, with two-speed supercharger. Fitted to the Hurricane II, this had a combat rating at 48.2 in manifold pressure (9 lb boost) on 100/130 fuel of 1,175 hp at 20,500 ft compared with 1,160 hp at 13,500 ft for the previous Hurricane engine, the Mk II. In January 1941 the Spitfire's Merlin XII was replaced by the Mk 45 single-speed engine, resulting in the mass-produced Spitfire V. The Mk 45 was rated at 1,315 hp at 16,000 ft at 54.3 in (12 lb boost), compared with the Mk XII's 1,280 hp at 10,500 ft. Though they missed the Battle of Britain, apart from a few dozen Mk XXs, the improved Merlins were crucial in keeping the Merlin fully competitive into 1941.

Inwardly, Hooker now considered that not much more could be done to improve the Merlin as a fighter engine. Small extra gains could be wrung from the induction system and supercharger, but not enough to warrant disrupting production. The future thus appeared to lie with the bigger Griffon and other new engines though meanwhile, there was a requirement for a turbocharged Merlin to power a special high-altitude version of the Wellington bomber. Rolls-Royce was reluctant to introduce turbos, which were thought to be

Left *Hooker's improved supercharger came on production during the Battle of Britain in the Mk XX and 45. This view shows the Rotax generator on the left side, Lockheed hydraulic pump driven off the left camshaft, and BTH or Hymatic compressor on the right.*

Below *Part of a wartime Merlin machine shop. This was at Hillington, Glasgow.*

unreliable, heavy, bulky, and to eliminate the useful ejector effect of the exhausts. As an alternative, Hooker suggested the use of two superchargers in series; he calculated it would be possible by this means to raise the full-throttle height of the Merlin to almost 30,000 ft. Moreover, he pointed out that no design effort was needed on the first-stage blower, as the supercharger of the 24-cylinder Vulture engine was just the size needed (the Vulture being rated at 1,000 hp at 30,000 ft). To test the idea Hooker rigged up a Vulture blower at one end of his electrically driven test plant and a Merlin 46 supercharger at the other end, and fed the outlet of one into the other. Results were so good that no further theory was needed.

There was one further item to be added. The high compression resulted in a rise in temperature of some 205°C as the mixture passed through the two stages of the supercharger, and to increase the charge density (and thus power) and avoid detonation it was necessary to cool the compressed mixture before feeding it to the cylinders. Accordingly an aftercooler was needed (this became incorrectly known as an 'intercooler', though this device would cool the flow between the supercharger stages). Some testing was done with an air-cooled intercooler, but it was so big it spoilt pilot view and increased drag from the bulged cowling. Nobody had ever made a water radiator with such performance in a small bulk, but Farnborough came up with a superb copper matrix using the same pressurized water/glycol mix as the cylinder blocks. The result was the Merlin 60, on bench test in April 1941 and flown in the Wellington VI three months later. Hives sent for Hooker and demanded to know the estimated full-throttle height. Hooker replied, nervously, '30,000 ft, approximately'. Hives handed him a piece of paper on which was written '29,750'. He said 'I've just had that figure from Dorey, taken on

the first flight of the Wellington'.

Thus, purely by adding a new and bigger supercharger upstream of the first—a technique later common with turbojets—the Merlin had been utterly transformed. Inevitably its length and weight had been slightly increased, but the gains were tremendous. Never before had anything remotely comparable been achieved with any aero engine, and never before had any non-experimental aero engine had a full-throttle height of 29,750 ft! Production of the Merlin 60 began in November 1941, but the whole programme was almost immediately cancelled and no Wellington VI went into service. But by this time a far more important two-stage Merlin was under development. At the first of his regular Monday meetings after the first flight of the Wellington VI Hives asked 'What would happen if we put this engine into a Spitfire?' According to Hooker, 'It was blindingly obvious that the Spitfire was the true home for the engine, and it had been left to Hs to suggest it. We all sat back aghast and silent. Dorey said "I don't know, but we will damned soon find out. I will start work on putting one into the Spit immediately".'

Spitfire III *N3297* was torn apart and rebuilt to take the new engine, while Rolls-Royce redesigned the Merlin 60 into the Mk 61. At last it was possible to bring in the two-piece cylinder block, which had been planned since March 1938 but kept out by the overriding need for production. The Mk 61 omitted the cabin supercharger drive fitted to the Mk 60, and had different gear ratios to the single shaft on which the two supercharger impellers were mounted. As rebuilt *N3297* had a longer cowling, four-blade propeller and symmetric radiators, that on the left housing coolant and oil radiators and that under the right wing housing coolant and intercooler radiators.

The increased performance of the Spitfire was all that had been hoped. With radiator shutters closed it reached 42,500 ft, a full 10,000 ft more than the Typhoon or Spitfire V, and the level speed was raised by 70 mph to 421 mph at 27,500 ft. From its first flight on 20 September 1941 the re-engined Spitfire behaved well, until the Assistant Chief of the Air Staff responsible for aircraft development said on 12 November 1941 that he wanted to cancel everything but Merlin 61 Spitfires. The first production Mk 61 was dispatched on Christmas Day 1941. Supermarine redesigned the Spitfire to take the new engine, the result being the Spitfire VIII. In typical British fashion this kept being side-lined while production surged ahead on the Spitfire IX, a complete lash-up of a Merlin 61 in a Spitfire V airframe, of which 5,665 were built, plus 1,658 Mk XVI which again had the old Mk V airframe but a Packard-built Mk 266 engine.

Ratings for the Mk 61 were 1,280 hp for take-off, 1,560 hp at 12,000 ft and 1,370 hp at 24,000 ft, weight being 1,640 lb. Whereas the best previous Merlin supercharger (Mk XX) had a peak pressure ratio of 3.1 and efficiency of some 66–70%, the two-stage supercharger of the Mk 61 and its relatives had a pressure ratio of 4.9 in high gear, combined with efficiency of 70–75%. It enabled 9 lb/sq in boost (48.24 in manifold pressure) to be maintained to 30,000 ft. With the intercooler cooling the charge to about 100°C the maximum power to 30,000 ft was almost exactly doubled, compared with early Merlins, from 500 hp to 1,000. The Mks 63A and 64 drove cabin blowers, while the 'all can do' Mk 66 of 1,720 hp had interconnected controls.

This unprecedented increase in high-altitude performance was almost entirely due to the aerodynamic capability of Stanley Hooker. He also noticed that an empirical formula had always been used in calculating the power developed at altitude by a supercharged engine. When he examined this formula Hooker discovered that it was far from accurate, and certainly did not reflect true conditions. It always tended to over-estimate the power, and the error grew sharply as the boost pressure was increased. This provided the solution to a problem that had been a thorn in Rolls-Royce's side since the mid-1930s. Aircraft designers, Sydney Camm in particular, had complained that supercharged engines did not give the power claimed; and when the prototypes of the Hurricane and Spitfire began flying, both were found to fall roughly 20 mph short of the speed predicted. Accordingly, Hooker organized a detailed and precise research programme which determined the exact consumption of fuel/air mixture of an engine under all flight conditions, as well as the power expended in driving the internal parts of the engine (including the supercharger itself). He also deduced a formula which gave, for any engine, the true rate of consumption of fuel/air mixture at all heights and speeds. For the first time ever, it became possible accurately to predict the power of an engine at any height and under any flight condition. Late in World War 2 a Merlin was tested in the high-altitude testbed at Wright Field in the USA—there was nothing like this in Britain—and it was found to behave exactly according to the calculations. Hooker said this showed 'The pen is mightier than the spanner'.

Development was not always directed at increasing power at high altitude. Since 1936 Merlins had been developed for naval aircraft, such as the Fulmar and (as a replacement for the Exe, described later) the Barracuda, and these needed maximum power for take-off and low altitudes. A typical example was the Merlin 32, with Coffman starter and four-blade propeller, which at a boost pressure of 18 lb gave 1,620 hp for take-off and had a maximum power of 1,640 hp at 2,000 ft. This powered the Barracuda II and Seafire II. In some theatres even the land-based Spitfire needed help at low levels.

Ronnie Harker visited the Middle East and found the tropicalized Spitfire VC, one of the most unspectacular performers of the Spitfire family, having a hard time against the Bf 109G and Fw 190. Local RAF workshops had tried to boost power by resetting the CSU (constant-speed unit) to 3,200 rpm, but this actually gave worse results than at 3,000. Harker cabled Derby asking how much should be machined off the supercharger impeller to get 18 lb boost at the typical combat altitude of 6,000 ft. The answer was 'three-quarters of an inch', and the resulting Merlin 45M was fitted in Spitfire Vs whose wings had been clipped by removing the tips. Together with an improved sand filter this gave 22 mph more speed, faster roll and an increased rate of climb. A complete wing of Spitfires was thus converted, to good effect.

Curiously, in Britain, when in October 1942 AFDU (Air Fighting Development Unit) clipped the tips of a Spitfire VB, the Assistant Chief of Air Staff responsible for aircraft development wrote, 'Such a major alteration is entirely unauthorized and should not have been undertaken. . . . This aircraft is not to be flown again, except to Boscombe Down who will test it to see if it can be applied to the Mk XII' (the XII is described later). Two weeks later Boscombe thought it was great, and from then onwards the LF (low-altitude fighter) versions of the Spitfire were numerous and important. But by 1943 the 'clipped, cropped and clapped' Spitfires were getting tired and were not popular, especially when flown against 190s at heights well above the 6,000 ft rated altitude of the Mk 45M.

At this point it is worth looking away from the engine and instead studying the gigantic build-up needed for production, service support and repair. In 1937, with Air Ministry backing, a vast Shadow Industry scheme was started to build engines in new government plants usually managed by car manufacturers; but this involved only Bristol

engines. Rolls-Royce chose to build its own factories, and the first was started in 1938 at Crewe, while the Derby works itself was several times extended. In 1939 work began on a further enormous new factory at Hillington, south of Glasgow, where yet another factory was later begun close by at East Kilbride.

On the second day of the war, at his regular Monday meeting, Hives said 'We must win; there's not much point in coming a good second'. It was expected that Derby would immediately be bombed flat. This never happened, and Derby's output soared to undreamed-of levels, even though many of the key staff and skilled men had to leave to form a nucleus at Crewe and Glasgow. Crewe got into production in 1940, and, after various union and Communist-inspired holdups, Glasgow came 'on line' in 1941. Both built mainly bomber engines. Nor was this all. Soon after the outbreak of war the Ford Motor Co was asked to make Merlins at its huge plant in Manchester. To the amazement of Rolls-Royce the car builder announced that the tolerances on the drawings were too wide, and that to achieve full mass-production with complete interchangeability of parts they would have to be tightened up! Ford took nearly the whole of 1940 redrawing the Merlin to their own tighter tolerances; then, from 1941, superb Ford-built Merlins poured from Manchester at over 200 a week. In practice, mating parts never exhibit all the extremes of dimensional tolerance, and Rolls-Royce's drawings were adequate.

Soon after the outbreak of war the British government opened negotiations with the US Ford Motor Co at Dearborn for production of the Merlin under licence, but these eventually collapsed. In their place discussions began with the Packard Motor Co at Detroit. This time there were no insuperable difficulties, and final agreement was reached in September 1940. Ellor and Barrington were sent from Derby to liaise with the US company (and carried such a crushing burden of work that Barrington died there, and Ellor soon after his return). With remarkable speed the Merlin XX was totally redrawn to third-angle projection, and equipped mainly with US accessories: the result was the Packard V–1650–1. The first two engines were started on their Detroit testbeds on 2 August 1941.

From the very start the specification of the Packard V–1650 included an interim form of the two-piece cylinder block. As noted previously, this had been recognized as desirable from early 1938, but the over-riding need for increased production prevented its incorporation in British Merlins until the Mks 22A, 45A and 61 in 1942. The two-piece cylinder liner flange was trapped between head and skirt, the two castings being held together by side studs, which contributed to top joint integrity. The main loads on the block were taken by the flexible cylinder holding-down studs through the head and skirt, the liners carrying no compressive load. On the old single-piece block the loads were taken through the cylinder liners, which contributed to liner distortion and also made the top joint 'feel' crankcase distortions. On the two-piece block the joint was dry, and a gas leak would go to atmosphere. The block was detachable, like the single-piece variety. It stiffened the whole engine and at the same time cured the maddening tendency towards water leaks for which the only previous palliative had been a thermostatically controlled cooling system to try to maintain a constant water/glycol temperature. Packard, able to start from scratch, had an interim two-piece block on its very first engines in August 1941. Packard also introduced an epicyclic step-up gear in the drive to the super-charger. The switch to US-supplied accessories resulted in few major alter-ations apart from the use of the Bendix injection-type carburettor. The V–1650–1 was used in the Curtiss P–40F and P–40L,

and as the Merlin 28 was supplied for Lancasters. Similar engines were shipped to Canada for Hurricane and Mosquito production. With the Mk 38, Packard introduced the full two-piece block design.

While Miss Shilling's neat orifice provided an excellent temporary solution to the problem of engine cut-out under nega-tive-g, Lovesey planned a longer-term solution in the form of a carburettor with the float chamber replaced by a flexible rubber diaphragm. In the event this found only limited application because of inconsistency between one diaphragm and the next (one complete batch failed merely because they had been stored near hot-water pipes and the rubber had hardened). In November 1942 this carburettor failed its Service trial, with the Spitfire VIs of 124 Squadron at North Weald, because it could not sense zero-g. A better answer was an anti-g version of the SU carburettor developed by Farnborough with RR participation. This had a modified float needle and ball valves which protected the jets from negative or high positive g. This worked well, and was fitted on new Merlins of single- and two-stage types and also retroactively. In 1943 Lovesey's 'universal' Mk 66 Merlin was fitted with a Bendix-Stromberg carburettor. This at last eliminated the float chamber and injected fuel at 5 lb/sq in through nozzles round a spider into the rotating guide vanes of the LP supercharger. Though complex it worked well, provided air was rigorously excluded, and it went on the Merlin 66, 70, 76, 77 and 85.

With the ever-increasing power of the Merlin it was becoming clear that it was desirable to eliminate the restriction of a carburettor choke tube in the air inlet. There was no possibility of significantly increasing the size of the carburettor air passages, and so the company went back to first principles and worked out a formula governing the relationship between fuel flow and the factors affecting it. The result-

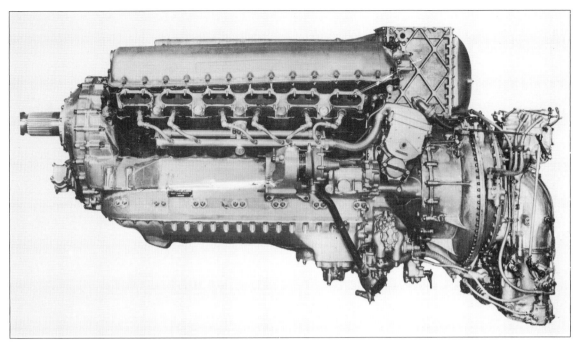

The extra supercharger and big intercooler box changed the outline of the two-stage engines. This is a Mk 66, similar to the Packard-built Mk 266, used in many Spitfires. Rating was 1,720 hp at low level and 1,580 hp at 16,000 ft. A Bendix fuel-injection carburettor is fitted.

ing formula showed that what was needed was a fuel pump driven at a fixed ratio of crankshaft speed, in which the stroke of the plungers was proportional to the boost pressure minus one-sixth of the exhaust back-pressure divided by the charge temperature. The result was the SU injection carburettor, governed by a stack of aneroid capsules, which injected a spray of fuel into the eye of the supercharger. This improved the supercharger pressure ratio by 7%, because of the sudden drop in charge temperature caused by evaporation. A little later this was supplemented by a Rolls-Royce vane-type pump with centrifugal governor control. These injection systems went on the later Mk 100 engines.

Early in the war development went ahead on the Meteor, a Merlin for armoured vehicles, and the Marine Merlin, for fast naval craft. It was to prevent explosions of

petrol/air mixtures in ship engine rooms that a flame trap was devised, based on the metal mesh principle of the Davy miner's lamp. This was introduced to the Merlin aero engines to prevent cut-outs or dangerous backfires caused by defective plugs, crossed plug leads, leaking inlet valves and other faults. It really proved its worth when running at high boost pressures, and there was at least one occasion when a Hurricane took off from Northolt at full throttle with plug leads crossed.

By 1943 one of the major development efforts was devoted to refining the mechanical design until the Merlin could be taken at random from production and run for 100 hours at 18 lb boost at 3,000 rpm. The first engine to be picked, a Mk 66 destined for a Spitfire VIII or IX, suffered a cracked crankcase at 27 hours. Progressively a strengthened crankcase was introduced,

Last of the major wartime families, the 100-series was based on the Mk 66 but with almost every part strengthened and with end-to-end oil feed. Many engines of this family gave over 2,000 hp at low level, while others gave 1,435 hp at 27,250 ft.

deep-top-land pistons designed, strengthened main bearings fitted and a totally new form of main and crankpin bearing lubrication devised with so-called 'end to end' oil feed, the oil being pumped in at both ends of the crankshaft. The result was the RM.14SM engine, which went into production as the 100-series, notably in the form of the Mks 113/114 which became familiar to the author as the power plants of the ultimate marks of Mosquito, with a high-gear rating of 1,435 hp at 27,250 ft, an amazing performance compared with the early Merlins. Even these were surpassed by the Mks 130/131 (identical except that the propellers rotated in opposite directions) which powered the de Havilland Hornets. These superb Merlins had a power at low level of 2,030 hp at 25 lb boost, and were notable in having downdraught induction from a slit in the wing leading

edge, low-pressure fuel injection through a single nozzle directly into the eye of the LP supercharger, big Corliss barrel-type throttles, and a beautifully clean installation. Whereas the first Merlins had a power of some 60 hp per square foot of frontal area, on the Hornet engines the remarkable figure of 340 hp/sq ft was reached. Another remarkable comparison is that the altitude at which 1,000 hp was available was increased during the war from 16,000 ft to 36,000 ft!

Last of the high-power Merlins was the Mk 140, for the Short Sturgeon, which had shunt-flow cooling, a Coffman starter for navy use, and drives to small contra-rotating propellers to absorb its 2,080 hp. Last of all the military production Merlins, the Mk 35 was a simple engine with single-speed supercharger rated at 1,280 hp for the Avro Athena and Boulton Paul Balliol trainers.

All were newly built, despite the acres of unused wartime production lying around in the early 1950s. Meanwhile, Packard had carried out their own development on the two-stage Merlins, the V–1650–7 being similar to the British Mk 68, and the V–1650–9 for advanced P–51 Mustangs having water/methanol injection and being cleared to 1,900 hp on 150-grade fuel. Last of the Packard Merlins, the V–1650–11, had the Stromberg speed-density injection carburettor and, with W/M injection, had a war emergency rating of 2,270 hp at 90 in (about 29.5 lb boost). These late-model V–1650s were also built by Continental. A feature of all US production was that, compared with British engines, they were scrupulously clean externally because of the virtual absence of the slightest oil leak. Today V–1650 Dash-9 and Dash-11 engines are being flogged to death at powers exceeding 2,500 hp in power boat racing. Another, carefully prepared, holds the world piston-engine speed record at 517.06 mph.

In late 1944 an RM.17SM Merlin was run at Derby for fifteen minutes at 36 lb boost on 150-PN fuel with water injection, recording an output of 2,640 hp. The bmep (brake mean effective pressure) was 404 lb/sq in, and the imep (indicated) no less than 535 lb/sq in. It would be foolish to claim these figures as world records for a piston aero engine, but the author knows of no higher figures. Rolls-Royce carried out much testing on fuels of their own blending containing as much as 11.5 cc/gal of TEL (tetra-ethyl lead), with which 25 lb boost could be used at low altitudes, giving tremendous performance to such aircraft as the Mosquito and Mustang in chasing flying bombs. Nitrous oxide injection was also used, notably for eight minutes of emergency boost for Mosquito night fighters and some FB.VI fighter bombers, again mainly at low level. A third special fuel contained 2.5 per cent MMA (mono-methyl aniline), and this gave such a boost to power that in July 1944 the whole of ADGB (Air Defence of Great Britain) was put on to this fuel, and it was subsequently widely used by fighters of 2 TAF and the US 8th and 9th AFs.

Towards the end of the war development began on civil transport Merlins, beginning with the Mk 500, based on the T.24 for Yorks and Lancastrians, and going on to the 620 and 720 series of two-stage engines for DC–4M North Stars and Tudors. The DC–4M went on until 1964, gradually overcoming extremely high overhaul costs and other shortcomings, one of which was noise, which in 1952 necessitated the introduction of an unusual crossover piping system which discharged all exhaust on the outboard side of the engine away from the passengers.

The common impression is that, except for 'hot rod' unlimited class racers and power-boat buffs in North America, development of the Merlin ceased in 1945. Nothing could be further from the truth! The total engineering effort on the Civil Merlin, especially the 620-series for the various sub-types of DC–4M and Canadair Four, was roughly equal to all that had gone before. Comprehensive performance charts were prepared, and approved by E. M. Eltis (later Director of Engineering), while David Huddie had a big team on the Civil Merlin for about three years. Part of the trouble was the need for a major extension in component life. Another was that Trans-Canada were a technically minded operator with forcefully expressed ideas, and another was that BOAC tended to think 'maximum continuous' at 58.5 in boost could be equated with 'cruise'. By the early 1950s the Merlin 626, with full-depth intercooler, was a smooth and reliable engine. Then, as late as 1963, an operator on Derby's doorstep, British Midland, took on a fleet of rather tired Argonauts and soon began burning out exhaust valves, losing power and even having the occasional catastrophic mixture explosion in the cross-over exhaust system.

Post-war commercial Merlins were polished silver, and Rolls-Royce had a job to keep the exterior as totally oil-free as the Packard-built engines. This is a Mk 626, standard engine for the Canadair Four (DC-4M2).

Their difficulties were certainly exacerbated by use of a detergent oil containing an additive which deposited sticky residue on the valve stems, preventing the normal random rotation of the valves (which Rolls-Royce had been at pains to ensure) so that the exhaust flame always attacked the same area round the tulip head. The airline called affected engines chuffers, from the noise they made when idling. The author rather became the proverbial meat in the sandwich by happening to write books about Rolls-Royce engines and British Midland at the same time, and it was hard to reconcile the two viewpoints!

Total production of the Merlin and V-1650 amounted to 168,040, made up as follows: Derby 32,377, Crewe 26,065, Glasgow 23,647, Ford Manchester 30,428 and Packard Detroit 55,523. Most of the British production was priced at approximately £1 per horsepower or per pound weight.

In 1938 a need was foreseen for a powerful engine for naval aircraft, notably torpedo bombers. Most oddly, the obvious application, the Fairey Barracuda, began life with the small Rolls-Royce Exe and then received the Merlin, not receiving the bigger purpose-designed engine until the end of the war. This bigger engine was the Type 37, later named Griffon. It was essentially a Merlin-style engine but with the capacity of the Buzzard and R, namely 6 in bore and 6.6 in stroke, giving a capacity of

2,239 cu in, or 36.7 litres. It is remarkable that, despite this increase in size of almost 36 per cent, the physical dimensions of most Griffons were similar to those of typical Merlins, and many were actually shorter and lower than two-stage intercooled Merlins.

The first Griffon dated from late 1934 and was to some degree an attempt to produce a Service engine based closely on the R. Indeed, it even had the racing engine's double-entry supercharger (but with a side inlet), a very similar crankcase, and rear magnetos and camshaft drives. By 1937 this had developed into the Griffon II, with camshaft drives moved to the front, a vertical water pump underneath and a downdraught carburettor leading to a normal single-entry supercharger. By the end of 1938 this was being refined into the Mk IIB, with an updraught carburettor, horizontal water pump and new rocker covers.

Harry Cantrill joined the firm from Armstrong Siddeley on 1 January 1939 and was immediately given the task of managing the development of the Griffon. The basic objective was 1,500 hp at low level, with the recommendation that the engine should be kept as compact as possible in order to make it easier for it to replace the Merlin in existing aircraft. By this time such red herrings as the ramp head were past history, and the Griffon soon became an excellent engine. Naturally, its existence

The first Griffon had cam-shafts driven at the rear, and rear-mounted mag-netos, and was virtually a modernized Buzzard or a detuned R engine Cantrill's redesigned engine was shorter, as subsequent pictures show.

served as a powerful spur to Cyril Lovesey and his team on the Merlin, and it is worth noting that, despite its far greater capacity, the Griffon never significantly exceeded the Merlin in power and never equalled the older engine in specific power on either a weight or capacity basis. This was partly because maximum rpm were always 2,750, not 3,000.

One of the major changes in the design of the Griffon was that a modified semi-float-ing coupling was interposed between the

This early production Griffon, almost certainly a Mk II, shows how the redesign reduced the overall length. The superimposed pair of 12-cylinder magnetos can just been seen between the front of the cylinder banks between the front drives to the camshafts.

crankshaft and the propeller reduction-gear input pinion, and the camshafts were then driven from the reduction gear instead of from the rear of the engine. In nearly all Griffons the magnetos were also at the front. This saved engine overall length and almost eliminated torsional vibration in the drives. The Griffon was also the first non-experimental engine to have the end-to-end oil lubrication, the main and big-end bearings all being supplied from inside the crankshaft. As noted earlier, this was to become standard on the later Merlins. Not least of the different features of the Griffon was that, compared with more than 99% of Merlins, the propeller rotated in the opposite direction. This resulted in single-engined aircraft tending to swing to the right on take-off, and this was disconcerting aboard a carrier because the ship's island super-structure was on the starboard side. The author remembers his concern not to forget to apply 'a bootful of left rudder' on his first

Griffon-Spitfire, which is just the opposite of procedure on Merlin-Spitfires. The Griffon also had a different firing order: A-block, 1–5–3–6–2–4, whereas the Merlin A-block sequence was 1–4–2–6–3–5.

Early Griffons were overweight, and Cantrill's team worked round the clock refining the design and lopping over 200 lb off! By June 1940 the Griffon II was on test, rated at 1,720 hp for take-off and with 1,495 hp available at 14,500 ft. The immediate application was the Firefly two-seat naval fighter, first flown in December 1941. The installation, with chin radiator and four-blade propeller, gave little trouble, and from the 470th Firefly the engine changed to the 1,815 hp Griffon XII. This was not the first Griffon aircraft in production, however. As early as 27 November 1941 *DP845*, a Spitfire VC later to be flown in many strange configurations, took to the air with a Griffon III as the first panic move to counter the excellent performance at low

One of the Griffon testbeds was this Hawker Henley, L3414. The neat engine installation was basically that of the Fairey Firefly I but with three-blade propeller.

level of the Fw 190. By this time a Griffon 60-series engine was being designed, with two-stage supercharger and intercooler, and this was proposed for the Spitfire XX planned to be available from July 1943.

After much argument it was decided to sanction 100 Spitfires based on the Mk VB, but with strengthened structures and clipped wings, to be produced as quickly as possible with single-stage Griffon engines for use as low-level interceptors to fight the Fw 190. In the event only 45 such aircraft were delivered, from December 1942, followed by 55 based on the Mk VIII airframe and thus having a retractable tailwheel and pointed rudder. All were called Mk XIIs, and had a Rotol propeller with four Jablo densified-wood blades with diameter limited by ground clearance. The engines were intended to be the 1,735 hp Griffon III or IV, but in the event the Griffon VI, rated at 1,815 hp at 15 lb boost, powered the Spitfire XII as well as the Seafire XV

and XVII, which were the first Seafires fully engineered for carrier service.

By 1943 the 60-series Griffons with two-stage supercharger and intercooler were beginning to come off production. The first Mark in service was the 65, rated at 2,035 hp at 7,000 ft and 1,820 hp at 21,000 ft, the weight being 1,980 lb (about 180 lb up on the single-stage engines). This engine powered the Spitfire XIV, which, just as the Mk IX was a hasty lash-up of the Mk V to take a two-stage Merlin, was a similar hasty lash-up of the Mk VIII to take a two-stage Griffon. The power was absorbed by a Rotol propeller which, because of the limitation on diameter, had five blades. The Griffon 66 had a cabin blower, for such aircraft as the Spitfire PR.XIX. The Griffon 72 and 74 were two-stage engines for the naval Firefly, rated at 2,245 hp at 9,250 ft. Last of the production fighter Griffons, the Mks 83 to 88 had drives for six-blade contraprops, which at last eliminated the

Typical of the engines of later Spitfires and Seafires, the Griffon 60-series family had a two-stage supercharger and intercooler. Remarkably, most were shorter (around 82 in) than equivalent Merlins, and the difference in power was much less than the difference in capacity might suggest.

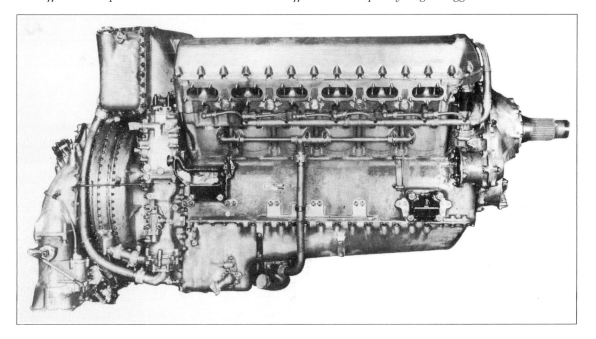

Today's Reno racers would have been interested in the project to fit a Griffon 65 Special amidships in a rebuilt Mustang. Flight stresses were transmitted through the tubular engine truss. Here engine No 1262 is seen in the beautifully finished metal mock-up at Hucknall.

severe torque problem on take-off. Rated at 2,340 hp at low level and typically 2,145 hp at 15,000 ft, they variously had either the Bendix-Stromberg fuel-metering carburettor or the Rolls-Royce injection pump, and powered the final Spitfires and Seafires. A slight visual difference in the final Seafire 47 was that the engine air intake was carried forward to the extreme front of the cowl just behind the propeller, as on Merlin-Mustangs.

Though the author approached them with some trepidation—partly because of the sheer size of the cowling looming ahead of the Spitfire XIV cockpit and the power implicit in five huge propeller blades—they were actually splendid engines, easy to start and, because of their balanced crankshafts, very smooth in operation. There were several little-known oddballs. One was the so-called Schneider Griffon, designed for minimum frontal area and with lateral air inlets. Another was a basically normal Mk 65 intended to be installed amidships in three much-modified Mustangs at Hucknall, with a long extension shaft under

the forward cockpit to a reduction gear and auxiliary gearbox which drove a Rotol contraprop and also auxiliaries including the Hymatic air compressor. One wonders if, had it flown, this aircraft—unkindly called Dorey's delusion— might have been a basis for a 500-mph record-breaker? There was also a Marine Griffon for fast naval craft.

The ultimate Griffon, not put into production, was the Mk 101 which had a three-speed supercharger. This engine caused seven dead-stick landings to the only Spiteful XVI, though it also drove this aircraft in full combat trim at 494 mph. Much more important was the Griffon 58, a specially prepared engine for the Avro Shackleton. Though it had only a single-stage supercharger it drove contra-rotating propellers and at low levels achieved an output of 2,455 hp with automatic water/methanol injection into the eye of the supercharger to permit 25 lb boost, the latter being immediately cut back if the W/M supply should run out. In 1949 the Shackleton first flew as a maritime patrol aircraft, and nobody had

As this book goes to press in 1988 the radar watch over British airspace is still borne aloft on the power of the Griffon 58. Features include a two-speed single-stage supercharger, electric starter and contra-rotating propellers. Shackleton engines have been designated Mk 58s for many years.

the slightest idea that the Griffon would soldier on in the Shackleton in the airborne early-warning role for another forty years! The last Griffon 58 to be delivered, for a South African Shackleton, was new in December 1955. The last to be put through major overhaul at the Glasgow factories was redelivered to the RAF in 1986. These are the last high-power piston engines to fly on front-line operational—as distinct from mere transport—missions with any air force in the world.

Chapter 6

THE LAST PISTON ENGINES

In 1935 the official outlook of the British government was still that a blind eye was to be turned to the activities of the Nazi party in Germany, flagrantly in violation of the Versailles Treaty, and that the German Chancellor, Herr Hitler, was to be appeased by every means possible. Certainly, no additional funds were to be earmarked for defence, and indeed the supposed popular policy was one of 'disarmament'—unilaterally, if need be. Yet despite this background the British Air Ministry gradually went into top gear to try to plan for a modernized and enlarged Royal Air Force, and Rolls-Royce, very much on company initiative, began the development of a remarkable range of new and ambitious piston engines.

To some degree this was done for competitive reasons. The income from the Kestrel enabled the Aero Division to expand its design and engineering strength until it was probably stronger, technically, than any other aero-engine company in the world. Moreover, though 'the Old Man' had departed, the team he left behind was imbued with his uncompromising standards of excellence to an extraordinary degree. Without wishing to denigrate the company's competitors, many have given it as their considered opinion that this, coupled with the colossal strength of character and

capacity for hard work of the key men at Derby, increasingly lifted Rolls-Royce into a unique position, where it could not only do more than its rivals but could also do it quicker.

Thus, despite the unpromising start to what was obviously going to be a prolonged development programme with the Merlin, the Derby designers spent the second half of the 1930s simultaneously also developing not only the Peregrine but also three other new engines, all technically complex, utterly dissimilar and presenting enormous challenges. They embraced new configurations, compression-ignition, air cooling, the two-stroke cycle, and sleeve valves, among other innovations!

Chronologically, the first to be sanctioned, in February 1935, was a design study for a new engine in the 1,000-hp class for the Fleet Air Arm. For shipboard use air cooling was preferred, but no thought was given to a radial. Frank Halford, under contract to Napier and de Havilland, was busy with attractive air-cooled engines of the H and inverted-V layouts, but Rowledge, who led the design of the new engine until its termination in 1936, once again picked the X configuration because of its compactness, and the fact that it enabled 24 cylinders to drive on a single crankshaft. The cylinders were 'over-square' but very small, only

Rowledge always liked the X layout, with many cylinders driving a single crankshaft. In 1925 he gave up the Eagle XVI, but ten years later he designed the Exe, with 24 tiny cylinders which, breaking with tradition even more, were air-cooled and fitted with sleeve valves.

4.2 in bore and 4.0 in stroke, giving a capacity of only 1,348 cu in or 22.1 litres. This was appreciably smaller than the Merlin, despite having double the number of cylinders. In the author's view this was too small, whereas an engine of twice the power might have been extremely important.

The cylinders were pressure air-cooled, and arranged in four banks at 90°. Each had a sleeve valve, and a general form very similar to that of the contemporary Bristol sleeve-valve radials, though much smaller. The original design rating (FS gear) was 920 hp at 3,800 rpm at 11,000 ft. Most of the agony of sleeve valves had already been overcome by Bristol, and with the experimental sleeve-valve Kestrel. From its first run in September 1936 the air-cooled engine ran smoothly and without trouble.

At first named Boreas, it was judged that this trespassed on the naming policy at Bristol, and so it was changed to Exe, a play on the engine's X configuration and also (though not considered at the time) adopting the name of a river, as was done with the company's later gas-turbine engines.

Though there were many possible applications, the Exe was associated primarily with Fairey aircraft. It was tested in a Battle, was the intended powerplant of the Barracuda torpedo-bomber, and was planned to power the production version of the F.C.1 civil airliner. The engine was easy to install, and the arrangement of its accessories was especially neat. Cooling air was taken in at a forward ram inlet below the spinner and ducted between the two lower rows of cylinders, subsequently

passing between the upper rows and finally out at each side at the rear. Cooling was extremely efficient, and installed drag almost zero, unlike the liquid-cooled engines of the day. By 1938, when flying started in the Battle, the Exe had been uprated to 4,200 rpm, giving 1,150 hp at 4.5 lb on 100-octane, and there was every indication that 1,500 hp would later be forth-

Left *The Exe had coil ignition (the four coils are prominent in the foreground) and this was expected to make for instant starting, especially in its civil applications. The sleeve drives passed along each side of the crankcase, and the Exe never suffered from the crankcase distortions that afflicted the Vulture.*

Below *This Exe-powered Battle proved so trouble-free that it soldiered on as the company's hack transport from 1938 until 1943, long after development of its engine had been cancelled. Its unique sleeve-valve air-cooled engine pulled it along rather faster than Merlin Battles.*

coming. Despite the excellence of the air cooling, a liquid-cooled Exe was also studied. A four-cylinder liquid-cooled X-unit was run in 1938 using steel cylinders with fabricated jackets, reminiscent of those of twenty years earlier, but the jackets kept cracking. Accordingly the cylinders were redesigned as cast aluminium blocks, and a complete liquid-cooled engine was made and tested, but not flown.

To the author's regret the decision was taken at the outbreak of war to discontinue both the air- and liquid-cooled versions of the Exe, despite the former's promise. So trouble-free was the Exe that the Battle testbed continued until 1943 as the company's hack communications aircraft. Cyril Lovesey has recorded how on one occasion

he visited a Spitfire squadron at Biggin Hill. On return to Hucknall it was noticed that oil was dripping from the cowling. On removing the panel, one of the cylinder heads was found to be hanging loose, held only by the ignition leads. The pilot had noticed nothing unusual. On the other hand when L. R. Stokes was about to fly the Battle his boss Captain R. T. Shepherd said 'Remember it's not a Merlin, Stokey, it runs out of oil before it runs out of petrol'.

Experience with the Exe had been so encouraging that a small design team—led by Dr S. M. Viale, who had designed for Anzani in 1912, then for Armstrong Siddeley and then headed the Rolls-Royce team on the 40-mm aircraft cannon—continued work on similar engines. Around

Potentially one of the greatest piston engines ever, and related to even more powerful successors, the Pennine had 24 air-cooled sleeve-valve cylinders putting at least 3,000 hp into one crankshaft. This was the last engine to have an epicyclic reduction gear.

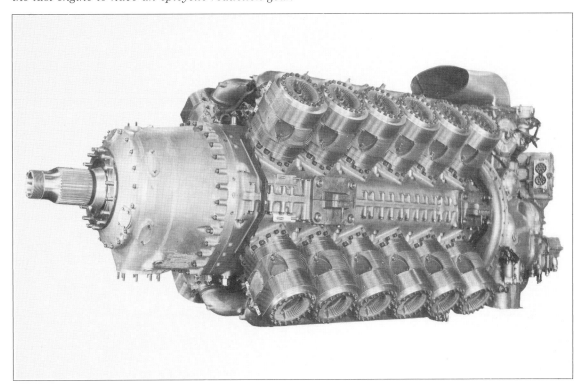

1942 the design was completed of the Pennine. This was again an air-cooled sleeve-valve engine with four rows of six cylinders set at 90°, but the cylinders were larger, with bore and stroke of 5.4 in (as in the Merlin) × 5.0 in, and capacity of 2,685 cu in (44.0 litres). While the Exe had a spur reduction gear, giving a high propeller axis, the Pennine had an epicyclic gear putting the propeller in line with the crankshaft. Accessories were grouped at the rear, the downdraught induction pipe having a Corliss barrel throttle and leading to either a single- or two-stage supercharger, and a low-pressure fuel injection pump. A conservative civil rating was 3,000 hp. Overall, the author rates the Pennine as potentially one of the best piston aero engines ever made, but during the war it never attracted any support. At last Rolls-Royce managed to get one on test in 1945, hoping it would find a market in post-war civil aviation, but by this time everyone was captivated by the

gas turbine and the whole project was abandoned soon afterwards. Moreover, an air-cooled intercooler would have been enormous. Possibly, if the Pennine had been started instead of the Exe, it might have been one of the most important engines of both the war and the subsequent peace. So far as the author knows, the only planned application was the Miles X airliner. Miles never had political clout and the Ministry assessment of the X assumed the use of traditional engines of much lower efficiency so we got the Brabazon instead.

In fact the Pennine team planned an even bigger engine with another 'mountain' name: Snowdon. This was never completed, but a lot of rig testing was done. It would have had 32 Pennine cylinders arranged in the form of front and rear X–16 engines sharing a common crankcase. All the 5,000-odd horsepower came out through a pinion amidships, driving shafts along each side, each driving a reduction gear to one half of

A production Vulture II, with front and rear casings over the reduction gear to a single propeller, front magneto ignition and two-piece rear downdraught air inlets.

the giant contra-rotating propeller. As in the Pennine, the carburettor group was fed by a downdraught inlet.

In contrast to the more unconventional projects, the Rolls-Royce Vulture, design of which was started in September 1935, was brought ahead rapidly to meet the needs of several important new aircraft for the RAF, but it was finally abandoned after hundreds had entered squadron service. The only unusual thing about it was that it was another 24-cylinder engine of X configuration, but in this case each cylinder block was a familiar one: that of the Kestrel. At least, the Vulture was originally four Kestrel blocks attached to one crankcase, but by the time it got into production it would have been more correct to describe them as Peregrine blocks. They were not spaced at 90°; instead, apart from having a single crankshaft, the engine literally comprised two V–12 engines, one upright and the other inverted underneath it, with the blocks accordingly spaced at 60°/120°. Dry weight was about 2,450 lb, and capacity was 2,592 cu in (42.48 litres). The engine had a large two-speed single-entry supercharger delivering mixture from the twin-choke SU carburettor to induction manifolds between the upper and lower pairs of cylinder blocks. At the front were the two 24-cylinder magnetos and an epicyclic reduction gear which put the propeller shaft on the engine centreline.

The Vulture first ran in late 1938, and was flight-tested in a Hawker Henley. It was earmarked for such important aircraft as the Avro and Handley Page bombers to specification P.13/36, the Vickers bomber to B.1/35 and the Hawker fighter to F.18/37. The fighter became the Tornado and was cancelled. The Vickers bomber became the Warwick, with various radial engines. The Handley Page bomber was redesigned with four Merlins and became the Halifax. Only the Avro bomber continued with the

The Henley used for early flight testing of the Vulture. Coolant was ducted to a large radiator well aft, but in the Manchester the radiator was under the engine.

Absence of black enamel shows this Vulture to be experimental, and the absence of the company name from the upper rocker covers indicates wartime. This particular engine had coil ignition, an updraught carburettor and redesigned asymmetric rocker covers.

Vulture, and the engine gradually proved to have major problems, which initially centred on lubrication difficulties in the twelve inverted cylinders. Nevertheless, the Vulture was type-tested in August 1939 at 1,800 hp for take-off, on 87-octane fuel. Production for the Manchester began in January 1940, the Avro 679 prototype having flown in July 1939.

By 1940 persistent trouble was being experienced with the connecting rods, and in particular with the four big-ends bearing on each crankpin. The crucial design fault was that, in a rare error, Elliott had arranged for the two halves of each master big-end to mate along a herringbone zig-zag, the two being then clamped by interference-fit bolts made of high-Brinell (non-ductile) Ni-Cr steel. Inevitably, the mating surfaces all fought each other, and fatigue was rapid. Some engines also burned out complete cylinder blocks because the flow of coolant had stopped. There were two coolant pumps in parallel, and it was possible for one to operate normally while the other suffered cavitation and delivered nothing. After much research the solution was found in the addition of a balance pipe linking the two pump inlets (over a decade later this

work was to provide direct assistance in the design of the bifurcated inlet to the Swift fighter, even though the Vulture problem had dealt with water and the jet problem with air).

The initial Vulture II was rated at 1,845 hp at 3,000 rpm at 5,000 ft and 1,710 hp at 15,000 ft, while the Vulture V, planned for the Avro-built Hawker Tornado and driving a Rotol or DH contraprop (both were flown), was rated at 1,980 hp. Continuing problems, notably with the conrods, forced rpm to be reduced to 2,850, but despite this in March 1941 a Vulture II was type-tested at 2,010 hp at 9 lb boost on 100-grade fuel. Moreover, by this time development Vultures, one having cylinders of Merlin 5.4-in bore, were being run at up to 3,100 hp, which was well beyond the level of power for which the engine had been designed. Despite this, the overall level of reliability of the engine in squadron service with Manchesters was dangerously low, and crew morale was badly affected. On top of the other problems, maintenance proved laborious, because of extreme difficulty of access to the 48 plugs and 96 valve tappets. Throughout 1941 Hives' regular Monday meetings pondered the future of the engine, and there were stormy arguments.

It was clear the Manchester would always be an also-ran, and that the Vulture would never forge ahead like the Merlin. Hives asked Avro to consider redesigning the Manchester wing to take four Merlins, as HP had done with the Halifax. Avro said they could do this, but could not at the same time handle the engine installation. Fortunately, back in 1938 Rolls-Royce had opened a Powerplant Engineering Department, initially under C. L. Cowdrey. When the latter went to Napier, Colonel Fell came back to Rolls-Royce from Armstrong Siddeley and managed the design of a standardized Merlin 'power egg' for the Beaufighter II. Though inner and outer engine installations were not quite the same, this already-existing Beaufighter Merlin package proved an admirable answer for the proposed four-Merlin Avro bomber. The latter, at first called the Manchester III and later the Lancaster, first flew on 9 January 1941. Its designer Roy Chadwick was at a loss to explain its unexpectedly good performance, which he thought might be due to the interaction of the underslung Merlin packages and the wing downstream. Everyone sighed with relief and the Vulture was cancelled in April 1942, with deliveries at 538. The engine had also powered the Blackburn B.20 retractable-hull flying boat, flown in March 1940.

One of the author's favourite quotations is attributed to 'Doc' (later Sir Stanley) Hooker, who described four-stroke engines as having 'one stroke to produce power and three to wear the engine out'. Though this was a tongue-in-cheek saying, there was more than a germ of truth behind it, and like many other companies Rolls-Royce kept thinking about what the two-stroke formula had to offer. By 1937 they could stand it no longer, but went to see Sir Harry Ricardo at Shoreham, who probably knew more about such engines than anyone else. Of course, the advantages of an engine that produces power on every downward movement of the piston are self-evident, but there are equally obvious drawbacks. Perhaps the chief disadvantage is that, whereas the four-stroke draws in fresh air and gets rid of virtually all its exhaust, the two-stroke cannot get rid of all the residual gas from each firing stroke but mixes some with the incoming supply of air. Expulsion of the burned gas can be improved by blowing air through the combustion space, and some of the best two-strokes are turbocharged diesels. Rolls-Royce took a long look at the two-stroke diesel, but the Air Ministry directed that the company should produce a spark-ignition engine.

Work began in 1937, with single-cylinder units soon on test at both Derby and Shoreham. Project engineer was Harry Wood, and the engine was given the name Crecy, which as a battlefield in France hardly fitted into any existing scheme. It finally settled as a 90° V–12, with liquid-cooled cylinders of 5.1 in bore and 6.5 in stroke, giving a capacity of 1,593 cu in (26 litres). Sleeve valves were fitted, together with spur-type reduction gear, direct fuel injection from a six-plunger pump at the front of each block, and a mechanically driven supercharger. Because of the high exhaust energy it was also planned eventually to fit a turbocharger or an exhaust gas turbine.

Ricardo and Wood got encouraging results from the single-cylinder testing, and the project was not terminated with the outbreak of war. In 1941 the first complete engine was on test, and its noise was awesome. Immediately various unexpected problems, mostly mechanical, reared their heads, though the design rating of 1,400 hp was attained from the start. Ricardo had designed an ingenious system of charge stratification from an injector in the centre of the head, and this appeared to work well. On the other hand, vibration and piston cooling, and to a lesser degree sleeve cooling,

Above *The best-known picture of a Crecy. In 1988 Andrew Nahum of London's Science Museum completed a detailed study of this engine.*

Below *A lesser-known Crecy, with many changes including a magneto mounted further back at an oblique angle (the plug leads are disconnected here). With 3,000 hp in sight, from an engine smaller than the Merlin, the Crecy team was sad to be stopped.*

An experimental Eagle, not quite complete. At the rear can be seen one of the four aftercoolers, beneath which is one end of the huge Corliss barrel-type throttle.

kept posing severe problems. To overcome torsional vibration in the drive to the supercharger a freewheel was inserted—which, said Lovesey, meant that the impeller actually ran at a higher speed than that dictated by the gear ratio! The Crecy was abandoned after a year of full engine testing, and with some reluctance. Just over 2,000 hp at 2,600 rpm had been achieved, and the intention had been to add an exhaust-driven gas turbine geared to the crankshaft, with which powers well in excess of 3,000 hp were predicted.

The Crecy was an engine of remarkable but probably unrealisable potential. Stanley Hooker thought it could never equal the Merlin in output per unit piston area, and Lovesey considered some of the claims of the Crecy team to be extravagant; but in many ways the two-stroke plus exhaust turbine formula ought to be hard to equal.

Suffice to say, in the 1950s Napier wasted a vast amount of effort on engines in this category, aiming at ultra-low fuel consumption and using valveless diesel cylinders.

In 1942, when the Crecy was dropped, there appeared to be a need for an engine more powerful than anything currently running. The Crecy team, plus others, were assigned the task of creating a totally new engine in the 3,500 hp class. This conventional four-stroke spark-ignition design was from the start a mainstream engine, developed by 'the First Eleven' under Lovesey, and it repeated the proud name of Eagle. Unfortunately, starting in December 1942 meant that the product emerged into a world fast becoming dominated by the gas turbine, and the new Eagle made no impact on the world scene at all.

In all essentials it was an enlarged Napier Sabre, but avoiding that engine's many pitfalls. The basis comprised a central crank-case to which were attached left and right monobloc castings containing lower and upper rows of six parallel cylinders, making 24 in all. Each cylinder had 5.4 in bore, again as in the Merlin, and a stroke of 5.125 in. Capacity was thus 2,808 cu in, or 46 litres. Each cylinder had a sleeve valve, in principle very like those of the Exe and Crecy, and each block was bolted through by 28 nickel-steel bolts. The basic premises were that not more than twelve cylinders should drive a single crankshaft, unlike the Vulture and Exe, and for reasons of flame travel the cylinder bore should not exceed 6 in. This meant two crankshafts, as in the Sabre, and they were linked to a two-stage two-speed supercharger with intercooling at the rear and, via a spur gear, a single propeller shaft at the front. Later the Eagle 22, for the Westland Wyvern naval strike fighter, was fitted with a new gearbox driving a contra-prop, at a ratio of only 0.2985. At the lower rear was a huge Corliss barrel throttle, lead-ing to the tandem nineteen-vane super-charger impellers and thence, via four aftercoolers (the correct term now being used), to the four cylinder banks. The five-plunger Rolls-Royce (SU) injection pump supplied metered fuel to the eye of the LP supercharger, and in all respects the Eagle rested on the massive experience gained with the previous piston engines.

The Eagle 22 of 1945 delivered 3,415 hp for take-off, for a weight of 3,900 lb. Rating in low blower was 3,500 hp at 3,500 rpm at 3,250 ft, and in full-supercharge gear, 3,020 hp at the same rpm at 15,250 ft. The Eagle was an impressive engine, and firing the Coffman cartridge starter unleashed awe-some power, but Rolls-Royce test pilot Cliff Rogers suffered two inflight failures in the Wyvern I which resulted in hairy dead-stick landings, in the second case on fire.

Hives told the author that, with the benefit of hindsight, it had been a mistake to embark on such a big reciprocating project, even allowing for the uncertain potential of turbo-

A production Eagle 22, showing the better outline of the casing over the spur-type reduction gear. Coolant from the junkheads passed through steam separators on its way to the header tank above the engine.

props. In fact the company embarked on an even bigger engine, the 100H24, in the 6,500 hp class! This was again to be a liquid-cooled H24 but with big sleeve-valve cylinders of 7 in bore and 6.65 in stroke, giving a capacity of 6,150 cu in. Fortunately this never got further than buying the materials for a single-cylinder test unit. Gas turbines were rightly seen as a better answer.

By 1950 Westland were at last in pro-duction with the Wyvern, with the Eagle replaced by the equally massive Armstrong Siddeley Python turboprop. This undistinguished engine was the sole outcome of a development programme started at Farnborough by Dr A. A. Griffith in 1926. It so happened that Griffith was the first person to be hired by Hives to see what might be expected from gas turbines, as related in the next chapter.

Chapter 7

THE FIRST JETS

The first man to work seriously on gas turbines for aircraft propulsion in Britain, and possibly in the world, was Dr A. A. Griffith. A curious loner, he had high academic qualifications but no conception of the team effort needed to design a real engine. In the early 1920s he developed a theory of axial-flow compressors and turbines, treating the blades as aerofoils. Among other things he discovered that an axial turbine should be of the free-vortex type, and calculated that he could design a good enough gas turbine to drive a propeller. Accordingly, in 1926 he proposed that work be started on what today would be called a single-shaft axial turboprop. (The idea of jet propulsion did not occur to him.) In 1927 tunnel testing began on simple cascades of aerofoils, but work was slow, and in 1930 Griffith was sent from the Royal Aircraft Establishment at Farnborough to do engine research at the Air Ministry Laboratory at South Kensington.

He had only been at South Kensington a short time when he was asked to interview a young RAF officer, Pilot Officer Frank Whittle, and give an opinion on Whittle's idea for a turbojet. Griffith ought to have seen that here was a totally new kind of aero engine with vast possibilities, opening up a new vista of flight speed and needing only the development of improved high-temperature materials for its realization.

Instead he poured cold water on the idea, scorned it because it was based on the centrifugal compressor, and gave the young inventor no encouragement whatsoever. Griffith's own ideas were for engines of far greater complexity, with multiple stages of axial blading. He had no conception of what was within the available state of the art. But after his meeting with Whittle Griffith began to think of how the gas turbine might be used for jet propulsion.

By the late 1930s Hives had heard repeated stories of Griffith's work, and also of the much more radical new engine which, against all the odds, had actually been built by Whittle, though he was still in the RAF. Hives possessed strategic vision of a kind almost universally lacking in British industry at that time. He recognized that Rolls-Royce had become perhaps the world No 1 in piston aero engines, and that this capability rested on its unrivalled team of design and development engineers. But he sensed that the company was going to need one or two rather different people with different skills. The first he hired was Stanley Hooker, not then an engineer at all but a mathematician and expert in supersonic aerodynamics, whom he weaned away from the Admiralty in January 1938. The results far surpassed any possible prediction; within weeks young Hooker had vastly improved the Merlin, and everything he touched seemed to turn to gold. The next visionary Hives hired was Griffith.

Griffith had little interest in anything except complicated gas-turbine designs of the turboprop or jet type. Hives appreciated that Rolls-Royce was already stretched to the limit developing the Merlin and other piston engines, but he had a feeling that in due course the gas turbine could well become the dominant kind of engine, and he judged that the company ought to have at least one engineer fluent in the new technology. He met Griffith in the spring of 1939, and the former senior Civil Servant was taken on the payroll in June of that year. As with Hooker, Hives did not assign the learned doctor any specific work. Rather, because he realized that even Rolls-Royce could expend its energies solving the immediate problems, he set him up in a self-contained office in the company's guest house, Duffield Bank, and told him 'Go on thinking'.

Don Eyre was attached to him as designer. Eyre had been the youngest of Royce's own team at West Wittering, and his drawings were things of beauty. Hooker used to say they 'sold Griffith's ideas just like Johnnie Walker sold Scotch whisky, and with the same soporific effect'. This is probably a fair assessment. For 21 years Griffith and Eyre worked together on ever more fabulous schemes, some of which were built and tested at great expense, without anything ever getting near the stage of becoming a commercial product. This is not to suggest any of the ideas were impractical; Griffith was indeed one of the world's greatest experts on the axial turbine. But the best that can be said of his ideas, looked at from a purely business angle, is that some were near misses.

Common sense suggests that when thrusting out into a totally new field of advanced technology it is a good idea to start off with rather basic, simple schemes,

in order to gain experience and learn the pitfalls. Instead Griffith's soaring mind kept leaping far ahead, and most of his concepts were more suited to the 1980s or the 21st century. It is perhaps sad that not even Hives was able to persuade Griffith to make haste a little more slowly and start off with a simple engine that could be built and tested successfully. Instead, Griffith was given a free rein, and he spent the whole of World War 2 thinking up ever more impressive engines in which hundreds of axial blades, including many of the double-deck type, served as turbofans, compressors and turbines working in complex flows of air and hot gas which in most cases went through two complete reversals of direction in passing through the engine.

The first study for a complete engine to reach an advanced stage was the CR.1, the designation meaning 'contra-rotating'. Dating from 1940, this was a typically ingenious turbofan of bypass ratio 7, described by its inventor in the following terms: 'Starting at the nose, the parts shown under the nose cowl, in order, are an electric starter, rotary fuel burner, and a fourteen-stage axial turbocompressor. Under the ring cowl are six [the version illustrated has eight] airscrew discs in tandem driven by integral turbine blades. Successive discs in both compressor and airscrew sections rotate in opposite directions, a feature which minimises rotational speeds and stresses, and completely eliminates mechanical transmission of power. The use of a very large number of small airscrew blades permits a very large thrust to be obtained without excessive airscrew weight, whilst the enclosure of the airscrew discs in a cowl avoids the necessity for varying the pitch. As with all jet propulsion systems, no figure for bhp can be quoted, but broadly it may be said that in take-off thrust and propulsive power in flight the unit is estimated to be equivalent to a fully supercharged piston engine and airscrew of at least 3,000 bhp.

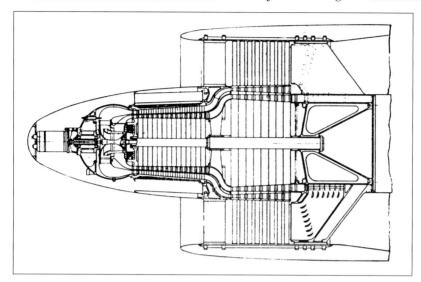

Griffith's series-flow contra-rotating CR. 1 turbofan with a bypass ratio of 7. Brilliant, and far ahead of its time – compare it with the Contrafan in the last chapter – it succeeded merely in diverting effort from engines that could be built and sold.

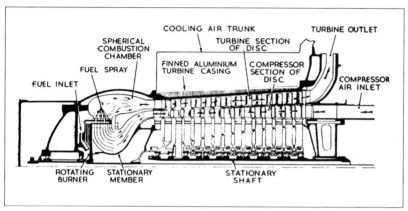

COOLING AIR TRUNK

TURBINE OUTLET

SPHERICAL COMBUSTION CHAMBER

TURBINE SECTION OF DISC

FUEL SPRAY

FINNED ALUMINIUM TURBINE CASING

COMPRESSOR SECTION OF DISC

FUEL INLET

COMPRESSOR AIR INLET

ROTATING BURNER

STATIONARY MEMBER

STATIONARY SHAFT

Detail of the 14-stage high-pressure section of the CR.1. This was actually built, but never even approached its theoretical performance.

Inclusive installed weight is expected to be less than 1,500 lb, ie less than one-quarter of the equivalent petrol engine installation. As a rough indication, cruising consumption may be put somewhere between that of a petrol engine and that of a diesel. High-level cruising is, however, much more favourable to long range than with a conventional powerplant, range at 36,000 ft being some 60% greater than at sea level. Practically any liquid fuel may be used.'

This description, written in April 1941, went on to suggest 'the possibility of a jump take-off, a flap being provided behind the power unit which could be lowered so as to deflect the slipstream downwards. An obvious further development is to use the flap for landing also, whereby ground speed might be brought practically to zero before touching down.' Much later Griffith was to be a pioneer of multi-jet VTOL schemes, which again were to be wholly plausible yet fail to be adopted. Rubbra and Lionel Haworth, two of the great mainstream designers at Derby, fell under the Griffith spell, and the decision was taken to build the fourteen-stage HP section of the CR.1. Each disc, with double-deck turbo/compressor blades, ran on its own ball bearings on a stationary shaft, and the fuel was injected centrifugally. The unit went on test on 3 March 1942. As might have been expected, the mass of leakage paths made it impossible to get anywhere near the predicted performance.

Accordingly Griffith switched his enthusiasm to the CR.2, an even more complicated engine with bypass ratio reduced to 2. In November 1944 Griffith described it thus: 'The engine components comprise a twenty-rotor contra-flow unit of the divided flow type in which rather more than half of the gas from the combustion chamber goes through an eight-stage power turbine to provide the useful work. The power turbine is coupled directly to a four-stage axial compressor or ducted fan. Part of the air delivered by the fan (about one-third at full power) feeds the intakes of the contra-flow compressor, which is therefore super-charged by the fan. The remainder of the fan delivery and the exhaust gas from the contra-flow unit and the power turbine pass through a common jet pipe to the propelling nozzle. As a result, both turbines work under practically the same pressure ratio as the contra-flow compressor. This minimizes leaks in the contra-flow unit and ensures freedom from surging. The propelling nozzle may be of variable area, and provision may be made for burning additional fuel in the jet pipe to increase the thrust. The combustion chamber is a development of the spherical type with rotary burner which has already been tested for CR application. Owing to the low speed and large number of stages the blade stresses in the power turbine are about the same as in the contra-flow turbine, so that the same gas temperature may be used in both. . .'

In the harsh real world Griffith side-stepped such questions as gas temperature by running his rigs on compressed air. Not until well into 1943 was any CR running attempted with a combustion chamber, even though by this time the CR.2 had a high priority and many engineers were assigned to it. Increasingly, the yawning

chasm between Eyre's beautiful drawings of Griffith's concepts and an actual engine that Rolls-Royce could sell became clear to everyone, even to such disciples as Haworth and Rubbra, and with great reluctance the complex contra-flow effort was brought to a close in 1944.

To Griffith's inexpressible chagrin their place was by this time being taken by the despised centrifugal turbojet of Whittle. The first direct contact between Whittle and Rolls-Royce came in January 1940 when Hayne Constant, Griffith's long-time associate at Farnborough, invited Dr Hooker to Whittle's small company, Power Jets Ltd, at Lutterworth. There, in a derelict old foundry, in an atmosphere filled with abrasive casting sand and with snow on the floor, Hooker saw the strangest and crudest engine of his life. Compared with the jewel-like Merlin it looked barbaric; yet, as it thundered away on its testbed, Hooker felt that he was 'in the presence of great power'. A brilliant aerodynamicist, Hooker carried out his own analysis of Whittle's engine, and in doing so 'came under the spell of Frank Whittle's genius and super technical knowledge'.

Hooker realized that the crudely simple engine at Lutterworth opened the door to the future. It eliminated reciprocating motion, and the three wasted strokes of the four-stroke cycle. It swept away the propeller and its heavy gearbox which posed a barrier to further advance in the speed of aircraft. In principle, it could burn any liquid fuel. Moreover, Whittle had also calculated the performance of any kind of turbojet or turbofan with the precision of Newton. Not least, having to incorporate a compressor with performance far, far beyond anything previously attempted, he simply set about the task of designing one. Whittle was well aware of the advantages of axial compressors but, said Hooker, 'with his infallible clear insight he chose a centrifugal. . . When, some years later, I was destined to take over from him, I was never able to improve his compressor—I made it worse on one occasion, but never better.'

Hooker and Whittle soon became friends, with great mutual respect. In August 1940 Hooker suggested that Hives should visit Power Jets and see this new engine. Hives asked 'What does it do?' to which Hooker replied 'It is giving 1,000 lb thrust'. 'That doesn't sound very much', said Hives, 'it wouldn't pull the skin off a rice pudding, would it?' Hooker had already foreseen this, and pointed out that, assuming 70% propeller efficiency, this was about the thrust of a Spitfire's Merlin at full throttle. Hives instantly pushed the bell to summon his secretary; he told her 'I'm going with Hooker to Lutterworth on Sunday'. This was the start of the company's work on gas turbines that could actually be produced.

Whittle was able to show visitors just one turbojet, which had been rebuilt so often it was, in his words, 'a running heap of scrap'. Hives said, 'I don't see many engines; what is holding you up?' Whittle explained how impossible it was to get new parts made, whereupon Hives said 'Send us the drawings . . . we will make them for you'. As they parted, Whittle emphasized how simple his engine was; Hives' classic retort was 'Don't worry, we'll soon design the bloody simplicity out of it!'

Hives asked Hooker and Haworth to keep in touch with Whittle. With Geoff 'Oscar' Wilde, Hooker soon helped solve the surging problem experienced by the Power Jets W.2 engine by testing its compressor on a specially built rig at Derby driven by a Vulture via a 5.67:1 step-up gear. This was the kind of test rig far beyond the financial reach of Power Jets. Hooker noted 'with envy and admiration', that Whittle's compressor had an efficiency within 1% of the design target of 80%.

On 12 January 1942 Hives invited Whittle to Derby to discuss the proposition that Rolls-Royce should build a Whittle engine.

Unfortunately, after this most amicable meeting each waited for the other to make the next move, and much valuable time was lost. Some months later, however, the Ministry of Aircraft Production (MAP) approved collaboration between the two companies. The situation had previously been appalling. Power Jets had invited the Rover Car firm to build turbojet parts under subcontract. Rover, however, went to the MAP behind Power Jets' back and sought, and eventually obtained, direct contracts. Thus, the net result was that Power Jets failed to get a much-needed subcontractor, getting instead a competitor for vitally needed materials and parts. Worse, the MAP had authorized Rover to handle production only on the understanding that no design changes would be introduced without approval of the MAP and Power Jets, but before long it was clear that Rover had no intention of honouring this agreement. Soon, not only was Rover allowed to make any design changes it liked—though it had no experience whatsoever, nor any gas-turbine technical staff—but Power Jets (Whittle's own firm) was forbidden to interfere in the design of production engines! Things went from bad to worse, and as 1942 dragged on the two firms were hardly talking to each other. The vital W.2B engine, for the F.9/40 Rampage (later renamed Meteor) twin-jet fighter, made hardly any progress at all. Rover had all the political clout, and big facilities at Barnoldswick and Clitheroe, plus Lucas at Burnley (all near the border of northern Yorkshire and Lancashire) for making jet engines, but totally lacked design and development capability. At Lutterworth poor Whittle had a brilliant and experienced team, but very limited facilities, and hardly any permission to do anything. And this during the darkest hours of World War 2!

For a start the MAP let Power Jets subcontract six turbojets to Rolls-Royce in spring 1942. The result was the WR.1,

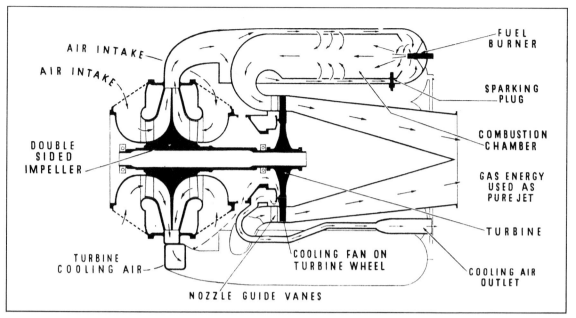

Simplified longitudinal section of the WR.1, the company's first Whittle-type turbojet. Air entered at the front and rear of the double-sided compressor, passed to the rear of the tubular combustion chambers and then, entering the inner flame tubes, travelled forwards again before making a final 180° change in direction to escape through the turbine and jetpipe.

basically like a W.2B but with a less ambitious compressor, of only 2.6 pressure ratio, designed mainly by Haworth according to the company's experience on superchargers. The engine was also slightly scaled up, to give a design thrust of 2,000 lb. One objective had been to see if a turbojet could be made completely reliable, and another was to gain experience among the gas-turbine design team being formed at Derby. Two WR.1s were tested by November 1942, but by this time the engine had been dropped as being outmoded. Instead Hives told the MAP he was willing to replace Rover, and at last get the Whittle engine into proper development. In the same month, November 1942, he went with Hooker to 'The Swan and Royal' at Clitheroe and had a wartime five-shilling dinner with S. B. Wilkes, Chairman of Rover. After the meal, in a sixty-second conversation which changed the world, Hives said to his guest,

'Why are you playing around with this jet engine? It's not in your line of business; you grub about on the ground, and I hear from Hooker that things are going from bad to worse with Whittle'. Wilkes replied, 'We can't get on with the fellow at all, and I would like to be shot of the whole business'. At which Hives said, 'I'll tell you what I will do. You give us this jet job, and I will give you our tank-engine factory at Nottingham'. From that moment on, Whittle's turbojet— one of the greatest inventions of all time, which could have played a major part in winning the war—ceased to languish in the doldrums and at last got proper facilities and effort behind it.

The author talked at length with Whittle and Hives about these momentous times. Hives was the only man in Rolls-Royce with the vision and executive authority to take the company into the era of the turbojet. While outwardly remaining loyal to Griffith, who never ceased to be convincing despite his inability to 'deliver', Hives recognized that in Whittle's simple engine lay the key to the future. He could see that after the war the world would be 'knee-deep in Merlins. We wouldn't be able to give them away. We simply had to be not merely "in" on the next generation—something to render the Merlin obsolete—but leaders of it'. For the immediate future, the task was to force through development of the W.2B and get it into production. Though the official date for the Rolls-Royce takeover was 1 April 1943 the company did, in fact, take over complete control from 1 January. Changes happened immediately.

Most of Rover's engineers and senior staff chose to stay and move to Nottingham or Solihull, but about twenty elected to join Rolls-Royce with the W.2B. Three were to be of vital importance. Denis Drew was to become responsible for all development and test equipment and instrumentation, almost all of it utterly unlike that used in piston engines. John Herriot, of the MAP Aeronautical Inspection Directorate, who had been appalled at the situation in Rover, was at last able to plan for production. Adrian Lombard, previously a car designer, proved to be one of the world's greatest gas-turbine engineers and was eventually to become a main board director and Director of Engineering of the Aero Engine Division. The changed spirit of the development teams—and indeed the performance of subcontractors, aware of the impatience of Hives and the pressures he could bring to bear—was nothing short of miraculous.

Hives had realized months earlier what ought to have been obvious to all the armies of officials who had unhelpfully busied themselves in Whittle's struggle: that the former Rover works at Barnoldswick, Bankfield Shed, was 'totally inadequate' as a production factory. He ordered that henceforth it was to be devoted entirely to research and development, under the man-

agement of Dr Stanley Hooker. Production, under Herriot, was to be centred at a new factory at Newcastle-under-Lyme. At a stroke this put about 2,000 people on to W.2B development, and things at last began to happen fast—as they should have done throughout 1941 and 1942. Total running time in December 1942, under Rover, was 37 hours. In January the figure exceeded 390.

In the first three months of 1943 almost all the major problems with the W.2B were solved, by the basic process of running engines to death and rectifying each failure as it occurred. In this period Hooker built up a powerful gas-turbine team, taking design and development engineers from Derby, including such future stars as Harry Pearson, Freddie Morley, Lindsay Dawson and Geoffrey Fawn. Les Buckler came from Derby to manage the Barnoldswick machine shops, and soon had a line of machines turning out turbine blades machined from rough forgings of Nimonic 80, a special alloy of nickel and chromium. Previously there had never been enough blades, and they had been made by hand by many different methods in a variety of materials. From spring 1943 there were not only plenty of blades but their quality was also improved. At last the design of the vital blades was also as Whittle wanted, by being skewed (twisted) through an angle of 5°. Whittle had been trying to get this change incorporated since 1941, but Rover had repeatedly refused, saying it would 'disrupt production'! As a result the W.2B passed its first 100-hour Type Test at full design performance of 1,600 lb thrust on 7 May 1943.

Flight development also proceeded apace with engines installed in the second E.28/39 aircraft and in the tails of two converted Wellington bombers. Rolls-Royce called the engine the W.2B/23, but soon changed this to B.23, and then RB.23, the RB standing for Rolls-Barnoldswick. The engine adhered closely to Whittle's original design,

Above _Rolls-Royce's first jet flying testbed was Wellington II Z8570. The engine under test, initially a Rover-built W.2B/23, was installed in the tail, with inlets immediately behind the elevators._

Right _Britain's first production turbojet, after a delay of much more than a year caused by the hopeless management situation prior to the takeover by Rolls-Royce, began to come off the line at the Barnoldswick factory in October 1943. The Welland I weighed 850 lb and was rated at 1,700 lb._

with a double-sided compressor, ten reverse-flow tubular combustion chambers, and single-stage turbine. Two RB.23s derated to 1,450 lb powered an F.9/40 Meteor prototype (*DG205*) on 12 June 1943, and in October the engine was cleared for production at 1,700 lb as the Rolls-Royce Welland I, the company having decided to name its gas turbines after rivers to emphasize the steady flow through such engines. The initial production batch comprised 100 Wellands, followed by seventy more, made at Barnoldswick. These entered service on 12 July 1944 with 616 Squadron RAF, the world's first combat unit—as distinct from a test unit—to be equipped with turbojet aircraft.

By this time Power Jets had developed a greatly improved engine, the W.2/500, but with the full agreement of Frank Whittle Rolls-Royce decided instead to build its own 'next' engine, the B.37. This was based on the Welland but incorporated a new compressor diffuser designed at Derby by Wilde to increase mass flow by 25%, a change which was matched by slightly lengthening the turbine blades. Another new feature was the use of straight-flow combustion chambers—sketched by Whittle long beforehand, and also studied by Lombard at Rover—which greatly changed the engine's appearance. Hooker omitted the cascade of curved inlet swirl vanes at each compressor inlet because they were rather fragile and, if they broke, tended to damage the engine as they passed through. To his surprise, their omission caused such a reduction in compressor efficiency (from

One of the first production Derwent Is, accepted on 3 October 1944 for a Meteor F.III. Rated at 2,000 lb thrust, the equipped weight was 975 lb. The ten combustion chambers were of the straight-through type.

78 to 73 per cent) that to get the design thrust of 2,000 lb the turbine gas temperature had to be increased from 754°C to 843°C. Hooker still doggedly persisted in leaving them off and the engine ran reliably, if much hotter, without them. The B.37 first ran in July 1943, passed its Type Test in November, and went into production as the Derwent I at the new factory at Newcastle-under-Lyme in April 1944. Including the fifty built at Barnoldswick, Rolls-Royce delivered 550 by the end of 1945, to power the Meteor III.

In the Derwent II Whittle's Type 16 compressor casing, with a tangential-exit diffuser case with cascades feeding seven large combustion chambers, increased thrust to 2,100 lb. The Derwent III incorporated giant suction pipes for boundary-layer control in the Griffith-wing Meteor and all-wing A.W.52 aircraft, and the Derwent IV had a larger compressor to give 2,450 lb. But suddenly Rolls-Royce was able to leapfrog to far higher thrust.

In April 1944 Dr Hooker visited the USA and was shocked to find General Electric were actually running two turbojets, one a centrifugal and the other an axial, each rated at 4,000 lb thrust. Immediately on his return he resolved to design a Whittle engine of 5,000 lb thrust. He eventually obtained an MAP contract for an engine of 4,200 lb, on the understanding that 5,000 lb would be the design target. He had already calculated that a mere scaled-up Derwent would have a diameter of 60 in, whereas a completely new engine might get under 55 in. Work began on 1 May 1944, and for the first time Rolls-Royce (Hooker, Lombard, Pearson and Morley) designed a practical gas turbine from the proverbial clean sheet of paper. The compressor was of 28.8 in diameter, compared with 20.68 for the Derwent I, to handle a mass flow of 80 lb/s. A small auxiliary impeller was added to cool the rear bearing and turbine disc. There were straight-flow combustion

chambers, as in the Derwent, but these were of a more efficient design and there were nine of them. The Derwent's Lucas fuel pump was retained, but now two were needed! The B.40 design was quickly refined into the B.41, later called RB.41 for Rolls-Royce Barnoldswick, and the engine was named the Nene.

The first engine was ready for test at 10.00 pm on 27 October 1944, less than six months from the decision to start design. Virtually the entire workforce had gathered for the occasion, and a big groan was heard when, having reached the correct cranking speed on the electric starter, the Nene failed to light up. It failed a second time, and it was clear that the igniter plugs had been incorrectly positioned (this aspect of design was inevitably hit-and-miss). Denis Drew unscrewed one, and thrust an oxy-acetylene torch into the hole. The engine lit with a muffled explosion, and flames appeared from collected fuel—just as on the very first light-up of Whittle's first engine on 12 April 1937. Within a few seconds, however, the Nene was running beautifully. Slowly the throttle was opened, and Hooker recalled 'when the engine passed the 4,000 lb mark the cheer must have been heard all over Barnoldswick'. It was around midnight.

The Nene had been designed with Whittle-type inlet swirl vanes, but Hooker insisted on omitting them at the start of testing. The instrumentation showed high turbine temperatures, and Hooker could see that it would be a long struggle to reach 5,000 lb. When he returned to the testbed a little later that morning, having snatched an hour or two's sleep, he was amazed to find the Nene giving 5,000 lb at the same gas temperature as at 4,000 lb in the small hours. Harry Pearson had had the vanes fitted, and the improvement was dramatic. Rolls-Royce had the most powerful aero engine in the world. A Nene flew in an American YP-80A Shooting Star fighter on 21 July

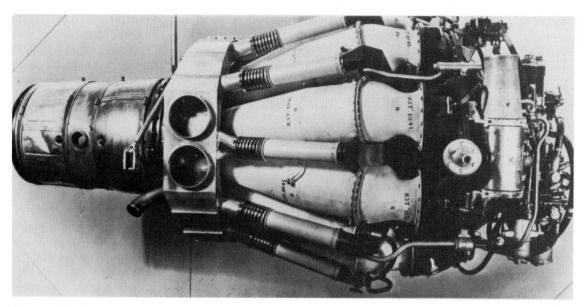

Above *The Derwent III was an oddball engine with a high-capacity bleed system to energize the boundary-layer control of the A.W.52 all-wing research aircraft. It retained the 20.68 in compressor, the Mk IV engine having a compressor enlarged to 21.7 in.*

Above right *A Nene 10, of which 1,000 were produced by Rolls-Royce Canada in 1953–55 to power Canadair T-33AN Silver Star trainers. It had a larger wheelcase for additional accessories.*

Right *This cutaway of a Nene shows the auxiliary compressor amidships feeding cooling air to the turbine disc and main bearing. Also visible are the concentric curved vanes guiding air into the front and rear of the main compressor. Their importance was discovered on the very first run.*

1945, but by this time the British government had little interest in aeronautical progress, and no attempt was made to rush ahead with Nene-powered aircraft. This was not the case in other countries, however, and when in 1946 the British government shipped 25 Nenes to Moscow—as a misguided gesture of goodwill—the engine was quickly put into massive production in the Soviet Union as the RD–45. From this was developed the VK–1 family, which later went into production in China as the WP–5, which is to this day an important front-line engine. In 1947 a licence to build an Americanized version of the Nene was obtained by Pratt & Whitney, establishing that giant rival of Rolls-Royce in the gas-turbine field, while other Nenes were made

in France, Canada and Australia. Later a few Nenes were even used in British aircraft, the Attacker and Sea Hawk naval fighters. The Nene also figured in early jet-lift research (Chapter 10).

In November 1944 Whittle came to see the Nene on test, and stayed for a celebration dinner at 'The Swan and Royal' at Clitheroe. He bewailed the lack of any application for this powerful engine, and suggested scaling it down to fit the nacelle of the Meteor. Lombard did the calculation on the table-cloth and got the amazing answer of 3,650 lb thrust! Hives was disconcerted, because Newcastle-under-Lyme was getting into production with the Derwent I at just over half this power, but he did not specifically forbid a go-ahead and the result was the

Above *The Derwent V resembled earlier Derwents in size only. A totally new design, it was produced by scaling down the Nene. Note the prominent right-angle elbows leading from the compressor diffuser to the nine combustion chambers.*

Below *Rolls-Royce conducted their earliest flight development of reheat jetpipes (afterburners) with the Derwent V engines of this Meteor. Britain lagged behind in such work, reflecting lack of interest by the user services.*

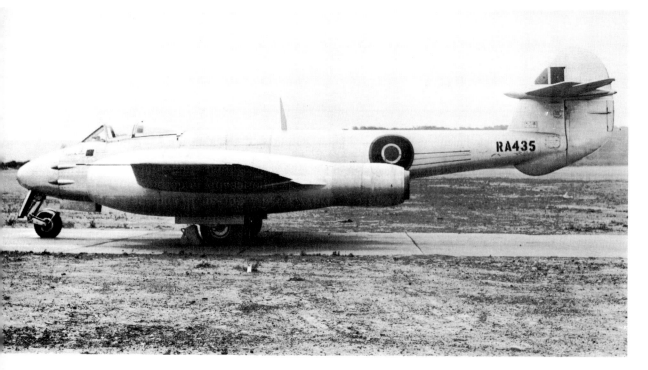

Above *With the original Tay, Rolls-Royce reached near to the limit of what could be done with the classic Whittle engine. In just ten years from Whittle's first run the thrust had been multiplied by almost ten, for considerably less than three times the weight.*

Below *A unique gaggle of testbed aircraft flying from Hucknall in 1947: Hornet F.I. PX288 (Merlin 130/131), Meteor F.I EE227 (Trent), Lancastrian VH742 (Nene), Meteor F.4 RA430 (Derwent development) and Vampire F.2 TX807 (after fitting with F.3 tail) (Nene).*

While licensed versions, or pirated copies, of the original Tay were mass-produced all over the world, the land where it was designed used just two. They were fitted in the V.663 Viscount, whose useful life was spent developing electrically-signalled flight controls for Boulton Paul.

Derwent V, first run on 7 June 1945. It began life at 2,600 lb but was swiftly developed to 3,500, and when Gloster test pilot Eric Greenwood flew a Meteor powered by two Derwent Vs on 15 August 1945 his comment was 'At last we have a real aeroplane'. In October 1945 Group Captain H. J. 'Willy' Wilson set a new world speed record at 606.25 mph, raised in September 1946 to 615.65 mph by Group Captain E. M. Donaldson, using engines with Nimonic 90 turbine blades rated at 4,200 lb thrust. Service rating of the Derwent 8, power unit of most Meteors, was 3,500 lb with small nacelle inlets and 3,700 lb with enlarged inlets. There were various experimental developments, including engines with primitive afterburners (reheat jetpipes).

By 1947 the classic centrifugal turbojet had been completely mastered, and the main design team at Derby added 0.5 in to the Nene compressor and made other changes to increase mass flow by some 60%, to 130 lb/s! The result was the RB.44 Tay, an outstanding engine that combined all that was best in the technology of Whittle and Rolls-Royce. Sadly, this saw even less usage in Britain than the Nene, being flown only in an odd conversion of the Viscount turboprop airliner on 16 March 1950. Other countries put the Tay to better use, massive production ensuing of the Pratt & Whitney J48 and Hispano-Suiza Verdon at thrusts of up to 8,500 lb with afterburner. At least this brought Rolls-Royce a good income from royalties.

Chapter 8

THE FIRST TURBOPROPS

In late 1943 Dr S.G. Hooker decided that work ought to begin on an advanced turboprop. Whittle himself had always recognized the importance of aircraft gas turbines more complicated than the simple turbojet, and had schemed various ducted fans and turboprops, while Dr A. A. Griffith had concentrated exclusively on such engines. Hooker judged correctly that none of Griffith's schemes would reach the production stage, and that the time was ripe for his own team at Barnoldswick to create an engine that could do so.

The result was the RB.39 Clyde, most of the drawings for which were produced by Lombard (hot end) and Lionel Haworth (the rest) in the first half of 1944. Hooker appreciated that with a turboprop there is every advantage in increasing pressure ratio (pr), and he considered a pr of at least 6 to be desirable. This was well beyond the capability of a single centrifugal compressor at that time, and he took a long look at two such compressors in series, as in the two-stage piston engines. Eventually a curious layout was adopted. A single-stage HP

The Clyde could have been a world-beater, produced in large numbers. Eleven of them showed tremendous potential in 3,200 hours of testing, but all Rolls-Royce got from this was experience with two-shaft engines.

(high-pressure) turbine drove a single-sided HP compressor scaled up from the Merlin 46 supercharger, via a tubular shaft. Down the centre of this shaft ran a long tubular shaft connecting a single-stage LP (low-pressure) turbine and an axial compressor and propeller reduction gear. The axial compressor was based on that of the Metropolitan-Vickers F.2/4 turbojet, an engine based on a design by RAE Farnborough but developed at Metrovick under Dr D.M. Smith. For the Clyde this spool was cut back from ten to nine stages. Pressure ratio of the LP spool was 2.65 at 6,000 rpm, and that of the HP spool 2.35 at 10,800 rpm, giving an overall pr of 6.23. The HP spool drove all accessories, and this alone was cranked during starting. There were eleven combustion chambers, arranged in a slightly skewed fashion to eliminate 90° bends in the flow path.

At first glance the Clyde looked like an axial turbojet and a centrifugal turbojet bolted end-to-end. It was the first two-spool, or two-shaft, aircraft gas turbine to be built anywhere. The author considered it extraordinary that the LP turbine, with but a single stage, should have had to drive both the axial compressor and the propeller; a more normal work split would have used one turbine to drive the tandem compressors and the other to drive the propeller. There was an auxiliary compressor as well as several major compressor air bleeds to provide large flows of cooling air for the turbine discs and other hot parts.

The first Clyde ran as a complete engine on 5 August 1945. Most of its component parts had been tested previously, and the only serious problem was that the two compressors were not correctly matched. This was soon rectified, and thereafter every predicted figure was exceeded. About 2,000 shp was reached on the second run, and the first engine probably exceeded the approved take-off rating of 2,560 shp. It was followed by ten further development engines, Nos 4

and 7 achieving 3,020 shp plus a remarkable 1,225 lb of residual jet thrust. By 1947 the No 9 Clyde was running with water/methanol injection at a rating of 4,200 shp plus 830 lb thrust, equivalent to 4,543 ehp. This tremendous advance in power was managed almost single-handed by J.P. Herriot, and in the author's view it is tragic that the Clyde was never treated as a potential winner for Rolls-Royce. Even the great uprating in power was accomplished purely in order to demonstrate mechanical integrity, and the capacity of the epicyclic reduction gear. The Clyde proved to be a powerful and reliable engine, and after a severe test to clear it for flight at 500 mph at sea level on full throttle—at which 3,000 hp static equated to 4,100 hp—a production order was placed for 100 engines for the Westland Wyvern. Hives refused this. He was polarized on the Avon turbojet, which he said would be 'the Merlin of the jet age'; he considered the Clyde would never be important.

For all its odd appearance, the only thing wrong with the Clyde seemed to be its grossly overloaded LP turbine. With two or three stages both power and efficiency would probably have been improved, and the world could have had an engine in the 5,000-hp class which would not only have been outstanding for the propulsion of large civil transports but which would also have had the swift fuel/propeller control response essential for military use, and especially for flying from carriers. Hives' refusal of what would have been the first of many contracts forced Westland to fit the Wyvern naval strike fighter—originally designed for the Eagle piston engine—with the Python instead, and this had a response time that was wholly unacceptable for carrier wave-offs. By chance, as this book went to press, the author received an 'out of the blue' letter from a one-time Westland man containing the statement 'If the Westland Board had been Total Aviation Persons they would have told the Ministry "The

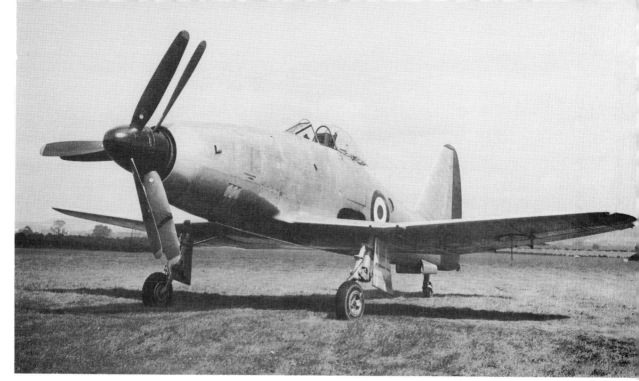

Seen here at Westland's Merryfield airfield, Wyvern VP120 was the only aircraft to fly with the Clyde. Sadly for the Wyvern, it had to go into production with the Python instead.

Clyde or nothing in our aircraft".' It would probably have been politically impossible to get the Clyde on to the Britannia, but if this had happened in 1950 the Britannia would almost certainly have entered service several years sooner and sold in much larger numbers. This is a highly provocative statement, but the author has no doubt of its validity.

Despite its world-beating potential, the Clyde was almost ignored. It was never installed in a big testbed aircraft, and did not fly until 18 January 1949, when it began a totally successful fifty-hour flight programme in Wyvern *VP120*, driving a Rotol six-blade contraprop. Certainly it was the first engine ever to have an approved Type Certificate (civil and military, the first for any turboprop) and a 200-hour time between overhauls, all before its first flight!

In fact the first turboprop in the world to fly was an odd lash-up based on the Derwent II turbojet. Back in May 1944 a regular production Welland had been equipped with a simple spur-type reduction

gear and the shaft power measured. In 1944 it was decided to do the same with a Derwent, and Rubbra and Haworth quickly designed a single-stage spur reduction gear on the front of a Derwent II with a cropped compressor, the turbine remaining unchanged. On the front was a flexible quill shaft to isolate the flimsy engine from feared vibration and other loads transmitted by the small 95-in Rotol five-blade propeller. Known as the RB.50 Trent, this was intended merely to gain experience quickly, and two were installed in Meteor I *EE227*, which was first flown by Gloster's Eric Greenwood at Church Broughton on 20 September 1945, just three months ahead of the American GE XT31. Nominal output of the Trent was 750 shp plus 1,300 lb thrust, and an adverse feature was that the centrelines of the propellers were well above that of the nacelles and jetpipes. Worse, when Greenwood throttled back, on the first landing approach, the propellers constant-speeded at high rpm and immediately went into the special 'zero pitch' used

Left *The Trent was a Derwent II turbojet (seven enlarged combustion chambers) cut down with a smaller compressor so that the turbine had spare power to drive a reduction gearbox and propeller. It was never intended as a production engine.*

Below *Meteor I EE227 was a lash-up like its Trent engines, but it made a useful contribution to learning how to interconnect turboprop throttle and propeller controls.*

for starting. This caused them to act as extremely powerful airbrakes, with the wing downstream completely stalled. The Meteor dropped like a stone, but quick application of full power averted a crash. This aircraft flew 47 hours, in which time much was learned about the throttle and propeller control problems of turboprops. The Trent was never considered as anything but a research tool, but the work was important in the rapid development of interconnected controls and propeller safety locks.

In 1946 a small team at Derby under Lionel Haworth designed a completely new and quite simple turboprop, the RB.53 Dart. Aimed at 1,000 hp, this met a Ministry requirement to power an odd trainer (Balliol and Athena) called for by the RAF with a single turboprop and three seats, the idea being that a second pupil could look over the shoulders of the side-by-side pupil and instructor. An engine in this class was also needed by the Brabazon IIB specification for a short-range turboprop airliner, examples of which were being built by Armstrong Whitworth and Vickers-Armstrongs.

Air Commodore F.R. 'Rod' Banks, by this time Ministry Director of Engine R&D, was one of the many who could not understand the RAF trainer requirement; and eventually the trainer went into production as the Balliol with a Merlin piston engine. But he was convinced the small turboprop would be needed for post-war commercial aviation. Hives was not enthusiastic about the Dart; his fixation on the Avon tended to make him think of all turboprops as small fry, and in a sense they were. Moreover, the leader in the field was Armstrong Siddeley, whose 1,000-hp Mamba had been started earlier and was doing well on the testbed. When the Ministry ordered two prototypes of the Vickers V.630 Viscount on 9 March 1946 the specified powerplant comprised four Mambas. Sir Roy Fedden was also fighting for this market with a neat axial engine called the Cotswold, and Napier entered the gas-turbine market with a 1,600-hp engine named the Naiad.

It was only the solid reputation of Rolls-Royce that got them a development contract for the Dart, Banks having a shrewd hunch they might come out winners in the end. He argued that the engine should be developed by the proven gas-turbine team under Hooker and Lombard at Barnoldswick, but by this time Hives had decided upon big changes. For one thing the vast Derby factory was running out of work, especially on the design and development side. He resolved to move the whole gas-turbine design effort from Barnoldswick to Derby. He was reinforced in this view by the desperate problems met with the axial Avon turbojet, which appeared to need all the help the mainstream designers at Derby could offer. Things came to a head when Marshal of the RAF Sir Charles Portal and and his entourage passed through Derby without stopping, on their way to visit Barnoldswick. Hives exploded 'We can't have that. Derby is the centre of Rolls-Royce, not Hooker's bloody garage at Barnoldswick!' So he dug his toes in and told Banks the new turboprop would be entirely a Derby engine. He thought it a suitable project on which they could cut their teeth. He hardly viewed it as a mass commercial product.

Haworth elected to use tandem centrifugal compressors as in the latest piston engines, and the LP and HP impellers were based on Eagle and Griffon practice. Mass flow was originally 15.8 lb/s, rising to 20.3 in the RDa.3. Each impeller had nineteen radial vanes preceded by curved steel guide vanes, and carefully profiled passages led the air from the LP diffuser to the eye of the HP rotor. The two compressors were mounted on the same shaft as the two-stage turbine, which had blades of Nimonic 80 retained in the discs by the newly standardized 'fir tree' type of root. From the HP compressor diffuser the air passed into

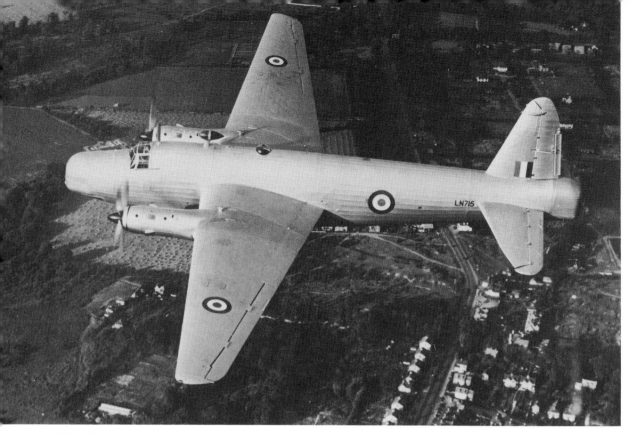

The Dart first flew in the nose of Lancaster NG465, but early development was done largely with this converted Wellington B.10. Later Viscount engines were fitted to BEA Pionair (DC-3) freighters to pile up hours on regular routes.

seven combustion chambers, arranged as in the Clyde at a skewed angle to reduce length and avoid the need for a right-angle bend in the flow. At the front of the main turbine/compressor shaft was a helical high-speed input pinion connected via three layshafts to a second stage of reduction gearing with spur gears, the overall ratio being 0.106. Thanks to experience with the Clyde and Trent, it was possible to get the interconnected fuel and propeller controls more or less right first time.

On the other hand, the Dart came out considerably overweight and down on power. When it first flew in the nose of Lancaster *NG465* in October 1947 it was rated at 750 hp, and looked a very bad bet in comparison with the technically more advanced Mamba. Captain Maurice Luby RN, Banks' successor, wanted to cancel the Dart, but Banks told him to hold off, saying 'Rolls will

get it right'. But by this time the troubled engine appeared to have no application. The RAF trainer had switched to a piston engine, and the Viscount (Mamba-engined in any case) was about to be cancelled because the obvious customer, BEA, announced it had no interest in it, and was instead buying a fleet of piston-engined Ambassadors.

Then Peter Masefield joined BEA as an exceptionally capable Chief Executive. He drummed into his Chairman, Lord Douglas, that the future had to lie with gas turbines, and that the Viscount should be supported. With commendable courage Sir Hew Kilner, Chairman of Vickers, and Sir Alec Coryton, Ministry Controller of Supplies (Air), kept the Viscount prototypes funded. And George Edwards, newly appointed Vickers' Chief Designer, went to see Hives, told him a lot of work was needed, and decided on the robust Dart rather than the Mamba for the first V.630. When this flew on 16 July 1948 it went like a dream. By this time the Dart was itself beginning to come 'out of the wood', and Haworth had already planned the RDa.3 (Dart 505) giving almost 50% more power. In 1949 Darts were type tested at 1,000 hp (No 11) and then 1,250 hp (No 4), and the RDa.3 rating was 1,400 shp plus 365 lb residual thrust, or 1,540 ehp. Flight development continued in Wellington *LN715* and a Dakota.

The greater power was immediately put to use by Edwards in stretching the now very promising Viscount to meet the needs of BEA. The result was the Viscount 700, with seating increased from 32 to 47/53. This flew on 19 April 1950, by which time Masefield had really got BEA to take an interest. On 29 July 1950 the smaller V.630 prototype, now with 1,380-ehp Dart 502 engines, began a month of regular scheduled service on BEA routes to Paris and Edinburgh. These were the first revenue services by any gas-turbine aircraft in the world, and the reaction of the passengers and crews was enthusiastic.

In the summer of 1950 BEA placed an order for twenty V.701 Viscounts, and not only was this order later increased but it was followed by many others. A key factor in the success of the Viscount was the fact that, like most of the company's engines at the time, the Dart proved capable of being repeatedly uprated. The initial production engine was the Mk 506, with the same RDa.3 rating as the 505 but improved compressor and turbine aerodynamics to reduce working temperatures and specific fuel consumption, the latter from 0.753 to 0.727. In mid-1955, by which time sales of the Viscount exceeded 100, the RDa.6 entered production with shrouded turbine blades, initially as the Mk 510 for the Viscount, with 0.093 reduction gear, and then as the Mk 511 for the F27 Friendship with 0.086 reduction gear matched to bigger propellers. This offered increased cruising power, with

sfc reduced to 0.689.

By 1956 the stretched V.800 Viscount was in production, and a year later this was uprated by being fitted with the RDa.7 Mk 520 engine encompassing a three-stage turbine with shrouded blades. Combined with mass flow increased to 22 lb/s, twin oil coolers and many other changes, the Mk 520 was rated at 1,700 shp plus 477 lb (1,890 ehp) and further increased cruising power. By 1959 the RDa.7/1 Mk 525 was in production, with mass flow of 23.5 lb/s and power raised to 1,800 shp plus 481 lb (1,990 ehp), with sfc of 0.680. The RDa.7/2 Mk 527, also of 1959, was rated at 1,910 shp plus 487 lb (2,105 ehp), with sfc of 0.665.

These mainstream Darts, for the V.810 Viscounts, F27 and 748, remained in production until 1987. From the mid-1960s the chief versions were the Mk 536–2 for the 748 and Mk 536–7R for the F27, the former rated at 2,080 shp (2,280 ehp) and the latter at 2,120 shp (2,320 ehp). Since 1982 Rolls-Royce has been selling kits for upgrading existing engines to Mk 552 standard, with improved compressors and turbine giving an 11% reduction in sfc combined with power increased to 2,330 ehp.

From 1960 there were numerous other Dart versions. For arduous carrier-based service in the Breguet Alizé the RDa.7 Mk 21 was developed, rated at 1,910 shp. For the AW.660 Argosy C.1 the RDa.8 Mk 102 was developed, rated at 2,470 shp (2,690 ehp). For the Japanese NAMC YS–11 and the Convair 600 and 640 conversions the RDa.10 Mk 542 was produced, with mass flow increased to 26.5 lb/s and pressure ratio raised from 5.6 to 6.35, resulting in a rating of 2,750 shp (3,025 ehp) with sfc of 0.556. Reduction gear ratio was altered to 0.0775 to match the 14 ft 6 in propellers. Most powerful of all production versions, the RDa.12 Mk 201 powered the RAF Andover C.1 (not other Andover marks), with take-off power of 2,970 shp (3,245 ehp). All later Darts were governed to 15,000

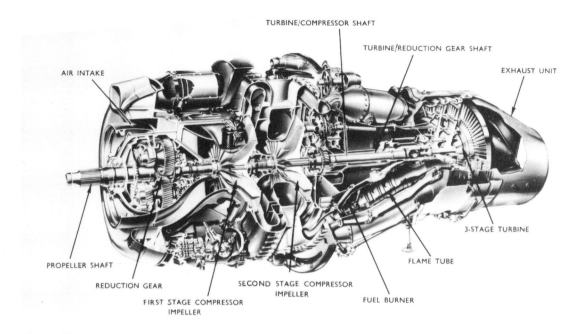

TURBINE/COMPRESSOR SHAFT

TURBINE/REDUCTION GEAR SHAFT

AIR INTAKE

EXHAUST UNIT

PROPELLER SHAFT

3-STAGE TURBINE

REDUCTION GEAR

FLAME TUBE

SECOND STAGE COMPRESSOR IMPELLER

FIRST STAGE COMPRESSOR IMPELLER

FUEL BURNER

Cutaway of a later Dart with three-stage turbine. Above the air inlet is the ducted oil cooler, the hot air from this being discharged upwards. The drawing suggests that the tandem compressors and propeller reduction gear are driven through separate shafts, but this is not the case, there being only a single drive shaft.

rpm, and had an automatic water/methanol injection system to maintain take-off power in hot climates.

Like so many aviation success stories the Dart began very haltingly. Throughout its life it has been considered a piece of agricultural machinery, long since overtaken by newer technologies, but the 7,100 engines delivered have flown nearly 120 million hours, far more than any other British aircraft engine. Unfortunately, Rolls-Royce remained uncertain of the size of the market for a successor, and failed to take decisions soon enough. As a result the two chief applications for late-model Darts, the 748 and F27, have been developed into aircraft powered by competitor engines.

To say that Haworth and his team cut their teeth with the Dart is an understatement. By the early 1950s the same designers had produced schemes for several much more advanced engines, almost all of them two-spool axial engines of the kind which even Griffith would deign to notice. In 1954 Haworth got the green light from Hives for one of these schemes, the RB.109. Broadly this was planned to begin life at 2,500 shp, to go on from where the Dart would have to leave off, but it was confidently expected that 4,000 hp would eventually be forthcoming. The immediate application was to power a large four-engined airliner wanted by BEA as the successor to the Viscount. Ministry pressure tried to get the airline to buy a version of the Britannia, claiming that the proposed V.950 Vanguard was duplicative and wasteful. But BEA's Masefield and Trans-Canada's McGregor insisted on the combination of Vickers-Armstrongs and Rolls-Royce, which had proved so good

Above *The most powerful civil Dart was the Mk 542, rated at 3,025 ehp. Externally it looked almost identical to the first Darts of one-third this power.*

Below *A water-spray icing test rig mounted ahead of a Dart 542 in Ambassador G-37-3. This mark of Dart drove a large four-blade propeller.*

Above *Servicing a Dart 536-2 of a 748 belonging to British West Indian Airways. The entire cowl folds back in four petals.*

Below *An RB.109, later to be named Tyne. In comparison with reverse-flow competitors such as the Python and Proteus its slimness was amazing, and so was its specific fuel consumption (in Imperial units, around 0.48 instead of 0.8).*

with the Viscount, so Ministry support for the RB.109 was forthcoming.

Though there was no pressure to accomplish this, because such engines are lost inside their capacious cowlings, the RB.109 was always a very slim engine, by far the greatest diameter being the annular inlet behind the propeller spinner, with an integral oil tank surrounding it. The LP spool comprised a three-stage turbine driving a six-stage compressor and the input pinion to the 0.064 double epicyclic reduction gear, the propeller shaft being driven by the forward (second-stage) planet-wheel spider. The HP spool comprised a single-stage turbine driving a nine-stage compressor. Overall pressure ratio was 13.5, and mass flow 41 lb/s at 15,250 rpm.

Like other new Rolls-Royce engines, the combustion chamber was of the can-annular type, and like the earlier Conway it contained ten separate flame tubes, but in this case each with twin coaxial burners. Another similarity with the Conway was the use of tip-shrouded air-cooled blades in the HP turbine (air-cooled blades are discussed

at greater length in the next chapter). Materials used included magnesium alloy for the inlet casing, light alloy for the LP compressor rotor blades, titanium for the first seven HP rotor stages, and steel for the compressor discs, stator blades, HP stages 8 and 9, and all casings. Accessories, driven from both the LP and HP shafts, were neatly grouped beneath the engine. Some versions made provision for water/methanol injection through holes in the first LP compressor disc.

The RB.109 first ran in April 1955, the author being a visitor on that occasion. It was immediately apparent that, instead of being developed to an ultimate goal of 4,000 hp, the new 'supercharged turboprop' (so called because of the tandem axial compressors) had begun its life at the higher figure and was going to go on from there. Weight was a little over 2,000 lb, and sfc about 0.52. It proved of intense interest to Douglas and Lockheed, who published details of proposed turboprop conversions of the DC-7 and L-1049, and Lockheed even ordered four engines, but these appli-

Initial flight development of the Tyne took place with the turboprop mounted in the nose of this Lincoln, with the jetpipe passing obliquely down beneath the cockpit. The aircraft demonstrated at the Farnborough airshow with the four Merlins feathered.

cations did not materialize. By summer 1956 the engine had been named the Tyne, and flight development began with a single engine mounted in the nose of a Lincoln (B-class registration *G–37–1*). In December 1957 two Tynes of RTy.1 Mk 506 type, as earmarked for the BEA Vanguard, began intensive simulated airline flying in an Airspeed Ambassador, joined in 1958 by a second. Many BEA Viscount captains had been Ambassador drivers, and were disconcerted to find themselves being overtaken by such aircraft until they realised its installed power had been doubled. The original RTy.1 rating was 4,220 shp (4,695 ehp), but by the time the V.951 entered service it had been raised to 4,785 ehp, with cruising sfc of 0.405. Trans-Canada's V.952s had the RTy.11 Mk 512 rated at 5,545 ehp and with cruising sfc of only 0.384, just half as much as early Darts! After a troubled start the Tyne established an excellent record in service, though with overwing jetpipes the passengers could see the unburned carbon which resulted in sooty

emissions and deposits. Very unfortunately the Vanguard, an excellent aircraft produced at low cost by Vickers, hit the market just as short-haul jets were all the rage and only 43 were sold.

Fortunately other modest sales resulted in the Tyne being a successful commercial programme. First to materialize was the Canadair CL–44D, a modified and re-engined version of the Britannia which began with the CC–109 Yukon for the RCAF (later Canadian Forces) and concluded with the swing-tail CL–44D–4 commercial freighter and stretched CL–44J passenger aircraft with 214 seats. These all had the 5,730-ehp RTy.12 Mk 515/10. The ten Short Belfast freighters for the RAF, likewise originally based on the Britannia, were powered by the 5,500-ehp RTy.12 Mk 101. But the most useful and enduring applications involved large twin-engined aircraft developed in international programmes. First to fly, on 21 October 1961, was the Breguet 1150 Atlantic maritime patrol aircraft, powered by 6,105-ehp RTy.20

A Tyne RTy.12 in the 5,700-hp class, as fitted to the CL-44 and Belfast. The more powerful RTy.20 engines of the Atlantique and Transall are very similar.

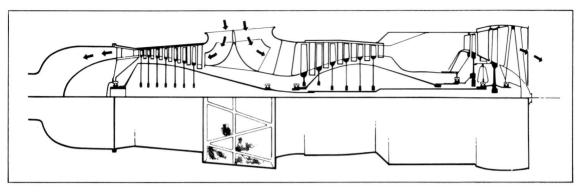

The RB.176 comprised a gas generator (right) aerodynamically similar to the RB.162 lift jet, with an LP turbine driving a second compressor (left) pumping air to the airframe. In its intended application the air was for rotor tip-drive pressure jets.

Mk 21 engines. Produced by the SECBAT five-nation consortium, the Atlantic had engines assembled in France by Hispano-Suiza (SNECMA subsidiary) with parts contributed by MAN (later MTU) of Germany and FN of Belgium, with support from Derby. The second aircraft, the Transall C.160 freighter, was a joint effort by Nord-Aviation, MBB and VFW-Fokker, with 6,105-ehp RTy.20 Mk 22 engines. The first flew on 25 February 1963. The RTy.20 engines have mass flow of 46.5 lb/s and pressure ratio of 14. Mk 101, 21 and 22 engines have water/methanol injection. Propeller diameters: Mk 506, 14 ft 6 in; Mk 21 and CL–44, 16 ft; Mk 22, 18 ft.

Deliveries of these engines were completed in the early 1970s, apart from a small batch of RTy.20 Mk 801 engines derated to 5,480 ehp for Libyan Aeritalia G222 transports. In 1980 production was resumed, initially for the 35 Transalls of the second series. In due course further engines will be produced for the Dassault-Breguet Atlantique 2. All will be similar to those delivered for the original versions of these aircraft. Meanwhile Rolls-Royce has carried out exhaustive studies of later gas turbines using the Tyne reduction gear, and of Tynes uprated to about 9,000 hp to drive propfans, as described in a later chapter. The Tyne is also one of the staple products of the company's Industrial and Marine Division which produces gas turbines for ship and hydrofoil propulsion, electricity generation and other surface applications.

One application of the Tyne that never got off the ground was the Rotodyne Z, the planned production version of the great compound helicopter developed during the 1950s by Fairey and cancelled by Westland in 1962. The main engines would have been ordinary Tynes rated at 5,250 shp, driving four-blade propellers. In the rear of each nacelle was to be installed a Rolls-Royce RB.176. This unusual powerplant was intended to provide compressed air for the fuel-burning pressure jets at the tips of the blades of the 104-ft rotor. It was also seen as a flap-blowing engine for STOL fixed-wing aircraft. As the diagram shows, it resembled a free-turbine turboprop with the reduction gear and propeller replaced by a seven-stage auxiliary compressor. The RB.176 represented the pinnacle of the contemporary art of the air-compressor engine. Since then there have been many attempts to achieve lift coefficients of 10 or more using powerful flows of compressed air, but nobody has produced a specialized engine to carry on where the RB.176 left off in 1962.

Chapter 9

THE FIRST AXIAL JETS

By 1945 Hives was champing at the bit to get a world-beating axial jet into production. Throughout the war Griffith had openly scorned anything with a centrifugal compressor, and inevitably this made Hives regard even the Nene and Tay as mere temporary stop-gaps. Tens of thousands of these centrifugal jets were made outside Britain, but the company that designed them hardly pushed them at all, and in any case from 1945 until 1950 suffered a near-desert in procurement of British combat aircraft. Hayne Constant at the National Gas Turbine Establishment and the technical experts at the Ministry all urged Hives to get cracking on axials.

Nobody doubted that an axial turbojet could give more thrust per unit frontal area, though in those days the difference was not great. The fact that an axial might even be heavier than a centrifugal of the same thrust was unknown, as was the likelihood that its throttle response—important for carrier wave-offs, for example—might be markedly more sluggish. In the longer term the axial was indeed to become dominant, except in the smallest sizes, but in the author's view Rolls-Royce went overboard on this type of compressor a little too precipitately. Certainly, nobody had any idea what they were letting themselves in for.

Britain had been building axial com-

pressors for aircraft gas turbines from 1936 onwards, but most had been purely experimental units of extremely pedestrian design. A fundamental measure of axial-compressor performance is the work per stage, usually expressed in terms of temperature rise dT. In the primitive British compressors dT was around $8°C$, so that sixteen or more stages were needed to get a pr of 3.5. The only compressors to do significantly better were those designed at Metrovick, for the F.2 Beryl turbojet for example, where Dr D.M. Smith would say 'We don't know why it's as good as it is'. As leaders in this field, Metrovick were given a Ministry contract for an extremely advanced turbojet to give 7,000 lb thrust with sfc of only 0.78. This became the F.9 Sapphire, but in 1947 it was transferred to Armstrong Siddeley in a Ministry move to cut down the number of aero-engine firms. The Ministry regarded the Sapphire mainly as a way of providing competition for Rolls-Royce.

Air Commodore Rod Banks, by now Director of Engine Research and Development, showed plenty of strategic vision in funding various new engines throughout industry despite the fact that the post-war government had little interest in any military hardware. There was, in fact, no need for an axial turbojet, except for a single project for a high-performance bomber to specification

B.3/45 to replace the Mosquito. Designer Teddy Petter left Westland and built up a new team at English Electric to create the new bomber. In consultation with Hooker he schemed a beautifully clean aircraft powered by a single giant centrifugal turbojet of 13,000 lb thrust which fitted neatly in the circular-section fuselage, but there were problems with the bomb bay, the centre of gravity and the inlets to the engine plenum chamber. With hindsight, the original bomber and its engine would probably have been developed with little fuss, but it was soon seen that this was the ideal vehicle for a Rolls-Royce axial engine. Hives had already nagged at Griffith to come up with a simple turbojet that could actually be put into production. Petter's bomber was recast with two axial engines of 6,500 lb each, at first in the wing roots and then, to simplify the inlets, moved outboard Meteor-style. The engine became the AJ.65, for 'axial jet, 65 hundred pounds'.

Hives was deeply conscious of the fact that the hub of the company was Derby. Here there were hundreds of fine engineers and skilled craftsmen who were rapidly running out of work on piston engines. Griffith had his own little cell, and Lionel Haworth dabbled with an axial jet (it was not built) and then designed the Dart turboprop. But the centre for gas-turbine work remained 'Hooker's bloody garage' 120 miles to the north. The aforementioned pressures to relocate the Barnoldswick team at Derby were powerful, especially since Derby possessed important test plant for complete compressors, and also, in a new technique, for testing turbines made of aluminium and run at normal temperatures. Because of his profound knowledge and long axial experience, Hives asked Griffith to carry out the initial project design on the AJ.65. In fact, Griffith had already started, under one of his personal project numbers. Predictably, he came up with figures based

An AJ.65, the axial turbojet that almost broke Doc Hooker's giant spirit. Points to note are the small size of the compressor in relation to the combustion chambers, and the large diameter of the single-stage turbine. This engine does have three blow-off valves along the top of the compressor casing to help the engine to get started.

on extreme optimism. His report described an engine of 6,500 lb thrust, to weigh between 1,200 and 1,500 lb, with a compressor handling 120 lb/s at a pr of 7 with an efficiency of 85%. Some unfortunate person then had the job of turning this project into a running engine. (Back in the war, when his CR1 hardware was bedevilled with internal gas leakages, running hot and totally failing to work, Griffith would murmur unconcernedly 'Isn't that a job for our young engineers?')

In this case the unfortunate person was Hooker. At that time nobody had any clear idea of the gigantic problems that would be encountered in trying to go from a pr of 3.5 to a pr of 7. Apart from its obvious aerodynamic and structural complexity, the axial compressor poses two problems which in the immediate post-war era were extremely difficult to solve. One is that the intermeshing rotor and stator blades, each roughly the size of a playing card, suffer tremendous mechanical and aerodynamic forces yet are cantilevered from their ends like tuning forks. From inlet to delivery the blades get progressively smaller, so they cover a wide range of resonant frequencies, and the power of the airflow is so great that a resonant vibration can snap off a blade, or a complete row, in a fraction of a second. The second problem is that, while the compressor may work well at full power, it can be almost impossible to get it started. While the starter is turning the engine over at low speed the pr across the compressor may be only about 1.5, which calls for blades at the downstream end only slightly smaller than those at the inlet. But the compressor has to be designed for the full-power condition, where Griffith specified a pr of 7, and this requires the cross-sectional flow area at the outlet to be less than one-quarter of that at the inlet. Thus, during starting, the air cannot get out at the delivery end of the compressor, so it cannot get in at the front. The angle of attack onto each row

of blades goes 'off the clock', the blades stall, flow breaks down completely, and there is a grave risk of blades being broken by the turbulence.

Ever since Whittle's compressor was first tested on the Vulture rig, Derby had made a practice of testing as many gas-turbine components as possible ahead of a complete engine build. Wilde tested the proposed AJ.65 compressor and warned that it would be stalled and surge on the engine which would not be able to start and accelerate. Also it did not attain the pressure ratio required at high speed even if it could be coaxed up to high speed. The surge line bulged far to the right in the middle speed range, into totally unstable flow areas, which made it impossible ever to get to the high-power regime. Hooker was warned, but did not know what to do about it beyond adding blow-off valves to let air escape from the middle of the compressor during starting and low-speed running. The air escaped through apertures cut in the stator root platforms and thence to atmosphere via simple spring-loaded poppet valves. The idea was to accelerate the air uniformly and reduce the angle of attack onto the blades of the first three or four stages, but at first these valves were ineffective because they did not let the air escape evenly all round the compressor.

On top of this intractable obstacle, Lombard discovered there was no way the engine could be built at anything like Griffith's weight. The best he could predict was 2,200 lb, or 50% over target. From the start Harry Pearson had been worried at the target pr, and this was downgraded to 6.3. Even this was a major challenge in 1946 for an engine with twelve compressor stages. Each stage was designed to give a dT of 20°C. Other features were eight Lucas-type combustion chambers and a big single-stage turbine. The first engine weighed 2,550 lb, was difficult to start, would not accelerate, broke its first-stage blades, and

Most people think the variable-stator compressor was pioneered by General Electric. Their experimental GOL-1590 (predecessor of the J79) first ran in 1954, but this variable-stator Avon compressor was on test in 1949. The Avon was made to work without it.

needed most careful coaxing to struggle to a thrust of 5,000 lb. Hooker called it 'a hell of a mess'.

To try to get some engine mechanical running experience, performance was ignored and the compressor cut back to ten and even to eight stages. Meanwhile intensive compressor testing in Derby had demonstrated that blade stalling and compressor surge could be alleviated by the application of variable incidence stator blades. Tests were first done with different sets of stator vanes set at different angles. This was followed by a compressor design in which the inlet guide vanes (IGVs) and the first four rows of stators could be swivelled to different angles. It is commonly thought that General Electric pioneered the variable-stator engine, but in fact it was patented by Wilde for Rolls-Royce and a complete variable compressor was on test in 1949. In the end, however, its complexity was avoided by using just variable IGVs and much

improved inter-stage bleed valves. When the engine was started, the VIGVs were in the almost closed position to unstall the blading. As rpm increased, a ram driven by fuel pressure progressively opened the VIGVs to the fully open position at full speed, and progressively closed off the bleed.

The AJ.65 was named the Avon, and the initial engines were known as RA.1s. They were still sick engines, and after a year of serious difficulty Hives lost patience. Early one Monday he burst into Hooker's office and said 'This jet job is too important to leave here in this garage. I am moving it to Derby.' Previously, everything Hooker had touched had turned to gold. Now, in an emotional flare-up, he broke with the man he had worshipped, and he left the company at the end of 1948. But the troubled Avon had to go on, and in the RA.2 it at last began to show signs of behaving properly. This engine had a compressor with the

An Avon RA.1, very similar to the AJ.65 but with the important addition of variable inlet guide vanes. The ring of black dots shows their outer bearings, and the small actuating ram can be seen above the compressor ahead of the blow-off valves.

inner diameter increased throughout, to reduce mass flow by 10%. This moved the surge line to the left, at last enabling the engine to go from the start to full power without passing through an unstable regime. Two RA.2s flew in the outboard positions of Lancastrian *VM732* on 15 August 1948. Later test flying took place in Meteor *RA491*, and though the RA.2 was derated to 6,000 lb test pilot Cliff Rogers called *491* 'a very sporty aircraft indeed'.

The only remaining worry was the turbine, which was stuck at a miserable 76% efficiency. At Derby the turbine rig office was run by Geoffrey Fawn, who was convinced a two-stage turbine would do better. The idea was at first opposed by Lombard— as are many 'not invented here' proposals— who claimed it would be heavier and increase moment of inertia, making throttle response sluggish. Wilde and Fawn continued with rig testing which gave promising results. Almost overnight Barnoldswick was eager to have the two-stage turbine, and the result was the RA.3, which at last reached

the design rating of 6,500 lb. The two-stage turbine increased efficiency from 76 to 85%, reduced engine diameter, reduced moment of inertia and saved 300 lb in weight! The RA.3 weighed 2,240 lb, complete with an electric or cartridge starter in the nose bullet, a compressor bleed to run the cabin pressurization and a shaft drive to a remote accessory gearbox. Sfc was an excellent 0.88.

At last the Avon could go into production for the Canberra B.2. War having broken out in Korea in June 1950, the government was thrown into a panic and tried to make up for the lost years by having the Canberra and Avon forced into mass production at several firms, regardless of cost. Avons were hustled into production not only by Rolls-Royce but also by Bristol, Napier and Standard Motors, having the salutary effect of forcing these companies to acquire the capability of making gas turbines and thus of eventually competing with Rolls-Royce.

The RA.3 Avon Mk 101 entered service with RAF No 101 Squadron. The author flew with them as a passenger in May 1951, the month in which they completed their conversion from the Merlin-engined Lincoln. On night exercises no fighter could get near them, and the only problem seemed to be finding jobs for redundant signallers, engineers and gunners.

From 1950 onwards the Avon was picked for many of Britain's most important new combat aircraft, as well as for all DH Comet airliners beyond the troubled Mk I, and also the French Caravelle short-haul jet. Fairly minor improvements resulted in the RA.7 rating of 7,500 lb, with a mass flow of 125 lb/s, most engines of this family having full anti-icing by hot compressor bleed and a triple-breech cartridge starter in an enlarged nose bullet. The first engine of this series to enter production was the Mk 109, for the B.6 and later Canberras, closely followed by the Mks 104 and 107 for the Hunter and Mk 105 for the Swift. The latter suffered numerous problems, one (shuttling of airflow between the left and right inlet ducts) having been mentioned in connection with the cooling system of the Vulture in an earlier chapter. More intractable was a tendency of Swift engines to shed their compressor blades, at a time when this was no longer an Avon characteristic! The cause obviously lay (it was thought) in the design of the Swift inlet duct, until it was noticed that all the affected engines came from one of the 'crash programme' licensees. This firm had introduced a seemingly trivial change in the machining of the compressor rotor blades, and in so doing had induced a fatigue problem.

The Swift soon ground to a halt, through no fault of its engine, leaving Rolls-Royce with a little much-needed experience of afterburning, which had previously involved various reheat Derwents and Avons flown in testbeds, but nothing to equal the massive in-service experience of rival American engines. Failure of the Swift also left RAF Fighter Command with no new British single-seat fighter except the Hunter, which was being cleared for production as the F.1 with the Avon 104 and F.2 with the rival Sapphire. Strangely, because in almost all respects the Sapphire aircraft was superior, the Armstrong Siddeley engine powered only a few Hunters which were progressively phased out of service. This left the Hunter with only the Avon, which was still prone to severe surging, and was also found to flame-out when the guns were fired. The result was to limit Avon-Hunters to below 25,000 ft(!) pending a solution, which eventually, in the Avon 121 (RA.21 rating of 8,050 lb), comprised automatic fuel dipping, the fuel flow being greatly reduced as soon as the gun trigger was depressed. Thus, by dogged persistence with both Avon and Hunter, the RAF by 1955 had something approximating to an acceptable day fighter.

The original prototype Hunter was modified for high-speed purposes and fitted with an afterburning RA.7R engine, setting a world record on 7 September 1953 at 727.6 mph. Just eighteen days later the prototype Swift F.4, with a similar engine, set a record in hot Libyan air at 737.7 mph. These engines were primitive, with just a single (maximum) reheat setting and a nozzle fitted with twin eyelid shutters which were either fully closed or fully open. They had no production application except in a handful of Swift FR.5 and F.7 aircraft. In Sweden, however, Svenska Flygmotor made similar engines under licence as the RM5, and these had a long service career powering the A32A Lansen. When the first RM5 went on test it gave about 2% more thrust than expected, and the reason was found to be that Flygmotor were producing blades to finer tolerances than the British blades. Rolls-Royce soon held the Swedish company in high esteem. The author was once amazed to see their vast underground cavern into which pumped-out water could return at high pressure, expelling air in a mighty hurricane which was used mostly for

The RA.7R was the company's first production engine with an afterburner. Compared with the RA.1 the compressor is larger, and anti-iced by bleed air taken through the large diagonal pipe, the two-stage turbine is of much smaller diameter, and there is a triple-breech cartridge starter on the nose.

testing ramjets. Rolls-Royce requested and received permission to use it to test an Avon at a simulated Mach number of 2, checking mechanical behaviour in a high-density airflow, because in the mid-1950s Mach 2 could not be simulated on any British engine testbed. Another foreign licensee was Commonwealth Aircraft of Australia. They built basic RA.7 Mk 26 engines for a locally built run of 112 Sabres whose re-engining caused such problems that the Australians vowed never again to tinker with an imported warplane. In 1961 this was to result in Australia choosing the Atar to power 100 French-built Mirage fighters, even though Rolls-Royce had designed, built and flight-tested a much superior version with the Avon.

On 16 February 1952 de Havilland flew the No 6 Comet airliner modified as the Mk 2X with 6,500-lb Avon Mk 502 engines. These were similar to Canberra B.2 engines but fitted with an electric starter and other changed accessories, and retaining bleed-air cabin pressurization. The Comet 2 never entered airline service, those on the production line being modified as Comet C.2 transports for the RAF with 7,350-lb Avon Mk 117s, setting a flawless record with 216 Squadron until April 1967.

Thus, by never giving up, Rolls-Royce turned the Avon into a fine engine, and the heartbreaking early years receded. But the rival Sapphire had the advantage of what seemed a less-troubled compressor, and when Armstrong Siddeley sought its rival's help in overcoming some Sapphire mechanical problems in 1950 the occasion was used to discover just how its compressor worked. One difference had long been obvious. Pressure-rise per stage is proportional to the square of blade velocity, and in the Sapphire the velocity was progressively greater towards the HP end of the compressor than in the Avon, because while in the Avon the casing tapered from front to rear, in the Sapphire the full diameter was maintained throughout. A less evident difference was that the aerodynamic loading of the Sapphire blades was much lower (it was in fact only 12° at the first stage), the blades being less sharply cambered aerofoils. Accordingly, the decision was immediately taken to redesign the Avon from stem to stern, so that what emerged was really a wholly new engine. The new compressor had fifteen stages, the first four being based on the light loading of the Sapphire stages. It was impossible to avoid some taper for a low drag installation but the diameter of the HP stages was considerably greater than before. Mass flow rose to 150 lb/s and pr to 7.45, starting problems being avoided by improved VIGVs positioned by a ram under the control of an rpm-sensing unit which also controlled high-capacity slide valves bleeding air from the casing. For the first time in a Rolls-Royce engine a can-annular combustion chamber was used, followed by a new two-stage turbine.

The Ministry of Supply issued the RA.14 with a rating of 9,500 lb, and the first of the new Avons went on test on 17 November 1951. It was some 400 lb heavier than its predecessors at 2,860 lb, but overall diameter was reduced from 42.2 to 41.5 in, which made it easier to fit four inside the wing of the Valiant bomber, the first application. The Mk 201 for this aircraft was type-tested in 1953 at 10,000 lb, with very few problems. De Havilland realized the new engine could transform the Comet, and on 14 July 1954 the Comet 3 flew with civil RA.26 engines of 10,000 lb. Similar engines powered the prototypes of the French Caravelle, which broke new ground in having the engines hung on the rear fuselage. F. B. Greatrex, Chief Installation Engineer at Hucknall, developed a pioneer noise-reducing nozzle in which multiple lobes increased the peripheral length and promoted rapid mixing at the jet boundary. Hucknall also developed the world's first practical thrust reversers, with a pair of internal clamshells which in the reverse mode shut off the jetpipe whilst uncovering cascades in the jetpipe walls which directed the gas diagonally forwards.

After studying afterburning engines Sir Sydney Camm at Hawker Aircraft decided to fit future Hunters with a non-afterburning Avon of the new family. Whereas the original RA.14 still had minor aerodynamic problems, the production RA.28 incorporated a new fuel control system with an overfuelling limiter, which made surging a thing of the past and at last swept away all handling problems. First of the 'large-bore' Hunters, the F.6 went into production with the 10,150-lb Avon 203, fitted with an IPN (iso-propyl nitrate) starter, which resembled a cartridge starter but drew liquid fuel from a tank holding enough for at least twenty starts. The Fairey FD.2 supersonic research aircraft flew in 1954 powered by an RA.14R with crude twin-eyelid reheat. By 1956 it had an afterburning RA.28, and test pilot Peter Twiss urged his firm to have a go at the world speed record. The Ministry, to whom the aircraft belonged, were extremely antagonistic, while Rolls-Royce agonised over the inlet and engine operating conditions.

In the event the record was gained by the unprecedented margin of 310 mph at 1,132 mph; with more fuel the figure could have been way beyond Mach 2, because that was the speed at the end of each run, with no sign of it levelling off. Other RA.28 applications included later Valiants, the Canberra PR.9 and Sea Vixen, while an odd application involving operation in the vertical attitude was the Ryan X–13 Vertijet. This used an ordinary Avon, and so does not figure in the next chapter, but it did incorporate compressor-bleed reaction jets to control the aircraft when hovering.

From 1951 Rolls-Royce devoted attention

With the 200-series the Avon at last began to go places. This RA.28 is typical of thousands of later Avons, with the new compressor and can-annular combustor forming a staggering contrast in relative sizes compared with the RA.1. The diagonal pipe in this case encloses an accessory shaft drive; the anti-icing pipe runs horizontally along the top.

to the development of air-cooled turbine rotor blades. Since Whittle's first engine, as rebuilt in 1938, the upstream nozzle guide vanes, or stator blades, had invariably been hollow and cooled by an internal flow. In contrast, the much more highly stressed rotor blades had had to be solid. Just like the exhaust valves of a piston engine, they represented the principal barrier to increased gas temperature, and thus to engine power.

By 1952 hollow air-cooled rotor blades were on test, but they were primitive and made from two aerofoils welded together at the leading and trailing edges. With a cooling airflow of about 1% of the total mass flow, the best reduction in metal temperature at a gas temperature of 977°C amounted to 150°C at mid-chord, falling to 105°C at the very hot leading edge and to much lower values at the thin trailing edge. Much of the

Canberra WD930 was used for extensive testing of noise-reducing nozzles for civil engines. This pattern, subsequently used on commercial Conways, was fitted to an RA.26 on the left side.

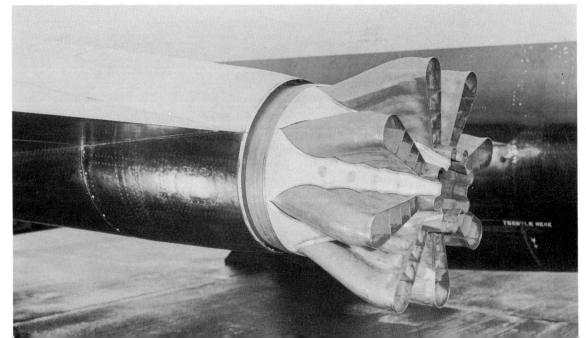

On the right side of the same aircraft was an RA.29. It is seen here flying with a multi-pipe nozzle, not used by Rolls-Royce but adopted by Pratt & Whitney and Boeing for the first commercial JT3Cs.

research was done on Avons, and in late 1953 an Avon was run with air-cooled blades fitted with small (4.6 gal/min) sprays adding water to the cooling airflow. The results were dramatic, the mid-chord metal temperature being reduced by 560°C. The increase in gas temperature which this would have made possible caused thermal problems elsewhere, and it was appreciated that increasing gas temperature is 'a long row to hoe'.

Though Rolls-Royce lagged behind Bristol in the introduction of cast blades, and behind the Americans in the introduction of DS and single-crystal blades (described later), it was the world leader in the introduction of wrought blades containing ever more complex and effective internal cooling airflows. The first such blades in production anywhere in the world were fitted to the RA.24, type-tested in July 1956 at 11,250 lb and put into production as the RA.24R Mk 210 for the Lightning F.1 with a four-stage afterburner, maximum thrust being 14,430 lb. Flygmotor produced a better afterburner for their RM6B, a licence-built Mk 48, which was fully variable up to 15,190 lb and powered the J32B Lansen and early Drakens. Dry Mk 202 engines, with a large bleed manifold for flap-blowing, powered the Scimitar. These engines had blades

which were initially rough forged as a 'tadpole', with various bulges on both sides. Circular holes were then drilled the length of the blade in the centres of the bulges. When the blade was forged to its aerofoil section the holes were squashed into narrow passages for the cooling air, but this technique was limited both by the available heat-transfer surface area and the air velocity.

The next idea was to start with a solid block of nickel alloy and drill it with a number of precisely positioned parallel holes. Each hole was then filled with a rod of mild steel and the block heated in a furnace and extruded through a die whilst being lubricated with molten glass. The result was a crude blade of sausage-like profile which was then machined to the accurate aerofoil profile, the steel being removed by hydrofluoric acid from the now very flattened holes. Such forged/extruded blades have been used in Speys and other engines, and every air-cooling hole can be located in the final blade to within plus or minus three thousandths of an inch, a tribute to manufacturing skills.

To bring this story up to date, rather than return to it in later chapters, the progressive introduction of Nimonic alloys with ever-greater heat resistance obviously meant

The RA.24 was the first engine in the world to go into production with air-cooled turbine rotor blades, in 1956. Without other significant changes this immediately added 1,000 lb to the thrust. The kinked pipe at 6-o'clock in the inlet discharges anti-icing air.

that forging became increasingly difficult. For many years Bristol had cast blades, using the same lost-wax process as the great Italian renaissance artists had done in making precisely repeatable sculptures. Rolls-Royce lost quite a few years through their fear that cast blades might be brittle, but perhaps felt they had reached the end of the road with forged blades on the early RB.211, in which each blade row cost about £10,000. These early RB.211s suffered unpredictable cooling because of microscopic variations between blades, which had to be replaced every 500 hours. The Company's first cast blades in the RB.211s of 1971 often failed after only a few hours' running due to inadequate cooling inside the blading aerofoils. Hooker gave Wilde the job of tackling this problem. Four things were done: better experimental methods were devised to assess cooling efficiency; the aerodynamic and cooling design calculations were integrated in the design stage; a new-style turbine design office was created to integrate aerodynamic, heat-transfer, material stress, geometry, vibration and life

prediction calculations; and a high-temperature demonstrator unit (HTDU) was designed to advance the turbine blade cooling independently of the RB.211 engine development work. These measures, coupled with the advances in materials and techniques for casting turbine blades, have improved dramatically both the performance and endurance (life) of the high-pressure/high-temperature turbine blades. Today the life in service of these blades exceeds 15,000 hours.

A cutaway HP blade appears in the chapter on the RB.211, and even more advanced blades have been run in the HTDU at a flame temperature of 1,827°C. This is well above the melting point of the metal of which the blades are made! Meanwhile, the blade's aerodynamic design has been vastly improved. According to RR's Simon Byworth, 'In the 1950s the design consisted of simple calculations of gas conditions half-way up the blade, performed with a sliderule and a few charts, and the blade profile was made up of circular arcs. Today gas conditions are calculated at up to thirteen radial stations, using a large computer, and the blade shapes are individually tailored to the real flow, using 3-D viscous-flow calculations with allowance for the boundary layer on the blade surface'.

To return to the Avon, this was expected to need replacing in the mid-1950s in large supersonic fighters, and a two-spool successor was designed. This engine, the RB.106—for which the author heard the unofficial suggestion that it should become the Thames—was in turn superseded by the even more powerful RB.128. Designed by Fred Morley, this got as far as rig testing of the complete compressor in 1956, but along with so many other things it was swept away by Duncan Sandys' infamous White Paper on Defence of April 1957 which said that the RAF would need no more fighters or bombers. The only people to gain were Orenda Engines in Toronto, who used a lot of RB.106 technology, including its pioneer elimination of IGVs, in their Iroquois.

Though the 'Sapphire-style' blades had been instrumental in avoiding aerodynamic problems in the first RA.14, by the mid-1950s far more was known about axial compressors and the low loading of these blades had become an embarrassment. With effective VIGVs and bleed valves it was found possible to go even further, and whilst increasing the loading on the blades to add also a zero stage, an extra stage inserted in front of the existing compressor. Such a change would naturally increase the overall pr, and thus reduce sfc, but its chief effect would be to increase the mass flow and thus increase the power, without necessarily any change in turbine temperature. Such a change could benefit both military and civil engines, but it was done first on the latter.

The result was the RA.29, developed initially as the Avon Mk 524 for the Comet 4. First run in late 1955, its sixteen-stage compressor handled 160 lb/s at the high pr of almost 10, and a new three-stage turbine

Cutaway of the civil transport RA.29/1, showing the 16-stage compressor (with a new blow-off valve group on top), annular combustor with eight flame tubes, surrounded by a bleed manifold, and new three-stage turbine.

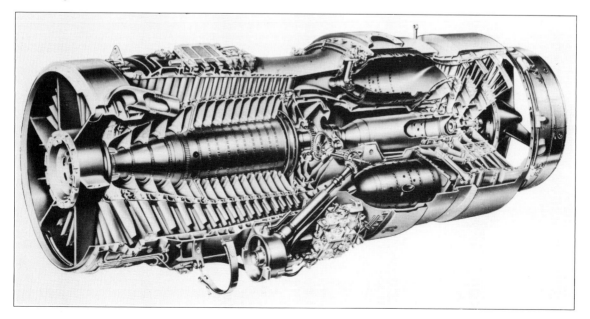

In 1960 General Electric put CJ-805-23 aft-fan engines into a Caravelle. Fearful of losing the Caravelle, Rolls-Royce quickly produced an aft-fan Avon, here seen on test at Hucknall. The fan has its own peripheral inlet duct. Note the large overhead ducts carrying away air from the compressor blow-off valves.

was fitted. This put up the weight to 3,340 lb. The take-off thrust was kept to 10,250 lb, but it was achieved at a very modest temperature, which not only resulted in an sfc of only 0.786 but also enabled the RA.29/1 to be the first turbojet in the world to be cleared to 1,000 hours between over-hauls (a time soon greatly extended). Subsequently the RA.29/3 Mk 527 was delivered at 11,400 lb for the production Caravelle III, followed in 1961 by the RA.29/6 in which a unique zero-zero stage, giving a seventeen-stage compressor, entered service with the Caravelle VI at 12,200 lb. This was followed by the Mk 533R rated at 12,600 lb and fitted with a reverser. These later engines weighed about 3,490 lb and had a two-position Greatrex nozzle for improved cruise performance, its area being varied by a single hinged flap. In 1960 a Caravelle was re-engined with General Electric CJ–805–23 aft fans, giving greater power and much lower sfc. In a quick response Rolls-Royce developed an aft-fan Avon, run outdoors at Hucknall at record low sfc, but in the end the Caravelle switched to an American front-fan engine, the JT8D.

The corresponding military engine was the RB.146, with a sixteen-stage compressor but retaining a two-stage turbine. The Mks 301 and 302 went into production in the 1960s for later marks of Lightning, fitted at last with an advanced afterburner with hot-streak ignition, infinitely variable thrust and an efficient multi-flap ejector nozzle. Typical ratings were 12,690 lb dry and 16,360 lb with maximum reheat. Similar engines went into production in Sweden as the Svenska Flygmotor RM6C for later versions of Draken, the Swedish after-burner giving a thrust of up to 17,110 lb.

The Avon was also developed by the Industrial and Marine Division at Ansty for ship propulsion, electricity generation and gas pumping, more having been sold for these purposes than any other gas turbine. The total number of Avons built by Rolls-Royce for aircraft propulsion was 10,433, and though this may seem unimpressive compared with over 168,000 Merlins it goes some way towards justifying Hives' conviction that this engine would be 'the Merlin of the jet age'.

By the end of World War 2 Hives had become rather disenchanted with Griffith's complex projects although they made all the sense in the world on paper. By 1946 the mainstream designers at Derby, trying to build up their previously non-existent experience on gas turbines, began considering various kinds of what were called bypass jet engines. These were two-spool axial turbojets in which a proportion of the air delivered by an oversize LP compressor was ducted past the rest of the engine, along an annular bypass duct surrounding the core, and expelled as a propulsive jet surrounding the hot gas jet from the core. Compared with an equivalent turbojet burning fuel at the same rate this resulted in the combined jet being bigger and cooler, and moving at a lower mean velocity, which in turn meant greater thrust (and thus lower sfc) and less noise. Today we call such engines turbofans, and they have almost ousted the turbojet from most markets, except those for supersonic flight.

Today we appreciate that for subsonic applications the best efficiency results from choosing a bpr (bypass ratio is the ratio of cool bypass airflow to that passing through the core engine) of from 5 to 15 or more. In other words modern turbofans have small cores driving large fans, the latter usually having only a single stage and thus behaving as multiblade ducted propellers, generating virtually all of the engine's thrust. Most unfortunately, the only application that

materialized in the immediate post-war era concerned the proposed V-bombers for the RAF, which happened all to be designed with their four engines buried inside the roots of the wing. The Ministry of Supply could see that the bypass formula was ideally applicable to a strategic bomber, and in 1948, accepting a proposal from Rolls-Royce, provided funding, the application to be one of the B.35/46 bombers which became the Vulcan and Victor. The buried installation inevitably militated against a high bpr, and the figure accepted was only 0.6. Then, because the Ministry called for greater thrust, the bpr was dropped to 0.3; in other words the engine was not greatly different from a turbojet, whereas for a decade Griffith had (with typical super-foresight) been arguing for bpr to be around 20.

The company designation for the new engine was RB.80, and it was later named the Conway (though according to 'Jane's' Rolls-Royce names were those of *English* rivers). It was designed to 575 mph at 50,000 ft, and the company's proposal offered a take-off thrust of 9,250 lb for a weight of 2,984 lb. This weight was appreciably less than that of the competing turbojet, the Bristol BE.10 Olympus. Throughout the 1950s the two engines were to compete, and Rolls-Royce considered they could show on paper that, had the reheat Conway been selected for such aircraft as the TSR.2 and Concorde, the result would have been either a lighter or a longer-ranged aircraft. From the outset it was appreciated that, because of the large flow of fresh air in the outer part of the jet, the bypass engine would be particularly amenable to afterburning and thus to the propulsion of supersonic aircraft. Sadly, Ministry policy was to ignore the great possibilities, and the Conway had only one limited production application in a British military aircraft.

Moreover, Ministry vacillation meant that Rolls-Royce had no sooner set about the design of each successive version of the

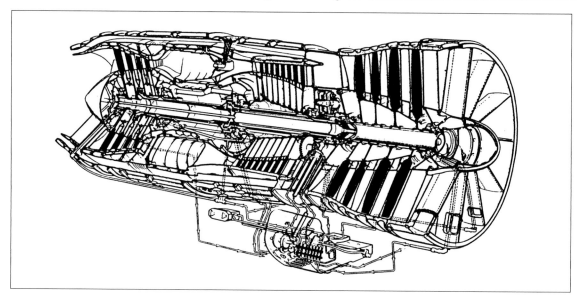

Proposed to the Ministry of Supply in October 1948, the RB.80—later named Conway RCo.2—was a remarkable engine for its day. Though bypass ratio was restricted by the wing-buried installation, it had titanium blades and discs throughout the rear HP stages, dovetail roots, and two-piece air-cooled HP turbine rotor blades.

Conway than it had to be dropped in favour of a more powerful model. Thus, while the original RCo.2 rating was 9,250 lb, subsequent versions increased the thrust in six stages to 21,800 lb! Even before a single engine had been built, the RCo.2 was overtaken by the RCo.3 of 11,500 lb, but a single RCo.2 was completed and run in August 1952, later achieving 10,000 lb thrust. It had a four-stage fan (LP compressor), eight-stage HP compressor, can-annular combustion chamber with ten duplex burners, and two-stage HP and LP turbines. The HP turbine blades were the first on any engine to be designed from the start with air cooling, and the discs, rotor blades and stators at the rear of the HP compressor were designed in titanium (though to save cost in the engine actually built these parts were steel).

Development engineer on the Conway was Lindsay Dawson. This pioneer bypass engine was in all design essentials very like jet engines of today, and it was a notable advance in aircraft propulsion. It proved of great value in providing experience of high-pr two-spool compressors, bearings for two-shaft engines, cooled blades in high-pressure gas flows, bypass ducts and many other new features. Flight development began using a single podded engine slung under an Ashton Mk 3 in 1954. Meanwhile the design team thrust ahead with the RCo.5 of 13,000 lb thrust, required under high priority for the Vickers-Armstrongs V.1000 strategic transport for the RAF. This outstanding aircraft was the obvious precursor of a superior long-range jetliner for the civil market. It was vitally needed, not so much for the RAF as to enable Britain to compete with the American Boeing 707 and Douglas DC–8. Alas, and contrary to all common sense, the whole project was cancelled in November 1955; but it was announced that the Conway engine was 'showing great promise' and would be used in a Mk 2 version

WE670, *an Ashton Mk 3, was used for the flight development of early Conway bypass engines. The test engine was carried in an underslung pod, upstream of which in this photograph is an icing spray grid.*

of the Victor bomber. Nationally, the cancellation of the V.1000 was a disaster of the greatest magnitude, but this was less obvious to Rolls-Royce which was eager to get its Conway on to the 707 and DC–8. It succeeded on both counts, but only to a very limited extent: a combined total of 69 aircraft out of 1,519 of both types built.

Hucknall soon learned that with axial jets there are likely to be inlet problems, and many aircraft programmes benefited enormously from the company's practice of trying whenever possible to test the engine in at least a mock-up of the installation. Seldom have the difficulties equalled those experienced with the Victor, and Lovesey has recorded how the obvious cure merely made things worse (the true cure was the exact opposite). Fortunately the Conway was quite a tolerant engine, and it gave few major headaches after 1956. The engines for the Victor B.2, 707–420 and DC–8–40 were all closely related, and were virtually new designs in comparison with their predecessors. Features included a seven-stage

LP compressor handling a mass flow of about 280 lb/s, a nine-stage HP compressor of titanium and steel giving an overall pr of about 14.1, a can-annular combustor with ten flame tubes each with a single burner, a single-stage HP turbine with air-cooled blades of the new forged type, and a two-stage LP turbine. The RCo.11 for the Victor was type-tested to the UK/US civil schedule in 1957 at 17,250 lb. It was air-tested in the very first Vulcan, *VX770,* but sadly this aircraft suffered catastrophic structural failure during a low-level display at Syerston on 20 September 1958. By this time the Conway had run true to Rolls-Royce form and grown considerably in thrust, and the production Victor engine became known as the RCo.17 Mk 201 of 20,600 lb. These are still in use in Victor K.2 tankers. For the 707 Rolls-Royce Hucknall developed a complete pod, with cabin-air turbocompressor above the engine, a multi-lobe Greatrex nozzle and reverser, the engine being the RCo.12 Mk 508 rated at 17,500 lb, followed by the 508A of 18,000 lb. The RCo.12 Mk 509 and

The world's first production turbofan was the RCo.11 Conway Mk 200 for the Victor B.2, rated at 17,250 lb. Later these were upgraded to RCo.17 Mk 201 standard at 20,600 lb. Note the huge anti-icing pipe, and the silver fuel/oil heat exchanger near the left engineer's right hand.

509A for the DC–8 was fitted into American pods, and supplied bleed air to cabin-air packs in the fuselage. Though the Conway made only such a tiny dent in the US jet market, it gave more thrust than the rival JT4A, had lower fuel consumption, was appreciably lighter (typically 4,500 lb against 5,100) and on take-off created much less noise and smoke. This was not lost on the competition.

By 1956 experiments were in hand on afterburning both downstream of the core and in the bypass flow, though these did not involve complete engines. The possibilities were impressive, but Rolls-Royce failed in its efforts to get such an engine adopted for the Republic F–105, Vought XF8U–3 and Hawker P.1121. Today the augmented turbofan is the accepted power-plant for supersonic fighters, but this was less apparent over thirty years ago. Not until January 1959 did anyone show interest,

A beautiful display exhibit of the Conway RCo.12 Mk 508A rated at 18,000 lb for the 707-420. Note the reverser (in reverse mode) and noise-reducing nozzle.

Last of the Conways, the 21,800-lb RCo.43 Mk 301 is fitted to the RAF's VC10 tankers and transports. As the engines are on the rear fuselage the reverser cascades blast the jets out above and below, whereas in the 707 engine illustrated opposite they eject to the sides.

and then it was the US Air Force for the TFX (F–111) programme. The Americans expressed doubt that an augmented turbofan was possible, so in one week Rolls-Royce put on a demonstration. Starting from scratch, a complete installation for a Conway was designed and built, giving 27.3% boost, and a few days later 47.5%. This was the first augmented turbofan.

Having effectively destroyed Britain's previously existing ability to compete with the 707 and DC–8, BOAC then took the foolish decision of asking British industry to start afresh and build a competitor, but matched to shorter runways. This inevitably penalized the economics, and quite unnecessarily because in the meanwhile the world's major airports were all enlarged at great cost to match the 707. To heap insult on injury, BOAC then publicly criticised the economics of the aircraft built to its specification, and demanded government compensation for using it (despite the fact that it was such a well-engineered aircraft it actually showed higher utilization and better profits than the BOAC 707s). The aircraft was the Vickers-Armstrongs VC 10, and it was ordered in May 1957 and flown in June 1962. It was powered by four Conways of an advanced design mounted on the rear fuselage. Initial production had RCo.42 Mk 540 engines, which introduced a new LP spool handling 367 lb/s, doubling the bpr to 0.6, and increasing thrust to 20,370 lb. The stretched Super VC 10 had RCo.43 Mk 550 engines with an eight-stage LP compressor increasing pr to 15.8 and airflow to 375 lb/s, giving 22,500 lb thrust. Similar Mk 301 engines power the RAF VC 10 transports and tankers. Plain nozzles are fitted to all versions, together with either two (outboard) or four reversers. The Conway was one of several fine Rolls-Royce engines which pioneered new technology but never gained a rewarding market, the total production amounting to 907 engines. It had the effect of catapulting Pratt & Whitney into the turbofan era, and also of showing Soviet designers exactly how such engines should be arranged.

In 1957 BEA woke up to the need for jets, and issued a specification for an eighty-seat airliner with a range of 1,000 miles—ignoring the fact that such an aircraft was already in production at Toulouse in the Avon-engined Caravelle. BEA opened negotiations in February 1958 for a totally new airliner with three turbofans grouped at the tail. The author cannot resist quoting the top Boeing man who, on learning about this British aircraft, the DH.121, said 'Three engines? Heck, that's the optimum worst.' That was before they sold 1,832 Boeing 727s. Maybe the Caravelle should have been bought for BEA, but the 121 aimed at greater speed and significantly better economy, carrying 111 passengers over a stage-length of 2,073 miles. The engine finally selected was the RB.141, later named Medway, and it was a 'clean sheet of paper' engine. Griffith continued to dream of a sensible bpr around 20, but a deep study which took pod drag of externally hung engines into account came up with the answer 'not greater than 1'. In the USA newly created NASA pushed for high bprs, but Britain's National Gas Turbine Establishment (NGTE) seemed to have no strong views. In any case, the BEA aircraft was supposed to be a short-hauler where bpr exerted less influence on operating costs. When everything was put into the melting pot and stirred, the bpr answer that emerged was 0.64. (See photo p 159).

The RB.141 was designed and on test with impressive speed. It was a good engine, with an initial rating of 13,790 lb, and large markets opened up for commercial and military versions with ratings up to 20,000 lb, or 30,000 lb with reheat. While Pratt & Whitney ran into terrible problems with the smaller TF30, Allison ran an augmented (afterburning) Medway with a reheat combustion efficiencyof 90% over the boost range from 70% down to 3%! British government interest was zero, because British combat aircraft had been decreed an obsolete concept three years previously. Then,

out of the blue, BEA decided they could be as eccentric as BOAC. They ordered the DH.121 to be cut down in size to 97 passengers, and in range to 921 miles. De Havilland and Rolls-Royce tore up all their work and started again on a much less capable aircraft. The result was the DH.121 Trident, powered by 9,850-lb RB.163 engines. Other markets vanished, the Swedes going to Pratt & Whitney (whose JT8D was very like the Medway) to power the Viggen.

When Freddie Morley designed the RB.163 it was a crash programme. There was no question of increasing bpr or making any major change other than to scale everything down. Of course, blade profiles, pipes, accessories and many other parts stayed the same size, and as the complex air-cooled HP turbine blades kept the same cross-section, the two-stage turbines were rather squashed together, which for a while caused a vibration problem. The company had paid for five Medways with its own funds, and Chief Executive Sir Denning Pearson said 'The 163 must go into more than one aircraft.' It did better, and to some extent its reduced size was a blessing, as it enabled it in due course to replace the Gyron Junior, J79 and Avon in three military types.

It was named the Spey, and first ran in December 1960. It had a four-stage LP compressor handling 203 lb/s, a 12-stage HP spool giving an overall pr of 16.8, the usual can-annular combustor with ten flame tubes, two-stage HP and LP turbines and simple non-mixing coaxial nozzles. In Trident engines an internal clamshell reverser and six-lobe noise-suppressing nozzle were added. The Spey was soon adopted for the BAC One-Eleven twin-jet at a thrust of 10,140 lb, water injection then being added and the Greatrex nozzle removed. The obvious need to upgrade the Trident as nearly as possible back to the DH.121 was then partially met with the RSp.4 Mk 510, with a five-stage LP spool handling 208 lb/s at a pr

Above *A Spey 511 being readied for despatch. Most Speys look pretty much alike, though this one has an internal clamshell reverser and is for a One-Eleven. Trident engines had six-lobe suppressing nozzles, and Gulfstream engines have target-type reversers.*

Right *The simple Greatorex nozzle reduced the aft (jet) noise spectrum of many hundreds of engines for civil applications. This is the five-chute noise suppressor for the Spey of a Gulfstream II.*

of 21.1. Weight increased from 2,200 to about 2,500 lb, thrust increasing to 11,000 lb with the Mk 510 and to 12,550 lb with later versions. The Mk 512–14DW remains to this day in licence production in Romania for the One-Eleven, and many Mk 511–8 (USAF F113–RR–100) engines remain in use in Gulfstream II, III and C–20A aircraft. After years playing off Rolls-Royce against Bristol Siddeley at 7,500 to 8,500 lb thrust, the Fokker F28 Fellowship was first flown on 9 May 1967, powered by an engine initially called Spey Junior but later known just as the RB.183. This is basically a simplified Spey with a four-stage LP compressor handling 199 lb/s with bpr of 1 and pr of 15.4, thrust being 9,900 lb at reduced rpm, making for a quiet and lightly stressed engine. The final RB.183 Mk 15N and 15P introduced a ten-lobe mixer nozzle.

Shortcomings of the original Blackburn Buccaneer naval strike aircraft led to the Buccaneer S.2, flown in May 1963. This was powered by two Spey Mk 101 engines, similar to the early airline Spey with a four-stage

LP spool but with turbine temperature increased to give a thrust of 11,030 lb. A special feature of this engine, which is still in front-line service, is a large bleed manifold to serve the extensive blc (boundary-layer control) system of the Buccaneer. The next military application also required a bleed manifold, for blowing the wing leading edge and flaps on the British Phantoms. In this application, however, major changes were necessary to operate at Mach numbers up to 2 and meet many other challenging demands. The Spey 202, for the Phantom FGR.2, has a five-stage LP spool with construction changed from drum to shaft/disc. To the rear is a large fully modulated afterburner with six rams driving the ejector-type primary nozzle. A Plessey gas-turbine starter is fitted. The Phantom FG.1 has the Spey 203, with ultra-fast afterburner light-up for carrier overshoots. After prolonged negotiations the People's Republic of China bought a manufacturing licence for the Spey 202, a deal which included the import of fifty engines from Britain. China built a large factory to produce the Spey, as an extension of the huge existing works at Xian (Yan Liang). By 1979 the Spey factory was fully tooled and in operation, and two Mk 202 engines were despatched to Britain and tested. They fully met the design performance, of 12,250 lb dry and 20,515 lb with full reheat augmentation, and passed a 150-hour type test with no trouble. Then nothing was heard for almost ten years, and the author eventually omitted to mention the Spey under 'China' in the annual *Jane's*. Suddenly, at the 1988 Farnborough airshow, a model appeared of the B-7 all-

As has so often been the case, the British government picked an American aircraft with a Rolls-Royce engine when it bought Phantoms for the RAF and Royal Navy. The Spey 202/203 did not produce the expected boost to the Phantom, but certainly gave a boost to Rolls-Royce.

weather two-seat attack fighter, powered by two Speys! The Chinese said 'Didn't you know, we are in full production, and the first B-7 will fly in November 1988'.

For the Nimrod maritime patrol aircraft the Spey 250 was developed, rated at 11,995 lb and fully navalized. The final production Spey, being made under licence in Italy with many parts supplied from Brazil, is the Mk 807 for the AMX attack aircraft. This essentially comprises the compressors and turbines of the Mk 101 in the structure of the RB.183, and with the bleed manifold deleted and a manual fuel control added. Rating is 11,030 lb and weight 2,388 lb.

In the competitive portion of the TFX (F–111) programme Rolls-Royce teamed with Allison to propose an augmented Spey derivative, the AR.168. Had this been chosen it would have been very unlikely to have suffered the prolonged engine/air-frame mismatch problems of the eventual winner, the TF30, but the latter did not suffer from the handicap of being 'foreign'. The TF30 was also chosen for the US Navy's A–7A Corsair II, and the result was not only a noticeably underpowered aircraft but one whose temperamental compressor was liable to surge and cause a flameout on steam-catapult take-offs. Even before the A–7 was in service, the USAF had awarded Rolls-Royce and Allison a joint contract for a more powerful and less sensitive replace-ment engine, and the result was the TF41, first run at Derby in October 1967. Based on the Spey, the TF41 has an enlarged five-stage LP spool handling 263 lb/s, and with the last two stages cut down to core size and called the IP (intermediate-pressure) compressor. Bypass ratio is 0.74 and fully equipped weight about 3,250 lb. The TF41 was ordered at 14,500 lb thrust for A–7Ds

Most powerful of the Spey family, the Rolls-Royce/Allison TF41 has a revised compressor handling a mass flow increased from about 203 to 263 lb/s. Large numbers are still serving in Vought A-7s.

for the USAF and at 15,000 lb for A–7Es for the US Navy, proving a vast improvement. Production of 1,440 engines was completed in 1983, but today Allison is proposing an uprated version with afterburner to give about 27,000 lb thrust.

Until the incoming government curtly cancelled it in 1965, Hawker were developing the P.1154RN supersonic STOVL fighter with twin vectored-thrust Speys, as described in the next chapter. Another vectored version, with a giant air-bleed system added, powered the NASA Augmentor-Wing Buffalo. For nine years from 1960 Rolls-Royce collaborated with MAN Turbo on lift/cruise engines derived or scaled from the Spey, again as related in the next chapter. Overall it has been an extremely successful programme, but almost from the start the old calculations of optimum bpr were totally discredited. Increasingly the civil Speys suffered from criticisms of unimpressive fuel economy and inability to meet new noise legislation. By 1965 the RB.225, a refanned Spey of much higher bpr, was in active consideration. Similar refanned Speys kept on being studied, while the company was preoccupied with the RB.211. After twenty years these bore

fruit in the Tay, with bpr of 3 (Chapter 17). Today the Marine Spey powers important warships, but excluding surface applications the number built still exceeds 5,500.

In 1947, following interest shown by the Air Staff in cruise missiles, which at the time were called pilotless bombers, the Ministry of Supply issued development contracts with three companies for suitable jet engines. Rolls-Royce studied a number of possible designs, but only one was flown (with two engines on the wingtips of a Meteor). The RB.93 Soar was an extremely simple engine, the main requirements being light weight and low cost. It had very few parts, including a fully annular combustion chamber, and its starting and control systems were almost non-existent. The overall diameter was 15.8 in, and a typical RSr.2 Soar weighed 267 lb and had a thrust of 1,810 lb. Another version of the same weight was type-tested at 1,860 lb, the T/W ratio of 6.97 being approximately double that of the best conventional axial jets of the day. Nothing came of the intended applications, but the Soar and related designs greatly assisted the later development of jet-lift engines, as outlined in the next chapter. A photograph of the Soar testbed appears on page 155.

Chapter 10

JET LIFT

Like many new ideas, jet lift occurred to various people working independently. Certainly one of the pioneers was Griffith, who as related earlier wrote a farsighted paper on jet-lift VTOL in 1941 and suggested achieving 'thistledown landing' by putting a 90° deflector flap behind the jet nozzle of one of his complex ideas for an engine. None of his schemes was built, but by 1944 various jet-lift projects were urgently being funded in Germany, necessity being the mother of invention! They included a rocket interceptor launched up a nearly vertical ramp (this actually got into production) and a curious machine, similarly standing upright on its tail, with a three-blade helicopter-type rotor carried on a ring around the mid-fuselage and turned at high speed by jets on the tips!

In 1947 the US Navy awarded Ryan a contract to investigate the problems of controlling an aeroplane at very low airspeeds, and this resulted in a free hovering flight by a remotely controlled test rig containing an upright Allison J33 turbojet on 31 May 1951. This work later led to the same company's X–13 Vertijet, powered by the engine judged to have the best combination of high thrust, low weight and man-rated reliability (in a very critical application, totally dependent upon engine thrust): the Rolls-Royce Avon 200-series. This again

was a tail-sitter (or tail-stander), a formula considered not feasible for practical use. The pioneer flat-riser aeroplane, in which the aircraft maintains a normal attitude, was the Bell VTOL (Vertical Take-Off and Landing, the first time this acronym was used), powered by two pivoted Fairchild J44 turbojets, which made its first free vertical flight on 16 November 1954. The first aircraft to hover with deflected jets was the Bell X–14, fitted with twin AS Viper engines on its first hover on 19 February 1957.

All this time, much was happening in Britain. From 1946 Fairey Aviation pioneered the technology of tail-standing VTOL fighters, beginning with remotely piloted gimballed-rocket models and going on to the manned FD.1 (Fairey Delta 1) powered by a Rolls-Royce Derwent 8 of 3,600 lb thrust. It was intended that this stumpy machine should have a swivelling jetpipe, to be developed by Rolls-Royce, plus four surrounding booster rockets, but none of these features was ever installed. Wisely, the Ministry cancelled this programme, but it did sponsor pioneer work on a jet-deflection flat riser. The aircraft was Meteor *RA490*, which had already completed valued research programmes before it was torn apart in 1953 by Westland Aircraft and rebuilt with major parts from no fewer than

The first TMR 'Flying Bedstead' in thunderous flight at Hucknall. Looking up at it, one can see that the aft Nene serves the large central nozzle and the front. Nene smaller nozzles on either side. The attitude control jets were fed by bleed pipes from all 18 compressor delivery elbows.

seven different marks of Meteor, plus giant nacelles housing Nene engines fitted with pilot-controlled valves which could switch the efflux to short jetpipes extending downwards at 70°. First flown in February 1954, the jet-deflection Meteor often flew at 75 knots, and once at 65.

In a parallel programme Rolls-Royce Hucknall built a much stranger device officially called the TMR, for Thrust-Measuring Rig, but which understandably became more commonly known as the Flying Bedstead. It comprised a steel-tube space frame standing on four small swivelling castors and carrying two Nenes, two fuel tanks and a pilot seat. The engines directed their jets towards each other, one having its jetpipe turned down through 90° directly in the centre of the rig and the other having its pipe bifurcated on each side and turned 90° down so that its thrust (or sudden loss of it) likewise caused no pitch or roll moment. When the pilot opened the throttles the whole contraption rose thunderously into the sky. Basically unstable, its attitude was controlled by four reaction jets on long arms, locally called 'puff pipes', one pair giving control in pitch and the other in roll, fed with compressor bleed air. This device, unlike anything seen in the sky previously,

lifted off restrained by loose tethers on 3 July 1953. Soon it and a companion were blasting round the sky at speeds approaching 100 knots, control being effected by bodily tilting the whole rig. Captain R. T. Shepherd said he enjoyed leading the test-pilot team!

Rolls-Royce were thus the world pioneers of height control achieved entirely by judicious throttle variation of jet engines and of attitude control achieved entirely by compressor-bleed jets. One TMR is still preserved at Hucknall. Within a month of the first free flight of a TMR in 1954 a new group was formed to design the first direct-lift turbojet, the RB.108. Thus began an effort which lasted nearly twenty years and put Rolls-Royce right in the forefront of a totally new and very challenging field of aircraft engines. Indeed, the work was belatedly picked up again in 1983, though today's ASTOVL proposals are based on engines which in various ways can be used for propulsion as well as for lift.

In designing the RB.108 it was at once appreciated that, while the engine resembled the Soar and related missile engines in being relatively simple, light and with no need for a long life, it differed in one crucial respect. During take-off and landing the

The Soar was the smallest aero engine Rolls-Royce ever made, weighing 267 lb. Two were flight tested on the wingtips of WA982, an otherwise standard Meteor F.8.

aircraft and its crew would be totally dependent upon the lift jets, so reliability had to be of the highest possible order—if possible, even better than for conventional engines. This involved not only the design of the engine but also its safe and stable operation in unprecedented conditions such as vertical mounting with air rushing at 90° horizontally past the inlet and with large air bleeds to control the aircraft.

Despite this severe demand, and the use of generally conventional design and materials, the RB.108 went well beyond the Soar in achieving T/W ratios up to 9.5. A typical weight was 270 lb, and thrust varied from 2,550 lb without air bleed down to 2,340 lb with 5.875% bleed and 2,150 lb with a bleed of 10%. The eight-stage compressor rotor had pre-machined aluminium discs orbitally welded into a rigid drum, the

The RB.108 was the world's first purpose-designed lift jet, though it used traditional materials. It was designed for vertical installation, pivoting on trunnions to tilt 30° fore and aft.

stator-vane assemblies providing circular stiffness to the very thin forged and machined casing. The combustor was of the light annular type pioneered with the Soar, but it had to be of more sophisticated design to achieve the most even exit temperature distribution possible, in view of the extremely high gas temperature employed and the overriding need for reliability. As in the Soar, a heavy starter was replaced by simple air impingement on the turbine blades, drawing air from a ground source or a previously running propulsion engine. There was no gearbox or shaft drive. Fuel and oil were supplied by bleed-air turbopumps, and the bearings had to be capable of survivng high-speed running with the total-loss oil system virtually dry, and without air cooling. The result was the introduction of spring-loaded ball bearings.

Spurred on by Griffith's grandiose visions of giant supersonic airliners borne vertically aloft by batteries of dozens of lift jets, Rolls-Royce determined to become world leader in the technology, and it assigned large resources at Derby and Hucknall to the RB.108 and its successors, and to their challenging applications. The first application comprised two examples of a VTOL research aircraft, fully funded by the Ministry to specification ER.143 and built by Shorts as the SC.1. Each had a battery of four RB.108s in the centre of the fuselage in a special bay with large louvred doors on top and the four nozzles open at the bottom. The four engines were installed substantially vertically but could be pivoted in unison through 30° to give a component of forward or rearward thrust. At the insistence of the test pilot, Tom Brooke-Smith, a fifth RB.108 was installed in the tail for propulsion. This was fed from a dorsal inlet and was tilted to suit the vertically-arranged lubrication system, the jetpipe then bending round to the horizontal. The lift jets were coupled into a high-capacity air bleed system feeding reaction control jets at the nose, tail and wingtips.

Flying began in the conventional mode with just the propulsion engine, on 2 April 1957. The second SC.1 began tethered hovering on 23 May 1958. Though small the SC.1s were extremely complex, with comprehensive autopilot and stability sub-systems, but major difficulties were few. Many of the problems had been solved in 1956 with a single RB.108 mounted in an identical, but smaller, lift installation in a Meteor FR.9, *VZ608*, which was also the first aircraft to investigate jet-lift ground erosion. The latter was quite severe with the SC.1, and on one occasion a heavy and unpremeditated landing was made when the upper surface of the fuselage became covered with freshly mown grass, blown upwards by the jets and sucked on to the inlet grills to starve the engines of air! Later an SC.1 carried out such advanced research as VTOL landing at night and in bad weather.

By 1959 jet lift was all the rage, at Rolls-Royce because of Griffith's vision of slender-delta SSTs and in many other countries because it was realized that in the missile age every military airfield is at risk. Using partly US funding, the NBMR–3 (NATO Basic Military Requirement No 3) was drafted in 1960 as the outcome of sixteen revisions of a requirement for a light strike fighter issued in 1959. After all the talking came an avalanche of exciting jet-lift proposals from many Western aircraft manufacturers, all seeking to win what looked like the biggest multinational warplane programme in history. It called for low-level attack at Mach 0.92 and supersonic speed at higher altitudes, plus jet-lift V/STOL to avoid the need to use vulnerable airfields.

It was a time for adrenalin to flow, as Chief Designers, Managing Directors, Air Marshals and Generals argued vehemently about the technicalities while dancing to the tune of the politicians. At the end of the day the 'technical winner' was declared to be Britain's Hawker P.1154, but the word

Above _Meteor FR.9_ VZ608 _had its main fuel tank removed and the centre fuselage turned into a lift-jet bay with a single RB.108 arranged in exactly the way four RB.108s were to be installed in the SC.1. Rolling it down the Hucknall runway, the engineers learned about erosion and ingestion._

Right _The RB.162 was the result of a deeper look at how a lift jet could be designed, and the result was a thrust/weight ratio of up to 16.1. Fastened to the glassfibre compressor casing are the oil bottle, able to deliver a shot of oil to the two bearings on each of five or six starts, and the high-energy igniter box._

'technical' was added at the insistence of the French who said they were going ahead with their Dassault Mirage IIIV anyway. The IIIV, powered by a SNECMA turbofan and lifted by eight completely new RB.162 lift engines, was politically favoured and even had strong support from the British Air Staff, which took on board Rolls-Royce's argument that only by employing separate lift engines could the propulsion engine be the correct size for cruising flight. Unquestionably, the political clout was all behind Rolls-Royce and the multi-engine formula.

Dassault had been sold on the idea of jet lift by the patient missionary work of Rolls-Royce's former test and liaison pilot Ronnie Harker. To prove the concept a Mirage III was rebuilt as the Balzac, powered by a Bristol Orpheus and lifted by eight RB.108s. This first hovered on 12 October 1962 and made a successful transition from jet-supported to wing-supported flight and back to a vertical landing on 29 March 1963, but it subsequently suffered two serious crashes. Undaunted, Dassault went ahead with the much bigger and more powerful IIIV.

Like all the other multi-engine projects this used the RB.162 lift jet, a remarkable achievement by the now highly competent lift-jet team at Derby. Handling double the airflow of the RB.108, it was not only extremely simple but stages 2 to 6 of the compressor rotor, the entire inlet ring and guide vanes, compressor casing and stators, nosecone and pressure-feed oil bottle were all made of resin-bonded glass-fibre composite. This material had never previously been used in such demanding applications, and it needed completely new standards of quality control as well as high-temperature resins for the delivery end of the compressor. Cunning joints between the halves of the casing permitted quick assembly/disassembly without bolts. A single-sided combustion dilution system was used, with simple splash-plate fuel nozzles.

The RB.162–1 weighed about 270 lb and gave a thrust of 4,409 lb, with 4,718 available in emergency following failure of any other engine in a group. In most applications it had a fixed nozzle and 10% bleed offtake. For the production Mirage IIIV the RB.162–30 series was developed with a thrust of 5,000 lb with little increase in weight, resulting in T/W exceeding 16. All eight lift jets were started together by a high-volume air bleed from the propulsion engine im-

One of Don Eyre's beautiful drawings which 'sold Griffith's ideas'. It shows a supersonic airliner with 24 RB.162s for lift, plus three more in the nose, eight lift engines mounted transversely at the back and two further tail engines feeding the reaction-control jets. Eight propulsion engines are housed in the fins.

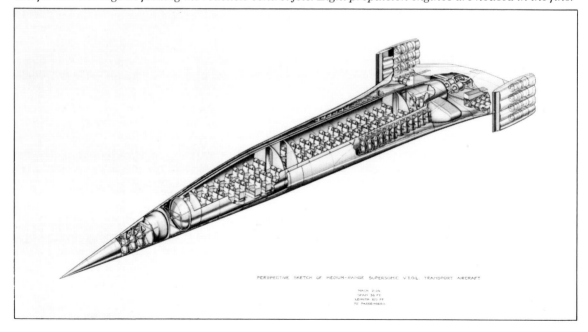

The Whitworth Gloster 681 transport for the RAF, cancelled in 1965, would have had four RB.142 Medway main engines, plus lift jets. Each main engine, rated at 18,290 lb, was to have had a switch-in deflector as seen here. Operating very much like the company's reversers, it enabled the engine to give thrust or lift.

pinging direct on the RB.162 turbines. The IIIV hovered on 12 February 1965 and went on to reach Mach 2.04, an accomplishment no other VTO aircraft has emulated. But it gradually became evident to almost everyone that aircraft of this type were probably not a practical proposition, and termination of the IIIV was made easier by loss of the second example in November 1966.

This still left the British P.1154, which gradually attracted the attention and support of the Royal Navy and RAF. Shortsightedly, the requirements of the two services diverged increasingly, and throughout Rolls-Royce attempted to get the single BS.100 engine rejected in favour of twin Speys with a complex system of ducting to avoid catastrophic asymmetric problems. Ultimately Rolls-Royce switched its allegiance to a Spey-engined version of the Phantom, and this probably influenced the customers and government in getting this to replace the P.1154RN in February 1964. The remaining P.1154RAF was likewise replaced by the Phantom in February 1965, keeping the RAF ever since tied to vulnerable runways for all its fighters.

Out of the wreckage of the totally mis-managed NBMR–3 competition came two European projects which for a further decade found work for Rolls-Royce lift jets. One was a purely German programme. Bölkow, Heinkel and Messerschmitt joined forces in the Entwicklungsring Süd to build a series of VJ 101C research aircraft from which it was hoped to develop the VJ 101D, a Mach 2 interceptor. The VJ 101C was an extremely neat supersonic machine with a fuselage and wing reminiscent of the F–104. The wing, however, was mounted high and carried on its tips large pods each housing twin RB.145 engines, with two more mounted upright in a lift jet bay in the fuselage ahead of the wing. Each tip pod could pivot from horizontal to vertical, so that its engines could give thrust or lift. The RB.145 was virtually an RB.108 with an added zero-stage and variable inlet guide vanes, and redesigned to serve as both a lift jet and a long-life propulsion engine, driving normal accessories, with conventional control and lubrication systems and an hydraulic starter. First run in 1961, it weighed 457 lb and was rated at 2,750 lb. EWR Süd built various ground and free-flight rigs powered by RB.108s and RB.145s before flying the first

Left *The right wingtip pod of the VJ 101C-X1, with twin RB.145 engines. The fixed-geometry inlet, designed for supersonic speeds, is shown translated forward to admit extra air for lift off, though the pod is horizontal.*

Below *To assist development of such aircraft as the VJ 101C Rolls-Royce built this 'Whippy Rig', which was used to investigate computer control of tip-mounted engines. The latter was a single RB.108.*

VJ 101C on 10 April 1963. The latter soon reached Mach 1.04 but crashed—due to an avionic fault on a conventional take-off—on 14 September 1964. The second VJ 101C had fully modulated afterburning RB.145Rs rated at 3,650 lb and was planned to reach Mach 2, but the programme was abandoned.

The other project lasted longer. The VAK 191B, originally called the Focke-Wulf Fw 1262, was the winner of a 1964 contest for a VTOL replacement for the Fiat G91 for West Germany and Italy. Originally Italy collaborated, feeding in its Fiat G95/4 project. Britain funded the RB.193 vectored turbofan, shared by Rolls-Royce and Bristol Siddeley in the ratio 2:1, but showed no interest in the aircraft. VAK was the German acronym for 'vertical reconnaissance and strike single-seater'. It attempted to get the best of both worlds by relying mainly on a central lift/cruise turbofan with vectored thrust, but avoided having this engine

'larger than necessary' by adding a lift jet in the forward fuselage and a second in the rear. The main engine was the RB.193–12, with a three-stage fan and two-stage IP compressor driven by a three-stage LP turbine, contra-rotating six-stage HP compressor driven by a single-stage HP turbine with cooled blades, annular combustor with large bleed ports for aircraft control, and four vectored nozzles. Mass flow was 203 lb/s, pr 16.2, bpr 1.12, weight 1,742 lb and guaranteed thrust/lift 10,163 lb. The lift jets were RB.162–81s with air-cooled turbine blades to increase thrust to 5,577 lb, later increased to 6,000 lb. Eventually three VAK 191Bs were built, the first beginning untethered hovering on 10 September 1971, but it fell into a number of design traps—such as poor STO performance and inability to carry heavy conventional weapon loads—and, having in 1968 been downgraded as a trials effort to support Tornado, the project

The second VJ 101C in hovering flight, with the fuselage lift jets working and the tip engines vertical. Later this aircraft had afterburning RB.145R engines.

To support the VAK 191B this rig, the SG 1262, was first flown in August 1966. Powered by a row of five RB.108s, it weighed 7,700 lb. It provided valuable data over a wide range of aspects of design and engineering. The location was Bremen airport, where the prototype Focke-Wulf 190 flew before World War 2.

was terminated in 1975. The same formula was, however, adopted for the Soviet Yak–38.

The RB.193 was actually a joint project with MAN Turbo (today MTU) of West Germany. So too was the last RR lift/cruise engine actually to run, the RB.153. Intended as the propulsion engine of the stillborn VJ 101D, the 153–17 was a slim and attractive turbofan of only 29.5 in diameter but no less than 166 in long with its unique afterburner. It had a four-stage fan, twelve-stage HP compressor, cannular combustor, two-stage HP and LP turbines, mass flow of 121 lb/s, bpr of 0.7, pr of 18 and dry weight (without jetpipe) of 1,430 lb. Ratings were 6,850 lb dry and 11,645 lb with full reheat. What made the RB.153 unique was that downstream of the afterburner was a vectoring nozzle. The nozzle itself was of the usual variable-area type with a multi-flap primary nozzle not compromised in any way. Upstream of it was inserted a section of jetpipe able to rotate, and connected at front and rear by diagonal joints. As this wedge section was rotated it caused the nozzle downstream to vector, the movement starting off sideways (the twin engines being handed to cancel out lateral components) and finishing in the 90° vertically downward position. The full range of movement took just one second.

To support the NBMR–3 aircraft NATO also ran an NBMR–4 competition for a V/STOL tactical transport. Apart from triggering off the former de Havilland team at Hatfield to come up with a succession of projects, the chief result of this competition was the German Dornier Do 31, which led to various test rigs and finally to two Do 31E flight articles. Main engines were two

Pegasus (Chapter 16), but under the outer wings were boxes housing eight RB.162–4s. These had no air bleeds and were arranged in line at an angle of 75° with a ±7.5° range of rocking movement and swivelling nozzles. Several of the unbuilt NBMR-4 designs featured RB.162s lying on their sides, with 90° nozzle deflectors, to enable a whole row to lie beneath the wing.

In the event none of these aircraft came to anything, but the RB.162 did find a useful application. Following the customer's foolish decision to shrink the Trident jetliner the Hatfield team did all it could to make it bigger and longer-ranged again, but they were restricted by the small Spey engine. In the final Tridents, the Mks 3B and Super 3B, take-off thrust was increased by adding a small booster turbojet in the tail, immediately below the rudder, fed by side inlets closed off by doors in cruising flight. The added 'fourth engine' was an RB.162–86, similar to the lift jets but with many glass-fibre parts replaced by light alloy and with a normal jetpipe and nozzle, and arranged for horizontal operation. The –86 was rated at 5,250 lb and weighed 520 lb, and gave little trouble in service.

When the Hatfield designers gave up work on the HS.129, their original NBMR–4 contender, they by no means stopped work on jet V/STOL transports. Among many other schemes, one stands out for the man-hours put into it; indeed, many still regret that it was never more than a 'near miss' in the world of commercial aviation, because it offered the prospect of an escape from the need to hurtle down long runways, an escape from queuing up to take off, and to some degree an escape from severe noise at airports. This aircraft was the HS.141, essentially a conventional 102/119-seat transport in the class of the 737 but distinguished by the addition of large sponson boxes along the lower sides of the fuselage. These housed (in the standard version) sixteen lift jets, eight ahead of the wing and eight aft, in compartments closed by doors in cruising flight. To meet the needs of civil operation these lift jets were turbofans of no less than 9.5 bpr, handling an enormous airflow with a jet velocity of only 640 ft/s, compared with 2,170 ft/s for the RB.162. Rolls-Royce investigated a series of such engines under the family designation of RB.202. The 202–25 was rated at 10,300 lb for early HS.141 studies, but natural growth led to the 202–31 rated at 13,000 lb for a weight of 850 lb. The gas generator was almost an RB.162, to which was added a three-stage LP turbine driving the big single-stage fan. Overall engine diameter, at 75.1 in, compared with the overall length (height) of only 45.4 in.

This non-starter has been described because it represented a pinnacle in an effort to build a jet-lift transport lasting more than a decade (1960–72) and appeared to have much to offer. It failed to be built because of the sheer difficulty of certificating a jet-STOVL airliner, and because such aircraft appeared likely to have considerably higher seat-mile costs than those needing long runways. But such considerations do not apply to military aircraft. The final fling in the story of specialized lift jets was the Rolls-Royce/Allison XJ99.

This third-generation lift jet was a truly remarkable further advance, being the kind of thing that results from an experienced team of engineers being given a real challenge. Obviously, by 1965 it was possible to aim higher even than the RB.162, but by this time Rolls-Royce had worked with aircraft companies on many proposals for jet-lift combat aircraft and this had brought to light extra design objectives. A great deal had been learned about installations, so that, whilst minimizing the weight and bulk, the power-driven doors above the lift engines could be made to turn the airflow smoothly downwards during an accelerating transition, with minimum pressure-disturbance at the inlet faces, whilst the engines

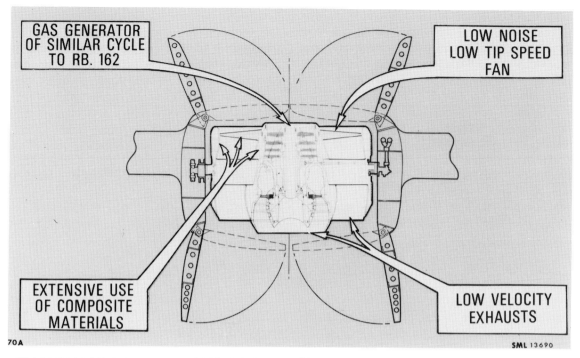

GAS GENERATOR
OF SIMILAR CYCLE
TO RB. 162

LOW NOISE
LOW TIP SPEED
FAN

EXTENSIVE USE
OF COMPOSITE
MATERIALS

LOW VELOCITY
EXHAUSTS

70A   SML 13690

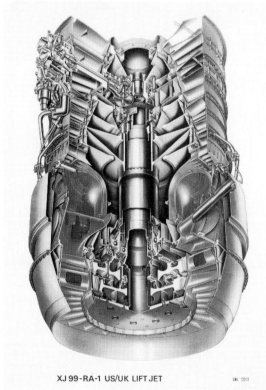

XJ 99-RA-1 US/UK LIFT JET

Above *Never built, the RB.202 was the company's answer to the need for a lift jet for civil transports. In 1968 design data included a thrust of 8,000 lb, weight of 470 lb, diameter of 58.5 in, length (height) of 34 in, and sfc of 0.45.*

Left *The Rolls-Royce/Allison XJ99-1 was on test twenty years ago, yet it still represents the pinnacle of achievement in direct lift engines. It could have formed the core of a very wide range of engines for propulsion as well as for lift.*

and/or nozzles could swivel to give forward or reverse thrust.

Equally significant was the realization that, for a supersonic combat aircraft, it is important to minimize fuselage cross section, and in practice this was found to mean that lift jets had to be made as short as possible. This required that the compressor had to achieve much higher work-per-stage, and the startling answer was to adopt contra-rotating intermeshing spools. This eliminated the need for stators, or for any variable stages. The concept was first used in the

RB.189, and this in turn was the basis for the XJ99, which was developed by Rolls-Royce and Allison under an inter-governmental Memo of Understanding of October 1965.

The simplicity of the XJ99 tended to mask its extremely clever design. The LP compressor had two stages and the HP four, all of mixed glass/metal construction and housed in a split metal casing. The concentric shafts were each driven by a single-stage air-cooled turbine, the entry temperature being 1,360°C. Absence of any turbine stators reduced the need for cooling air, and the turbine characteristics improved compressor stability. The annular combustor, surrounded by a large air bleed manifold, was shorter than in any previous engine designed by Derby and possibly in the world; overall engine length was 44 in. Dry weight was about 440 lb and normal thrust rating 9,000 lb. Among many new technologies explored with this engine were the use of abradable linings for seals and blade-tip rubbing paths, and exceptional operating stability in a most challenging environment without the use of variables. Engine response seemed almost instantaneous, and of course the twin-shaft layout almost exactly cancelled out gyroscopic effects. On the other hand, ground erosion was severe; it was simulated by tests with an afterburning Avon.

The only application for this impressive

The EWR-Süd/Fairchild Republic AVS was perhaps not the best way to create an advanced V/STOL warplane. At take off it would have used four XJ99s plus the deflected main engines, which might have been RB.153s or GE1/10s.

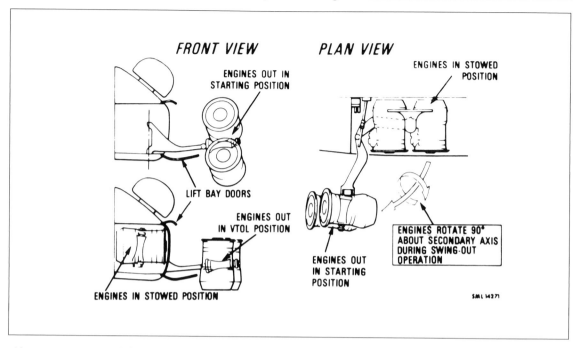

Almost every part of the AVS aircraft (model picture, previous page) had variable geometry. This certainly extended to the XJ99 lift jets, which swung out in pairs on each side of the forward fuselage. Fuel, control and instrumentation lines would have been inside the cantilever arms.

lift jet was the US/German AVS (Advanced Vertical Strike), to be developed by Fairchild Republic and EWR-Süd. A very complex machine, this was to have two pairs of XJ99s which were to swing out from bays in the fuselage as shown in a diagram. Probably wisely, this 'US/FRG' was cancelled in 1968. The XJ99, or Rolls-Royce RB.198, is not dead, however. In 1987 it was resurrected as the lift engine of the Grumman D754 AEW (airborne early warning) RPV (remotely piloted vehicle). This unique aircraft could roar aloft from confined spaces or from small ships carrying a powerful phased-array surveillance radar. The XJ99, today reported as purely a Rolls-Royce engine, would be mounted on the D754's centre of gravity and provide power for vertical take-off and landing at the beginning and end of missions lasting up to fourteen hours.

To conclude this chapter, 'jet lift' can be construed as including the propulsion of large ballistic rocket missiles, and Rolls-Royce was the only British company to enter this field. In 1955 the British government began funding the development of what it called an LRBM (Long-Range Ballistic Missile), with the code name Blue Streak. Sensibly, it encouraged main contractors to license technology pioneered in the United States, and in the field of propulsion Rolls-Royce obtained a licence in 1955 from the newly formed Rocketdyne Division of North American Aviation. This covered the technology of large rocket engines fed by turbopumps with liquid oxygen and kerosene.

Blue Streak was powered by a Rolls-Royce RZ.12 propulsion system comprising a pair of RZ.2 engines mounted on gimbals in a common bay. Based on the Rocketdyne

S–3, but with thrust chambers having the less-efficient straight-sided conical form instead of a curved bell, the RZ.2 was about 126 in high, had a nozzle diameter of 44.4 in, weighed 1,520 lb and was rated at sea level at 137,000 lb originally, later developed to 150,000 lb. Static testing took place at a vast establishment at Spadeadam Waste on the Scottish border, managed by Rolls-Royce. The missile was cancelled in April 1960, but it was then used as the first stage of the multinational European ELDO Europa I and II launchers, ten of which were flown flawlessly before termination in 1970. Most of the extensive instrumentation and equipment at Spadeadam was sold to India.

Chapter 11

THE RB. 211

For many years this large turbofan has been Rolls-Royce's most important single programme. Like several of the company's greatest engines, it began with a sea of troubles. So severe were these that no engine could be delivered, and the result was bankruptcy of the company. Gradually the RB.211 was cured of its faults and cleared for service. The core was then redesigned, and the resulting Dash-524 family progressively improved out of all recognition, and today the latest versions have the best fuel efficiency, and performance retention, of all the competing big fan engines. Meanwhile, the original Dash-22 core served as the basis for what has been regarded as a separate family of engines, the Rolls-Royce 535, described in Chapter 17.

Unlike the United States, where both the USAF (in Project Forecast) and NASA conducted far-ranging studies into propulsion requirements looking twenty years ahead, leading to the huge TF39 engine, British aviation customers have always conspicuously avoided any kind of strategic planning. Instead, large resources in manpower and facilities have been devoted to short-term studies leading to major manufacturing programmes which, after being repeatedly altered, were usually either allowed to wither or were cancelled by any change of government. In such an environment an engine-maker has to carry out his own long-term studies almost *in vacuo*, and this was certainly the case with Rolls-Royce. In 1961 the company recognized that its pioneering Conway had lost the turbofan battle to Pratt & Whitney's hastily contrived JT3D, partly because of the latter's higher bpr. For the future, it appeared that there would be a need for a subsonic turbofan, mainly but not exclusively for civil applications, much larger than any previous aero engine and with a bpr of about 5. Recognizing the impact the USAF TF39 engine would have on civil aviation, Rolls-Royce began detailed investigation of high-bpr engines and soon came to the conclusion that there were significant advantages in the three-shaft layout in which separate turbines drive the fan (and LP compressor, if any), IP compressor and HP compressor. Such an arrangement appeared to reduce the number of compressor and turbine stages needed, making for a shorter and more rigid engine, and facilitate the use of a giant fan of high bpr. The three-shaft layout also eliminated variable stators, and allowed for future thrust growth by supercharging the core (at the expense of lower bpr), and enabled approach noise to be alleviated by reducing fan speed while increasing core thrust.

Prior to the conceptual work carried out under the leadership of G.L. 'Oscar' Wilde, various rigs tested components of a planned future engine of more modest bpr. In July 1966 a complete demonstrator engine was run, 53 weeks after the start of work. This engine, the RB.178–16, had only two shafts but afforded valuable experience in the design and performance of the gas generator and other components. Many further studies followed, and later in 1966 one of these, the 45,000-lb RB.178–51, was proposed to power the projected A300 Airbus. The rival was the Pratt & Whitney JT9D, an engine already being developed for the Boeing 747. When the American engine was proposed by P&W in partnership with Bristol Siddeley and SNECMA it appeared to be an almost certain choice, and to prevent this Rolls-Royce bought Bristol Siddeley in October 1966.

Growth of the A300 called for increased power, and by early 1967 the proposed Rolls-Royce engine was the RB.207–03, rated at 47,500 lb. But by this time a possible market was opening up in the USA in the DC–10 and Lockheed L–1011 TriStar trijets, which needed an engine in the 37,500–40,000 lb class. Chairman Sir Denning Pearson and Managing Director David Huddie considered that, while the A300 appeared politically contrived, nebulous and a doubtful prospect, either of the US trijets would be a sure-fire winner certain to sell in large numbers. Almost all the effort was therefore switched to a smaller engine, the RB.211. In March 1968 Lockheed and its launch customers picked the Rolls-Royce engine, which technically and financially appeared simply too good to refuse. The British company entered into a contract to supply Lockheed with RB.211 engines flat-

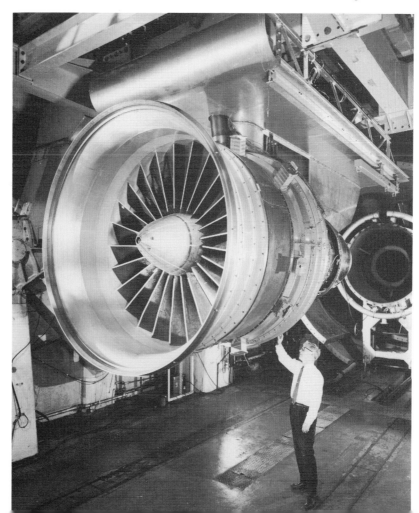

The first form of RB.211, into which so much effort went and on which perhaps too many of the company's hopes rested. This engine was RB.211-06.

rated at 39,576 lb to 90°F, to a timescale and price that were challenging in the extreme. The big RB.207 was 'put on a back burner', and in any case in December 1968 the Airbus was cut back in size and recast as the A300B. For this Rolls-Royce proposed an engine in the 45,000-lb class called the RB.211–28. The A300B was not thought as important as the L–1011, and after the British government pulled out of the programme in March 1969 the European aircraft went ahead with the General Electric CF6–50 engine, which had been picked for the DC–10. Rolls-Royce made little effort to stay in the programme. It concluded that there was no way it could develop engines for the L–1011 and A300B simultaneously, and the US transport appeared the obviously preferable choice, with 181 launch orders (though fifty of these were for a British financial group, Air Holdings, intended for resale to genuine customers).

In 1969 the L–1011 brochures described the engines as RB.211–23–02 three-shaft turbofans, each with a guaranteed rating of 38,300 lb, but later that year this was described as a derated engine, the standard model being the RB.211–22 rated at 40,600 lb for service in 1971. For 1973 the RB.211–40/41 was under study, rated at 43,040 lb (this was also offered for the proposed BAC Three-Eleven), while for future long-range L–1011s a 1.06 scaled-up engine, the RB.211–56, was proposed with thrust levels starting at 52,500 lb. The Dash–56 was to be ready for delivery in October 1972.

The RB.211–22 first ran on 31 August 1968, and seven were on test by May 1969. Much bigger than anything seen previously at Derby, it demanded colossal expenditure on plant and test facilities. Fortunately, Rolls-Royce already had tremendous experience of commercial gas-turbine operation, much of it on advanced two-spool engines, and it determined to make the RB.211 the best airline engine in the world. Particular attention was paid to squeeze-film bearings

to reduce vibration and avoid failures, to welded discs for perfect integrity, to modular construction and multiple borescope access to ease maintenance, and to every other advanced technology that experience had shown to be desirable. These features have served the company well, fully endorsing the decisions of the designers.

The three spools of the RB.211 comprised a single-stage fan driven by a three-stage turbine, a seven-stage IP compressor driven by a single-stage turbine, and a six-stage HP compressor driven by a single-stage turbine. The enormous fan, of over 85 in diameter, appeared to be the ideal application for CFRP (carbon-fibre reinforced plastic) composite material, produced by Rolls-Royce Composite Materials at Avonmouth under the proprietary name of Hyfil. Each of the 25 rotor blades was formed by bonding together about twenty laminates of Hyfil comprising high-modulus carbon fibres stuck together in a matrix of resin. The result was a perfect blade, very broad and of sharp-edged lenticular profile, with a tip speed of over 1,500 ft/s and more than half the area supersonic. (In contrast the rival JT9D needed 46 blades, much narrower, made of titanium with a density of 0.163 lb/cu in compared with Hyfil's 0.058, appreciably weaker and with efficiency degraded by two rows of blunt snubbers or mid-span shrouds along each blade.) The fan operated at a pressure ratio of about 1.55, supercharging the core from a pr of about 16 to an overall figure of 25, higher than in any previous engine and calculated to result in outstanding fuel economy.

At the same time, and again for fuel economy, the HP turbine was designed to operate in gas at 1,250°C. Though only 150°C hotter than the Conway, this made quite a difference to the design problems because creep strength of the rotor blades is halved for every extra 25°C of metal temperature. The HP blades were the only cooled blades in the engine, and they were forged in a new

Nimonic nickel/chromium alloy with tip shrouds to reduce gas leakage. It was planned that at some future date cast blades would be substituted. The combustion chamber was of the annular type, with all joints butt-welded and with advanced fully machined cooling rings superior to the wiggle-strips used in the Spey. Downstream atomizing burners were fitted. Bypass ratio was 5, and the calculated dry weight was 6,353 lb.

To fly the RB.211 the two left-hand Conways were removed from a VC10 and replaced by a single RB.211. This aircraft first flew on 6 March 1970. By this time it was evident that the engine was not giving anything like its design performance, and the initial flight rating was about 33,000 lb. There were problems almost everywhere, but the most distressing one did not significantly affect performance. The Hyfil fan blades had been designed to withstand the impact of the usual nominal 4-lb bird, fired into the front of the engine during a full-power run. To enable the blades to withstand the impact the soft composite was protected by a leading-edge sheath of hard nickel, and in early tests this appeared to work well. Lombard delighted in bashing them against steel roof trusses. To gain service experience, first-stage blades of Conways in British Airways service were replaced by similar blades in Hyfil and left to see how they got on. The results did not reflect the more demanding duty of the much larger, thinner, supersonic blades of the RB.211. After a few weeks of tropical rain and hailstorms, the edges of the blades delaminated and resembled black toothbrushes. As for the full-size fan blades, these buckled and bent under the 4-lb bird impacts. Prudently a titanium fan had been designed as a fallback programme, and with great reluctance this had to be substituted. It had 33 more slender blades with midspan snubbers, at a stroke eliminating one

An early engine with carbon-fibre fan blades on flight test in the VC10 in 1970. It was supposed to give the same thrust as the pair of Conways opposite, but in fact it gave only 75% as much.

of the chief advantages the British engine had over its rivals.

Worse, the engine was in any case considerably overweight and down on power. For the first L–1011 five Batch 1 engines were delivered, cleared to 34,000 lb at TET (turbine entry temperature) of 1,167°C. This got the TriStar off the ground on 16 November 1970, but since the start of the project three years previously the outgoings each week had been beyond anything in the company's experience, and it desperately needed income from sales of RB.211s. But all that was happening was that the factory was filling up with bits of RB.211s that could not be certificated and might well have to be scrapped.

The situation soon assumed crisis proportions. On 31 October Sir David Huddie, MD of the Aero Engine Division, resigned. On 11 November the Chairman resigned (continuing as non-executive Deputy Chairman). Hugh Conway became MD, and tough Ian Morrow chaired the executive committee. Stanley Hooker was asked back from retirement to try to cure the RB.211, and he was appalled at what he found. His biography recalls 'The first thing I did was to call in the performance engineers to give me a run-down on the reasons for the shortfall in engine performance. I was disturbed at the lack of data, and the scrappy nature of the analyses. They claimed that the efficiency of the HP turbine was 65%. To that I said "Rubbish, turbines can't be made that bad. It takes a genius to get above 85 per cent, but it also takes a lunatic to make one worse than 75 per cent." I then enquired about the speeds of the three shafts. Again I was bemused to find that these were way off the design values. It is always possible to adjust shaft speeds by altering the areas of the nozzle guide vanes which swirl the gas into the turbines. We went to work and calculated the changes in NGV area necessary to achieve the correct shaft speeds.'

When he reviewed this chapter, John F.

Coplin added here, 'It is important to remember that a gas turbine is a highly interactive machine. Any aerodynamic or leakage losses beyond those allowed for in any one component cause the remainder to operate at off-design conditions, which increases the losses throughout. Shaft speeds also mismatch, making the whole problem worse. Moreover, nearly all measurements are without meaning. Traditionally we developed engines by putting in one change at a time, and confirming by measurement that the benefit is in accordance with prediction. When an engine is badly adrift from its predicted performance this technique is impractical. With the RB.211, much of the problem was caused by scores of small leaks. Every compressor blade root fixing allowed compressed air to leak back, wasting work and spoiling the internal airflow as these leaks re-entered the gas path at lower pressure.

'Sir Stanley Hooker and Freddie Morley motivated everyone to cure every possible cause of leakage. Sir Stanley also insisted on the engine being rematched, to enable the shafts to run more nearly at their design speeds. But perhaps the most important factor was the way the two partners lifted the confidence of the engineers, and of the company and Government in those engineers. The result was a complete transformation of engine performance. Successively the more effective cures for leakage were replaced by well-thought-through detail designs, while those unnecessary were dispensed with. Events proved that the engine did not need radical redesign. Freddie Morley ensured that, wherever possible, each improvement was achieved by modifying existing finished parts. This resulted in a saleable engine at the earliest date and for far less scrap cost than had been feared.'

On 4 February 1971, just as the engine incorporating the improvements was about to run, Lord Cole had to declare Rolls-

Royce insolvent. Overnight the Government purchased all the company's assets, and also dismissed the company Board with the exception of its own three nominees. It did this to safeguard British defence, and explicitly refused to buy the RB.211. On the same day the improved engine went on test. It showed the predicted performance, at a stroke increasing thrust from 34,000 lb to over 40,000. The Government appointed a small committee to advise it on the technical and financial viability of the RB.211. Following the Hooker-Morley modifications in a refined form, the RB.211 came 'out of the wood'. The Government then made Lockheed an offer it could hardly refuse: 'accept a heavier and more expensive RB.211 delivered late, or we will cancel'. Lockheed accepted, and incidentally got an engine, the RB.211–22B, that was considerably better than the original design, and, at 42,000 lb, was also more powerful. Initial deliveries were of the Dash–22C, rated at 42,000 lb to 18.9°C or 38,750 lb to 28.9°C,

and this was the engine with which L–1011 scheduled operations began on 15 April 1972. The Dash–22B, rated at 42,000 lb to 28.9°C, was certificated in April 1973, and all –22C engines were later brought up to –22B standard.

At last the restructured Rolls-Royce (1971) Ltd was able to receive income from sales of RB.211s, but it was evident that it was in a position of marketing disadvantage. Whereas both trijets had been planned on the basis of engines of under 40,000 lb thrust, anyone with experience in the marketing of commercial transports could see that these aircraft would grow to meet customer demand for more range and payload, and that much more thrust would be needed. Pratt & Whitney had a programme for progressive development of the JT9D up to the region of 60,000 lb, and a version rated at 53,000 lb was certificated in December 1974. Meanwhile, back in 1969 General Electric had announced the CF6–50 in which, by redesigning the core to handle

Engine 10.001, the first to be certificated and come off production in 1972. It was designated RB.211-22C. Note the titanium fan blades, and accessories mounted not on the core but on the fan case.

Above *In August 1974 the RB.211-22B, the only model available, switched to a new 11° afterbody, seen in the foreground. This saved 'at least 1.5%' in cruise fuel consumption, and elimination of the hot-stream spoiler reduced weight and maintenance costs.*

Right *Principal differences between the original 42,000-lb RB.211-22B and the 50,000-lb RB.211-524 as redesigned by Hooker. This also shows how the engine is installed in its nacelle, with the airframe bleed pipe above and the shaft drive to the accessory gearbox underneath the fan case.*

a greater mass flow, and slightly increasing turbine entry temperature, thrust was to be increased from the 40,000 lb level to an initial 50,000, with much more to come. The US engines were thus going to get all the propulsion business for the 747, DC–10 and A300B, while the 42,000–lb RB.211 was going to prevent Lockheed from increasing the capability of the L–1011. Hooker accordingly set about the task of designing the RB.211–524, doing very much what GE had done with the CF6–50 in order to increase thrust to the 50,000 lb level. Hooker said this task, which involved many design and performance engineers and much paper and computer effort, but no expensive hardware, was almost light relief from the stressful task of knocking the Dash–22C and 22B into shape. It was evidence of positive long-term planning; but its realization seemed a pipe-dream.

Rolls-Royce (1971) Ltd was inevitably a company where expenditure was tightly controlled by the Government. With hindsight, it is obvious that to keep on selling RB.211s Rolls-Royce simply had to develop and certificate the Dash–524 version, and that, the longer this was delayed, the worse would be Lockheed's position and the fewer the number of engines that would be sold. Lack of a high-thrust version would virtually guarantee that the RB.211 would never get on to the 747 or other aircraft. By 1972 the design of the Dash–524 was com-

Right *The three configurations of RB.211 nacelle afterbody. Without changing the engine, the 11° afterbody reduced weight and complexity and improved cruise fuel consumption by over 1.5%. The 15° afterbody, standard since 1976 reduced weight and drag further, giving an overall range improvement of up to 5%.*

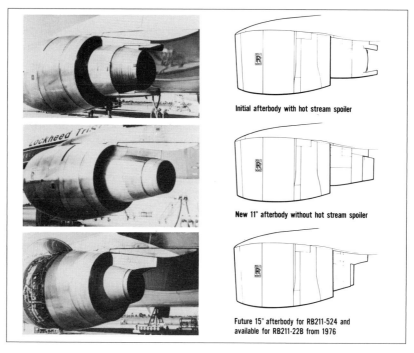

Initial afterbody with hot stream spoiler

New 11° afterbody without hot stream spoiler

Future 15° afterbody for RB211-524 and available for RB211-22B from 1976

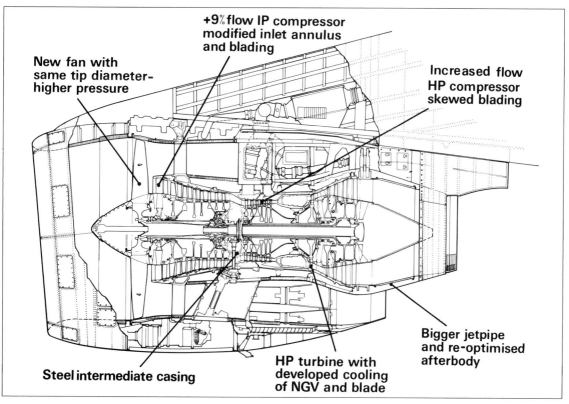

+9% flow IP compressor modified inlet annulus and blading

New fan with same tip diameter-higher pressure

Increased flow HP compressor skewed blading

Bigger jetpipe and re-optimised afterbody

Steel intermediate casing

HP turbine with developed cooling of NGV and blade

plete, and the prospects looked exciting, but it had to remain a mere project. Then in September 1972 Sir Kenneth Keith—a big man in every sense of the word—was appointed by the Government as the new Chairman. In many ways he was cast in the mould of Hives, with capability, capacity for hard work and powers of leadership that soon became a legend. He had the stature to tell Hooker to go ahead on the RB.211–524, and the first of the redesigned engines ran on 1 October 1973.

To some degree the –524 was planned as an optimized engine based on the –22B and suffering from none of the earlier engine's deficiencies, but many important sections of it were completely new. Since it develops about 75% of the thrust, the fan was obviously an item demanding the most careful scrutiny. Roy Hetherington discovered that a fan could be designed with the same 85.5-in diameter but handling a greater airflow with significantly higher pressure ratio. This required a pod inlet with increased capacity. Downstream of the fan the flow was divided with a reduced bpr (4.4 instead of 5), the flow through the IP compressor being increased by 9%, with a modified inlet annulus and new blading. Further downstream came a redesigned HP compressor with skewed blading handling the increased airflow. The combustion chamber was not at that time modified, but the HP turbine NGVs (nozzle guide vanes) and rotor blades were redesigned to handle slightly higher gas temperatures whilst actually reducing the metal temperatures. Finally the jetpipe was enlarged, without increasing weight, the afterbody being shortened, and the core flow spoiler (to reduce thrust and noise during landing) was eliminated.

If Hooker had not persisted in designing the Dash-524, even though no funds were then available to make it, the RB.211 would probably no longer be in production. This is a typical RB.211-524B.

Though Hooker aimed at 50,000 lb, the initial thrust certificated at about 1,252°C was 48,000 lb to 28.9°C. This was quickly overtaken by the –524B fully rated at 50,000 lb, and this was certificated in December 1975 by the CAA, and validated by the FAA in March 1976. Orders, however, were slow to come in. A crucial one was the decision of British Airways in 1976 to buy six 747-200s with the Rolls-Royce engine, thereby continuing Boeing and Rolls-Royce as the favoured suppliers to Britain's national airline. The same customer also ordered a new long-range version of the TriStar, the L-1011-500, with the –524B engine, and Saudia ordered an 'extended-range' model called the L-1011-200. The latter, and the British Airways 747, both entered service in 1977. Many airlines watched keenly to see how the British engines would perform in the 747, and in the case of Qantas of Australia the margin in fuel burn between the RB.211 and rival US engines was enough for the airline to switch its big 747 fleet gradually from the JT9D to the RB.211.

One reason why Qantas changed horses was because it had faith in Rolls-Royce's ongoing programme to keep the RB.211 competitive. For a start the basic –524 was better than prediction, and whereas the TET planned for the 50,000-lb rating was 1,347°C, the type test was achieved at only 1,277°C. On this basis Rolls-Royce planned a long series of improved and upgraded engines stretching far into the future, using a valuable group of special test rigs such as the HTDU (high-temperature demo unit), ACET (advanced core engine technology), ALPS (advanced LP system) and QED (quiet engine demonstrator). These, coupled with rapidly expanding use of computers, transformed the entire face of Rolls-Royce design, development and general engineering capability. In the author's view, a disaster such as the original RB.211 can never happen again. Since the late 1970s each new engine or variation to come out of Derby has been a smash hit, and the only cause for regret is that the RB.211 never 'got aboard the Airbus', where it could have carved out a significant share of 600 wide-body airliners.

Developments of the RB.211 fall broadly into four groups. One, the Dash–535 family, has been regarded by Rolls-Royce as a different engine and is therefore discussed in Chapter 17. A second group comprises improvements to the original Dash–22 family. A third comprises improvements to the original –524/–524B, both this and the preceding group being effected mainly by field modification of engines in customer hands.

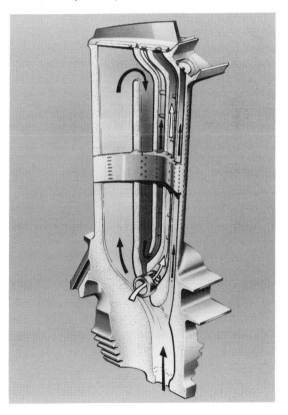

A cutaway RB.211 high-pressure turbine blade, showing the complex air-cooling pathways and the numerous holes through which air escapes to form a cooling envelope. The basic alloy is directionally solidified.

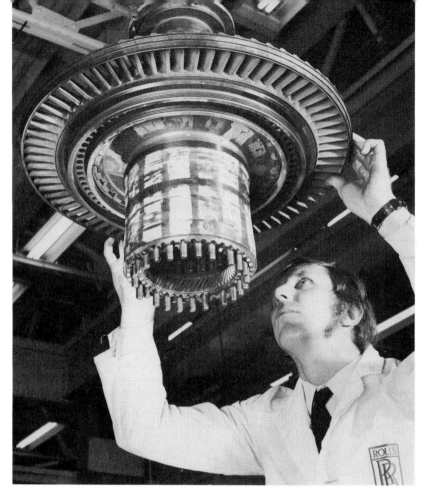

A key element in the development of the RB.211 and other recent engines has been the High-Temperature Demo Unit. Its small air-cooled turbine, seen here, has been progressively improved to stay about 150°C ahead of production engines. It develops about 25,000 horsepower.

The fourth group comprises the successive new versions with designations from –524C to –524L. In true Rolls-Royce fashion the RB.211 has been developed out of all recognition. The early vicissitudes are now ancient history, and the only enduring feature of the RB.211 that could be subject to criticism is that, instead of being much lighter than its competitors, it is heavier. Most versions weigh over 9,800 lb, compared with about 9,200 lb for the GE and P&W engines. Against this can be set significantly better performance, especially in the matter of fuel burn, and very much better performance retention over the periods of years that each engine remains installed without removal. Moreover the latest and most powerful version is actually lighter than its rivals.

The –524 first flew, on the left wing of the prototype L-1011, on 10 April 1976. Two days later the first production engine, for a British Airways 747, was despatched to Boeing. At that time the Derby engineers were already working on improved versions. In fact there eventually became so many sub-types, with such suffixes as 'Improved' or 'Upgrade', that in 1987 the designations were simplified. The following is a condensed description of versions marketed up to 1989:

524–02: Baseline Dash–524 engine, for L–1011–200; entered service at 48,000 lb in 1977.

524B–02: For L–1011–200 and –500 Mk 1, as 524–02 but with interrupted-spigot HP turbine disc, PS1 bleeds (some engines having PS1 VIGV control), a re-optimized convergent/divergent cold nozzle, hot convergent flared nozzle and new (103 Mk 8) FFR (fuel-flow regulator); rated at 50,000 lb with sfc unchanged.

524B2–19: For 747-200 and 747SP, increased-area cabin offtake, different bleed air system and modified reverser; rated in 1978 at 50,000 lb.

524C2–19: For 747-200, with PS1 VIGV control, additional combustor diffuser offtake (which modifies the HP turbine cooling to HP3 air), Waspalloy radial bolts in the HP/IP turbine bearing housing, and a 102 Mk 6 FFR; rated at 51,500 lb with sfc unchanged.

524B3–02: For L-1011-500 Mk 2, new fan blades and shaft moved 2.9 in forward with composite nosecone, redesigned fan case with longer Armco blade containment and lighter decambered OGVs to suit the forward fan, modified IP compressor, almost complete new fuel system with 104 Mk 1 FFR, and new pod with short inlet, improved noise-attenuation and composite access doors; in May 1980 rated at 50,000 lb with sfc 3.5% lower than 524B.

524B4–02: For L-1011-500 Mk 2, with high-capacity IP/LP turbine module and HP3 pre-swirl, new turbine suspension, and choice of metal or composite pod doors; rated February 1981 at 50,000 lb with sfc 4.8% better than 524B.

524D4–19: For 747-200, with increased-efficiency fan, new IP compressor with modified VIGVs, thicker discs and new blades in IP1 and 2, combustor with thicker OGV case, lightweight reverser, acoustically lined hot nozzle, increased-capacity gearbox and IDG (integrated drive generator), oil cooler and 105 Mk 2 FFR and new amplifier; 53,000 lb with sfc 4.8% lower than C2.

524D4 Upgrade: For 747, polished fan blades with clappers de-scissored and improved tip clearance control, skewed HP compressor with polished aerofoils and improved abradable lining, improved-integrity combustor with no diffuser offtake and low-pollution liner, and new IP turbine with multilean NGVs, variable-work blades and reprofiled bearing fairings; sfc 2.5% below D4, same rating.

524B4 Improved: 1987 revision for L-1011-250, with polished fan with tighter tip clearance control and smoothed OGVs with polyurethane coating, new intermediate-case bearings, new combustor locating dogs, new HP turbine with improved blades and disc and 92-off drive arm and ceramic cement, and completely new IP turbine with D4 Upgrade features plus reprofiled stators, honeycomb seal segments with revised sealing strips and ceramic cement; sfc 6.7% better than B4.

524D4–B19: For 747, with new intermediate-case bearings, new frequency limit on HP6 blading, otherwise as D4 Upgrade.

524G–19: For 747-400 and 767, completely new 86.3 in fan with 24 wide-chord hollow blades (535E4 technology) and new disc, shafts, annulus fillers and spinner, totally new fan case with 56 supercritical bypass OGVs, titanium torsion box, new front bearing and with front flange 2.7 in forward, new rear case and many other changes, a new IP spool with brush seals, VIGV optimization, fewer drain holes, improved abradable lining and improved surface finish, a new intermediate case with new HP, IP and LP bearings, an HP spool with new HP1 and HP6 blading, modified offtakes and smoothed abradable lining, strengthened combustor outer casing and OGVs, new HP turbine with optimized tip clearance, disc rear-face labyrinth seal and new material (MARM 002) NGVs, new IP/LP turbines with blanked firtree roots, MARM 002 NGVs, strengthened LP3 blades and improved seals, lightweight reverser with carbon-fibre translating cowl, multi-lobed forced mixer to common nozzle of conical titanium with new tailcone, totally redesigned nacelle and pylon, totally new digital electronic control system (with optional engine-condition monitoring), and increased-speed gearbox driving 90-kVA IDG. Deliveries of the –524G began in May 1988, ready for entry into service on the 747-400 in March 1989. The first G to be delivered was the 500th RB.211 to be des-

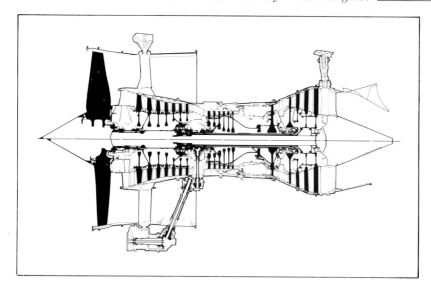

Left *Comparative longitudinal sections of the 524D4 (lower half) and 524G (upper half), showing the newer engine's wide-blade fan and integrated mixer nozzle.*

Right *Rolls-Royce artwork is justly famous. It has never reached a higher standard than in this cutaway of the RB.211-524G.*

Below *The beautiful fan, with wide snubberless blades, at last restores to the RB.211-524G the clear advantage Rolls-Royce had hoped to enjoy with the carbon-fibre blades of the first RB.211. In the author's opinion, it is a tragedy this super engine is likely to be restricted to Boeing airframes.*

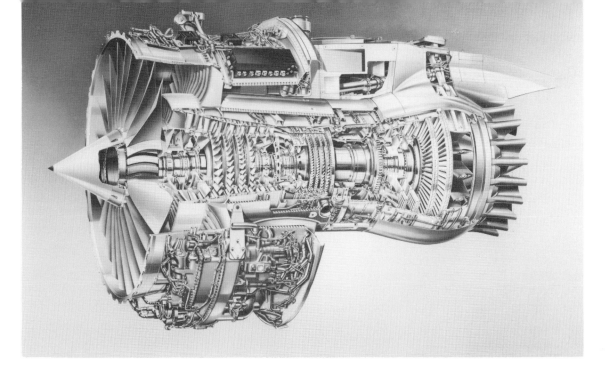

Below *The first RB.211-524G to be despatched to Boeing (in May 1988) was the 500th RB.211 to be sent to Seattle. It is the engine choice of British Airways, Qantas, Cathay Pacific and Air NZ for a total of 58 B.747-400s.*

patched to Boeing. Rated at 58,000 lb, the G-19 has cruise sfc 8.8% better than the D4.

524H-36: For British Airways 767, as G-19 but with increased combustor and HP turbine cooling. Overall pr raised from 33 to 34.5. To be certificated November 1989 at 60,600 lb.

524L: Originally designated 211-700, this major redesign promises to be demonstrably better than anything the competition can do, and to be the optimum engine for the advanced 747s, 767s, A330s and MD-11s to year 2000. The 211J airflow is the limit to what the existing pod inlet can swallow, so the L introduces a new and extremely attractive pod matched to a fan of nominal 95 in diameter. Thanks to the Rolls-Royce wide-chord snubberless fan blade this fan handles a slightly greater airflow than the CF6-80E1 fan of 96 in diameter or the PW4060 of 99 in, and this makes a major difference to pod weight and drag. The new fan has 26 (not 24) blades of totally new construction. Instead of a honeycomb core the hollow titanium blades are stabilized by an integral series of corrugations like oblique spar webs produced by SPF/DB (superplastic forming and diffusion bonding), each blade being inflated within its die by hot argon under high pressure. This superb fan starts life handling just over 1,916 lb/s, which increases bpr to 5 and alone gives a significant improvement in sfc. To drive it the core has been redesigned with an eighth IP stage and upgraded HP spool handling greater airflow, and this greater airflow enables the new four-stage LP turbine to generate the increased power needed despite running at reduced speed matched to the greater fan diameter. Many of the new features read across to the G/H and E4. The L was expected to grow from 65,000 to perhaps 73,000 lb, but only a month after its launch, on 5 October 1988 on the occasion of signing a deal with KHI of Japan under which

Kawasaki takes about a 10% share in the -524 family, it was stated that the 524L will be certificated in 1992 at 67,500 lb and will have growth capability to over 80,000 lb. Not least of the achievements in this superb engine is a total engine design weight slightly *less* than that for the G/H/J! Thus, instead of being the most fuel-efficient but the heaviest of the competing big engines, the 524L promises to be the lightest.

Launching the RB.211-524L will probably cost something like £300 million. As this book was being written, in late-1988, the British government had not replied to the company's request for launch aid, but on 10 June 1988 the project took a giant step forward when the new engine was offered for both the A330 and the MD-11. Jim Worsham of Douglas pointed out that this was the first Douglas jetliner to be offered with RR engines since the early DC-8-40, while the Airbus President, Jean Pierson, said how pleased he was as a European to be able to offer (he did not add 'at last') a Rolls-Royce engine on an Airbus. To the author, both aircraft look like being winners, and the powerful -524L can only be good for both. The launch order was for MD-11s, placed in February 1989 by Air Europe.

Since 1973 more than 670 RB.211-22 engines have been delivered, logging over 17 million hours. At the start of 1988 Rolls-Royce reported that a Dash-22B was still hung under the right wing of a TWA L-1011-100, having since 9 April 1982 made over 5,300 take-offs in over 20,000 flight hours without removal. Also, more than 660 RB.211-524 engines have flown about 11 million hours. They too have established an outstanding record, and, as the author has rather belaboured, the only cause for regret is their very limited range of applications. The only market today is as an alternative engine, picked by a small group of customers, for the 747 and 767. In February 1984 an

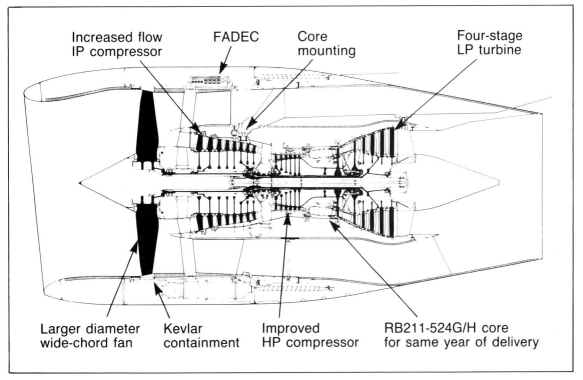

Increased flow
IP compressor

FADEC

Core
mounting

Four-stage
LP turbine

Larger diameter
wide-chord fan

Kevlar
containment

Improved
HP compressor

RB211-524G/H core
for same year of delivery

Planned for certification at 67,500 lb in 1992 the RB.211-524L represents the biggest single advance in the RB.211 programme since the original -524 of the mid-1970s. A key feature is the fan, markedly more efficient than those of competitor engines. These are the chief differences between the L and the G/ H models.

unusual agreement was signed with General Electric in which Rolls-Royce took a share (up to 25%) in the development, manufacture and marketing of the CF6-80C2 (a head-on rival to later RB.211s) while the US company took the same share in the 535E4. In December 1986 the increasing competition between the CF6-80C2 and later RB.211s resulted in the agreement being amicably terminated, but with the possibility of an ongoing subcontracting relationship on either or both engines.

Since 1974 the Industrial RB.211 has been important in pipeline pumping and electricity generation. Rated at 39,300 gas horsepower, it can (for example) replace two Avons and save about £4,000 a day. Such units around the world have logged over 1 million hours.

Since this book was written, the 524L has been named the Trent. Thanks to its superior performance, it quickly became the number one choice of engine on the A330. In April 1989, Cathay Pacific selected the Trent at ratings due to climb from 67,500 lb at entry into service in 1993, to 72,000 lb a year later and to 76,000 lb in 1996. TWA A330s will use the 72,000-lb rating from the start to enable them to carry a full payload from California to Europe.

Chapter 12

THE DE HAVILLAND ENGINES

Between 1960 and 1966, in one way or another, Rolls-Royce absorbed all the other established British aero-engine companies. In most cases the process took the form of a merger by mutual consent, the giant at Derby merely agreeing to assume responsibility for service support of engines produced by a firm which, for whatever reason, was running down and would of itself soon leave the aviation industry. The final takeover, in 1966, was quite different. In that year Rolls-Royce plunged deep into its pocket and simply bought out its only significant British competitor. For a while this gave Rolls-Royce an untidy structure, but gradually personnel were assimilated or departed, factories were integrated or sold, and engines from the vanished companies eventually passed into history. At this point in the book it is chronologically sensible to outline the various takeovers, and briefly describe the engines which came under the general heading of Rolls-Royce.

A particularly famous name was that of de Havilland. The early history is slightly convoluted, in that Captain de Havilland and Major Frank Halford first produced a series of air-cooled piston engines under the name Cirrus, which eventually passed to Blackburn Aircraft Ltd which was another of the firms taken over by Rolls-Royce (Chapter 14). By 1927 a completely new range of air-cooled piston engines had been started under the even more renowned name of Gipsy, which—as described in the author's *World Encyclopaedia of Aero Engines*, published, like this volume, by PSL—accounted for a total of 27,654 engines. Early work was centred at Stag Lane, Edgware, but in 1946 all production was transferred to the former LAPG Halifax plant at Leavesden, near Watford. Stag Lane remained the centre for design and development.

Two years earlier, in February 1944, the de Havilland Engine Co was formed, with Halford as Chairman overseeing the design work of an excellent team led by Chief Engineer Dr Eric S. Moult. Over the next decade this team produced the Goblin and Ghost centrifugal turbojets, the mighty Gyron supersonic axial turbojet and its 0.45-scale offspring the Gyron Junior, and a range of HTP and HTP/kerosene rockets including the Sprite, Super Sprite and a family of Spectres. In 1958 a licence was obtained for the General Electric T58 turboshaft in the 1,000-hp class, the first Anglicized de Havilland Gnome version being run on the bench on 5 June 1959 with a Lucas fuel system and Hawker Siddeley Dynamics control computer.

In January 1960 the assets of de Havilland Holdings (which included the engine com-

Above *A typical Gnome H.1400-1 turboshaft engine for a Sea King. Its jetpipe shows that this is a left-hand engine. The large tube curving round behind the inlet is the oil tank, and the black unit at upper centre drives the array of variable-stator linkages.*

Right *Gnome H.1400-1 engines on the production line at Leavesden. The nearest has its annular oil tank fitted.*

pany) were purchased by the Hawker Siddeley Group. In November 1961 DH Engines became the Small Engine Division of BSEL (Bristol Siddeley Engines Ltd), with HQ at Mercury House, Knightsbridge, London, and with all design and manufacture centred at Leavesden. In October 1966 BSEL was purchased by Rolls-Royce.

Leavesden, and the Halford Laboratory and test site at Hatfield, became the Rolls-Royce Small Engine Divison, and initially carried on as before under Divisional Chairman Hugh Conway, who had previously been BSEL Managing Director. In 1970, however, it decided to divest itself of the business in small piston engines. The stock of Gipsy and Blackburn spares was sold to Hants & Sussex Aviation, at Ports-

mouth. Civil overhauls were transferred at once, Ministry overhauls followed in 1975, and in April 1983 Hants & Sussex became the design authority for these engines. Spares manufacture and service support continued for the Ghost, Goblin and Gyron Junior, though this had dwindled to a very low level. The Artouste and Nimbus are discussed in Chapter 14.

This left just two Leavesden engines of importance. Support for the Gnome and Coupled Gnome has continued to this day, and the Gnome H.1400–1 continues in low-rate production for Sea King and Commando helicopters, and for re-engining Swedish KV 107–II helicopters. The new BS.360 was restyled RS.360 and finally named the Gem, as related in Chapter 18.

DH, BSEL and finally RR produced the Coupled Gnome H.1200 powerplant for the Wessex Mks 2 and 5. It gave the helicopter a welcome power reserve of about 1,000 hp.

Chapter 13

THE ARMSTRONG SIDDELEY ENGINES

Starting as the Siddeley Autocar company in 1902, ASM (Armstrong Siddeley Motors) was a founder member of the Hawker Siddeley Group. In 1959 it underwent total merger with Bristol Aero-Engines to form BSEL (Bristol Siddeley Engines Ltd) which, as related in other chapters, later absorbed DH Engines and Blackburn Engines.

When Rolls-Royce bought BSEL in 1966 the former ASM factories at Parkside, in central Coventry, and Ansty, east of the city, were both actively engaged in aero work, though it was a minor proportion of the whole BSEL Power Division. Parkside provided support for Cheetah piston engines into the 1970s, and for the Double Mamba turboprop with twin independent power sections which was finally withdrawn as powerplant of the Gannet AEW.3 in 1978, just four years before these aircraft were to be desperately needed in the South Atlantic. Parkside was also home for the M45 turbofan described in Chapter 16, and still had some years to run supporting the Sapphire 202 turbojets of the RAF's Victor K.1A tankers. Ansty had been the centre for ASM's widespread work on rocket engines, which had begun under Sid Allen in 1946. Early work centred on liquid oxygen and alcohol, but later combinations included lox/kerosene and finally HTP (high-test peroxide) and kerosene. Active rocket pro-grammes included the Gamma, Stentor and BS.605, as described in Chapter 16.

In 1967 Rolls-Royce formed IMD (Industrial and Marine Divison) with HQ at Ansty and with a former ASM man, W.H. Lindsey, as Director of Engineering. Val Cleaver was General Manager, Rockets. IMD's main business was described in its title, the provision of aero-derived gas turbines for electric power generation, pipeline pumping, marine propulsion and other surface applications. IMD also took over responsibility for operating the Spadeadam Rocket Establishment, where Rolls-Royce RZ.12 engines were tested (Chapter 10).

Lindsey had been the technical kingpin of ASM, being Chief Engineer from 1950 onwards. Back in 1934 one of the great RR men, Colonel L.F.R. Fell, had left Derby to join ASM as Chief Engineer. Like Hives, he had realized that what was needed was more brain-power (though ASM's ultimate boss, Lord Kenilworth, the former John Siddeley, had no conception of the need to undertake any kind of research or long-range planning). Fell asked the Engineering Department at the University of Cambridge if they could recommend anyone. The answer was 'Look in your own works, you can't find anyone better than young Lindsey, who is getting practical experience as an apprentice in your shops'! Together with

Bill Saxton, Lindsey built up a strong team on piston engines and then on axial jets and turboprops (though credit for the Sapphire's compressor, mentioned in Chapter 9, was due to Dr D.M. Smith of Metrovick). One feature for which the ASM team could claim credit was vaporizing burners, mainly of the 'walking stick' type in which a premixture of liquid fuel and air is injected into a curved pipe inside the primary zone of the combustion chamber.

The early ASM gas turbines—ASX, Python, Mamba and Adder—stemmed from the protracted work on axial compressors undertaken by the Royal Aircraft Establishment, but in 1950 Saxton and Lindsey began the design of an engine on the proverbial clean sheet of paper. Named the Viper, it was supported by the Ministry because it was needed to power the Australian Jindivik radio-controlled target. It was therefore planned as a simple short-life engine, cheap enough to be shot out of the

sky on its first flight. It is very doubtful that anyone thought for a moment that the Viper would mature as a long-life engine for piloted aircraft and sustain an unbroken production run to at least 1990!

The original Viper had a neat eleven-stage compressor handling a mass flow of 32 lb/s with a pressure ratio of 4.0, an annular combustion chamber with twelve pairs of walking-stick burners, a single-stage turbine and external (electric or air-jet) starting. It weighed 365 lb and gave a thrust of 1,640 lb, which was probably a record thrust/weight ratio at the time of the first run in April 1951. It was handed to Viper Chief Engineer John Marlow and went from strength to strength.

The first manned applications were the Percival Jet Provost, flown on 26 June 1954, and the Folland Midge, prototype of the much more powerful Gnat, flown two months later. By this time a Canberra was flying with a tip-mounted Viper ASV.7R with

A Viper 11, as fitted to large numbers of trainers. Length 64 in, weight 570 lb, and thrust 2,500 lb.

afterburner, and a pair of similar engines powered the very first Dassault Mirage in 1955. By the time of the Rolls-Royce takeover in 1966 about 2,500 Vipers had been delivered, mainly for military trainers but including some executive jets. The 200 series (Viper ASV.11), rated at 2,500 lb, was used in the Jet Provost, SOKO Galeb, HAL Kiran, Jindivik and (as a take-off boost unit) Shackleton MR.3 Series 3. Vipers were added to the Shackletons in 1966, the year RR took over. Unfortunately, while the added turbojets eased the strain on the Griffon piston engines, they increased the strain on the wings, and this mark of Shackleton was soon withdrawn with fatigue damage.

The Viper 22–1 was built under licence by Piaggio in Italy, for the very successful Aermacchi MB.326, starting an Italian connection which has grown with the years. The Viper 500 series introduced a zero-stage which increased mass flow to 52.7 lb/s with pressure ratio of 5.6. This was the launch engine for the DH.125 executive jet, at 3,120 lb thrust, and also powered trainer and light attack aircraft. In addition to Piaggio the Mk 22–1 was licensed to CAC of Australia and Atlas of South Africa, and Piaggio and Atlas also produced the Mk 540 for the MB.326GB and Impala.

In 1967 the Viper became a staple product of the Rolls-Royce BED (Bristol Engine Division), though, while development moved to Bristol, production continued at Parkside. The Mk 600 introduced a two-stage turbine, and with a rating of 3,750 lb for executive jets and 4,000 lb for trainers became the dominant version by 1970. In July 1969 an agreement was signed with Fiat, under the terms of which the Italian company handles development and production of most items to the rear of the compressor other than the turbine rotors.

Today the Viper 601 powers BAe 125–600s, the Mk 632 powers the Super Galeb,

A Viper 521, with zero stage, fitted to the Bristol Siddeley 125 which later carried the proud 'RR' logo on its fin. Weight 730 lb, thrust 3,170 lb.

Pushing a Viper 680 into an Aermacchi MB.339 at Rolls-Royce Bristol. When the rear trunnions have picked up the fuselage rail the crane can be disconnected.

MB.326K and MB.339, the Mk 632–43 (licensed to Piaggio) powers the MB.339A and derivatives, and the Mk 632–41 has been produced in Romania and Yugoslavia for the IAR–93A Orao 1. The Mk 633 has an afterburner of the two-gutter type, with hot-streak ignition and a variable nozzle, and is rated at 5,000 lb. This version, also produced in Romania and Yugoslavia, powers the IAR–93B Orao 2.

The latest, and probably last, version of the Viper is the Mk 680, which has a dry thrust of 4,450 lb. This has not been devel-oped in partnership with Fiat or Piaggio, though it is used in the Italian MB.339B and C and the MB.339K Veltro. Its weight, 790 lb, is the same as that of the Mk 601 and 632. Total Viper production is well in excess of 5,000, and a very high proportion of these are still in service.

The Sapphire, a first-class turbojet which deserved to have more applications in Britain, was serving only in the last few Victor K.1 tankers in 1966. Rolls-Royce played only a support role for this engine.

Chapter 14

THE BLACKBURN
AND NAPIER ENGINES

In 1924 Major Frank B. Halford created the first Cirrus four-cylinder in-line air-cooled engine, using components from one bank of an Airdisco V–8, the much lightened and otherwise improved derivative of the war-time Renault (some of which were made by Rolls-Royce). Later Cirrus engines were inverted, but in 1927 Halford started again with the first Gipsy, the Cirrus being taken over first by Hermes and in 1934 by Black-burn Aircraft at Brough, near Hull. Cirrus production continued during World War 2, but immediately after the war Blackburn produced a range of totally redesigned engines of which the most important was the Bombardier, an inverted 4-in-line with cylinders of 4.8 in bore and 5.5 in stroke (389.12 cu in, 6.524 litres) and a magnesium-alloy crankcase and direct fuel injection. The first production version was a civil engine with an electric starter, rated at 180 hp, but the chief version was the military Bombardier 203, derated to 173 hp on ordinary MT petrol and fitted with a cartridge starter. Small numbers of Cirrus and Bombardier engines were supported from Leavesden after 1966.

In 1952 Blackburn bought a licence for Turbomeca's range of small gas turbines, and promptly infuriated *le patron* Josef Szydlowski by undertaking a great deal of unnecessary redesign., Not much was done with these engines except for the Artouste turboshaft, which was used as the basis for an APU (auxiliary power unit) used in small numbers in the Victor B.2, CL–44, Trident 1, Belfast and RAF VC10 C.1. Surviving examples of these APUs are supported to this day.

In 1957 Blackburn decided to carry out further development of the Artouste, and produced the A.129 by adding two axial stages ahead of the centrifugal compressor (as was being done by Turbomeca). The first A.129 ran as a turbojet in July 1958, and in August 1958 the definitive turboshaft engine first ran with an added free power turbine, with blades machined into a single slab of Nimonic alloy, driving through a two-stage gearbox at the rear to power the Saro P.531–2 helicopter. Initially rated at 840 shp, the A.129 was further developed into the Bristol Siddeley Nimbus rated at 968 shp, and this went into production as the Nimbus 102, flat-rated at 685 shp for the Westland Scout, and as the Nimbus 503, flat-rated at 710 shp for the Westland Wasp. Both are still in service and are supported from Leavesden.

D. Napier & Son was a pioneer of high-quality cars, and from 1917 it was famed for the superb Lion aero engine. In the 1950s its small staff at Acton Vale, London W.3, worked on a mass of complex piston

Line maintenance on the Nimbus 503 of a Wasp of 529 Squadron, temporarily ashore in the Far East.

engines, compound gas-turbine/diesels, tur-boprops, helicopter tip-drive compressors, combined convertiplane engines, ramjets and rockets! Predictably, none became a profitable product except for the last engine to be developed, the Gazelle free-turbine turboshaft for helicopters. Almost Russian in its conservative design, its main feature was that it was intended to be installed in any attitude from horizontal to vertical. In the original Bristol 191 appli-cation, which ultimately led to the Westland

Belvedere, two were mounted far apart in an almost vertical attitude. In the Westland Wessex a single Gazelle was installed at an angle of 39°.

Features of the Gazelle included an eleven-stage compressor, fitted with blades of Napier's much-favoured DTD.197A alumi-nium-bronze and handling a mass flow of about 16 lb/s at a pressure ratio of around 6, six flame tubes encased in a single casing wrapped closely around the tubes, a two-stage compressor turbine, single-stage free

Orphaned by the demise of D. Napier & Son, this Gazelle Mk 165 is still serving in a single-engined Wessex. The jet exits through four nozzles.

power turbine, and an epicyclic reduction gear with an integral torquemeter surrounded by two pairs of exhaust stacks. The first run was on 3 December 1955, and the design output of 1,260 shp was soon achieved. Dry weight of the first version was 928 lb, much of this being accounted for by the big magnesium-alloy inlet casting which drew in the air radially (for comparison, the roughly comparable GE T58 weighed about 300 lb). The first production versions, with IPN (iso-propyl nitrate) starters, were the Mk 101 rated at 1,610 shp for the Belvedere and the Mk 161, again with IPN starter, rated at 1,410 shp for the Wessex, with an opposite-rotation turbine. Later versions have Rotax gas-turbine starters, and are flat-rated in Wessex helicopters at 1,540 or 1,600 shp.

Napier Aero Engines became a subsidiary of Rolls-Royce in 1960 and quickly lost its identity. Support of Gazelle engines has since been handled direct from Derby.

Chapter 15

THE BRISTOL ENGINES

Despite being one of the largest firms in the British aircraft industry, the Bristol Aeroplane Co was slow in developing gas turbines. At the same time, it did little to develop its established piston engines after World War 2, though, despite this, large orders were received for the 14-cylinder Hercules in the 2,000-hp class (also made under licence by SNECMA in France) and the 18-cylinder Centaurus of 2,500–3,000 hp. These famous sleeve-valve radials saw long service, the Varsity (RAF) and Noratlas (Armée de l'Air) soldiering on into the 1980s and civil Hercules still being in use. These engines have been supported by Bristol Engine Division and SNECMA.

The first Bristol gas turbine was the Theseus, a complex turboprop intended to set a new standard in low specific fuel consumption. It never went into production, but led to the Proteus, a bigger and even more complicated turboprop. When Dr S.G. Hooker went from Rolls-Royce to Bristol in 1948 Chief Engineer Frank Owner told him 'We set out to make the most economical turboprop in the world, regardless of the weight and bulk. So far we have achieved the weight and bulk'. In mid-1950 Hooker became Chief Engineer, and one of his first acts was to redesign the Proteus completely. Unfortunately, at this time the Brabazon and Princess were still active

applications for the Coupled Proteus, so the reverse-flow layout had to be retained. Air entered well aft of centre, passing radially inwards and then forwards through a twelve-stage axial compressor, at the end of which was a centrifugal compressor which turned the air radially outwards again, to pass through a diffuser turning it to the rear and thence through eight long but thin tubular combustion chambers, and out to the jetpipe via a two-stage compressor turbine and two-stage power turbine. The latter was mechanically independent and drove via a long shaft through the centre of the engine to the compound epicyclic reduction gear and thence the propeller.

By far the most important application of the Proteus was the Britannia, a few examples of which remained in active operation until 1987. The civil Proteus 755 and military Proteus 255 weighed about 3,850 lb and were rated at 4,445 total equivalent horsepower. This engine pioneered the use of turbine rotor blades precision-cast by the lost-wax method, which was used on almost all subsequent Bristol engines. Today the RR Industrial and Marine Division supports numerous Proteus used in warships, air-cushion vehicles (hovercraft) and in electricity power generation.

In 1946 preliminary work began on a turbojet, the BE.10, later named Olympus.

A superb two-spool engine, it had a single-stage HP turbine driving an eight-stage HP compressor, a single-stage LP turbine driving a six-stage LP compressor (overall pr 10.2), and a can-annular combustion chamber with ten flame tubes. Early engines weighed about 3,500 lb, and on the first run on 16 May 1950 Dr Hooker took the throttle himself, absolving the usual tester from responsibility. He deliberately banged it wide open, to the amazement of everyone including Roy T. Hurley, President of Curtiss-Wright, who was visiting in connection with a licence. At first Hurley was not very impressed, because the thrust-meter needle stuck at about 5,000 lb, until Hooker pointed out that there were two such meters each recording half the thrust.

Early versions of the Olympus were rated at 9,140 to 9,750 lb, but the first production version for the Vulcan B.1 was the Mk 101 rated at 11,000 lb. Subsequent Vulcan B.1 engines were the Mk 102 at 12,000 lb and Mk 104 at 13,500 lb. Nearly all had been brought up to Mk 104 standard when Rolls-Royce took over. Back in 1955 the Olympus 6, or Mk 200 series, had brought in a new compressor with only five LP and seven HP stages, while handling the far greater mass flow of 240 instead of 180 lb/s with pr of 12.

Starting life at 9,750 lb thrust, the Olympus has, in this Mk 621 form, been in airline service for over 12 years at nearly 40,000 lb. In fact its core is one of the most powerful anywhere, with a mass flow 20–25% greater than the biggest turbofans.

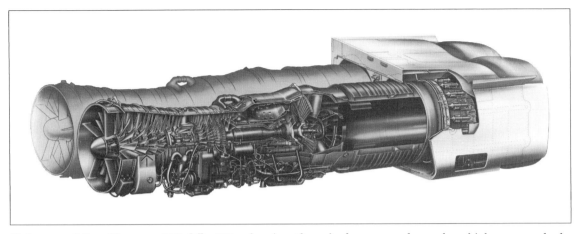

Cutaway of the Olympus 593 Mk 621, showing the afterburner and nozzle which are made by SNECMA. The overall thrust/weight ratio of 5.6 is outstanding in view of the fact that the whole engine is titanium, steel and refractory alloys, and stressed for Mach 2.

This was designed for 16,000 lb thrust, entered service in the Vulcan B.2 as the Mk 201 at 17,000 lb and was developed with a zero-stage into the Mk 301 rated at 20,000 lb! The Mk 301 finally passed out of RAF service in late 1986.

For political reasons the government decreed in 1959 that the RAF's new strike/reconnaissance aircraft, the TSR.2, would be ordered only from merged groups of companies. Accordingly Bristol Aero-Engines, the special engine company formed when the Bristol parent reorganized in 1956, was merged with Armstrong Siddeley Motors to develop the Olympus 22R, or Mk 320. This was basically a Mk 301 restressed for supersonic operation at low level and fitted with an advanced afterburner with a fully modulated convergent/divergent variable nozzle. This engine was rated at 19,600 lb dry and and 30,610 lb with maximum reheat. The whole programme was abruptly cancelled in April 1965, eighteen months before the RR takeover of Bristol Siddeley, but by this time the same basic engine had been selected to power the Concorde Anglo-French SST (supersonic transport).

The original Concorde engine was styled Olympus 591/2, and in 1964 was closely similar to the TSR.2 engine, though from the outset SNECMA of France was involved to preserve work-sharing agreements. Like the TSR.2 engine it had an HP turbine with aircooled cast blades, and this was increased in diameter and otherwise improved to form the 593/3 of 1965. Then came the 593D in which, by adding a zero-stage on the front of the LP spool and removing one from the HP spool, the mass flow was increased sufficiently to raise dry thrust from 22,700 lb to 29,300 lb. Then the 593B with simple reheat and a modified nozzle reached a Stage-0 rating of 32,825 lb and a Stage-1 rating of 35,080 lb. This led direct to the production 'Olympus 593 Mk 601' (surely a lunatic designation) at 38,050 lb, raised in 1977 after two years of airline service to the Mk 621 rating of 39,940 lb. Airflow is 410 lb/s and pr 15.5, weight being 5,793 lb. RR Bristol Engine Division was responsible for the main engine and SNECMA for the afterburner, noise-attenuating variable nozzle and reverser. How many other turbojets have had their thrust multiplied by 4.4 times?

Most powerful Orpheus, the BOr.12 was rated at 6,810 lb, raised to 8,170 lb by a simple reheat system.

Last of the engines to be considered here as 'Bristol', the Orpheus was developed from 1953 as a purely company-financed venture, because Bristol was (obviously rightly) convinced that there was a need for an extremely simple turbojet of light weight and small frontal area, initially to power what were then called 'light fighters'. The design was done singlehanded by Bernard Massey, who had previously worked on the auxiliary generating plant of the Princess. Freed from that ordeal, Massey turned in a brilliant design in a matter of a few weeks, using the seven-stage LP spool from the Orion turboprop and driving it by a plain uncooled single-stage turbine via a tubular shaft of such large diameter that no centre bearing was needed. Another novel feature was that each of the seven flame tubes in the can-annular combustion chamber incorporated in its downstream end one-seventh of the ring of turbine IGVs (inlet guide vanes). The result was a robust, efficient and troublefree little engine which quickly gained reasonably large markets.

The first Orpheus ran at 3,000 lb thrust on 17 December 1954, and in the following year was type-tested at 3,285 lb, first flying in the prototype Folland Gnat on 18 July of that year. Production Gnat fighters were powered by the Orpheus 701 rated at 4,520 lb, which was also used in the Jet-Pak booster pods for Indian C–119s. The Mk 703 of 4,850 lb still powers the Hindustan HF.24 Marut and Gnat-derived Ajeet, all Indian engines being licence-built by Hindustan Aeronautics. The 800-series, with increased-capacity fuel pump, was the preferred engine for the 1956 NATO light-fighter contest and was thus funded largely by the US Mutual Defense Assistance Program. The contest winner was the Fiat G91, for which large numbers of Mk 803 engines rated at 5,000 lb were produced by Bristol, by KHD in Germany and by Fiat in Italy. The BOr.12 was an attempt at a growth engine which could also have a simple afterburner, with ratings as in the caption (above), but Bristol let its development lapse. The Mk 805, derated to 4,000 lb, powers the Japanese Fuji T1F2 trainer. To power the RAF's Gnat T.1 trainers the Orpheus 101 was developed, with de-icing and an improved turbine, rated initially at 4,230 and later at 4,520 lb. All these have been supported in service by RR Bristol Engine Division.

Chapter 16

THE BRISTOL SIDDELEY ENGINES

In 1966 Rolls-Royce took over a large number of engine programmes then active at the various locations of BSEL, several of which have already been described under the names of Bristol Siddeley's precursor companies. Of the remainder, by far the most important was the Pegasus. This was a brilliant pioneer of jet lift, remains unique in the Western world and, when common sense sinks in to the minds of those who must plan to win any future war, it must lead to a new generation of engines for warplanes that could actually survive beyond the first few minutes of such a conflict by not being parked on airfields.

Briefly, the Pegasus is a basically conventional turbofan which discharges its fan air through one pair of left/right nozzles and its hot core jet through a second pair of left/right nozzles. All four flows initially curve out at 90° on each side and then terminate in short nozzles which turn the jet through a further 90°. These nozzles are mounted on circular bearings and are all driven in unison by chains from duplicated air motors to point anywhere within an arc of 98.5° to give forward thrust, vertical lift or reverse thrust for braking. The engine is installed so that, in the lift mode, the resultant thrust of the four jets passes through the aircraft centre of gravity. The result is the only engine in the world suitable for single-engined jet-lift aircraft. In practice, such aircraft usually operate in the STOVL (Short Take-Off, Vertical Landing) mode, to gain payload by using wing lift too.

This remarkable engine stemmed from a suggestion for a rather clumsy jet-lift aircraft put forward in France in 1956 by aircraft designer Michel Wibault. Bristol Aero-Engines gradually simplified the lifting system into a single two-shaft turbofan with the four rotatable nozzles. This engine, the BE.53/2 Pegasus 1, first ran at a rating of 9,000 lb thrust in September 1959. At this time, apart from the controversial TSR.2, the very idea of a military aircraft was taboo in Britain (were they not obsolete?) so it is extremely fortunate that the engine was ever built. It was funded 75% by the US Mutual Weapons Development Program, which happened to think that military aircraft might continue to be needed, and 25% by Bristol, whose courageous Sir Reginald Verdon Smith had made a habit of sticking his financial neck out in the face of ministerial obstruction. At the same time Hawker Siddeley showed equal courage in agreeing to fund two prototypes to be designed around the new engine, and these were designated Hawker P.1127. Two years later the Ministry agreed to assist with finance, provided that it was understood that the P.1127 was a pure research aircraft and had nothing to do with the forbidden idea of a new military aircraft!

Originally, in the BE.48 engine project, it had been intended to save money by using the first two stages of an Olympus LP spool as the fan (LP compressor) and an Orpheus HP compressor and combustion chamber. In the event, a new fan was designed with two stages overhung ahead of the front bearing, which was novel. It was then decided to use hot bleed air from the HP spool to power the 'puffer' reaction control valves at the extremities of the P.1127 for control at low speeds, and this demanded a new HP compressor with a bigger airflow. To reduce the gyroscopic couple effect the two shafts rotate in opposite directions. The resulting Pegasus 2 ran at 11,000 lb and powered the P.1127 on its first hover in September 1960. A year later the Pegasus 3 was giving 13,500 lb, with an eighth stage on

the compressor and a second stage on the HP turbine. In June 1962 the Pegasus 5 ran at 15,500 lb thrust, with a new three-stage fan with no inlet guide vanes, variable inlet vanes ahead of the HP compressor, an annular combustion chamber, and air-cooled blades in the first HP turbine. This powered the Hawker Kestrel and Dornier Do 31E.

Development continued, and in 1967 the first Harrier production engine, the Pegasus 6 Mk 101, began bench testing at 19,200 lb, with flight life extended from 50 to 300 hours. This engine introduced a new all-titanium fan, with part-supersonic blades, air-cooled blades in both HP turbine stages, a revised combustion chamber with water injection, a modified fuel system, and with vectoring nozzles containing two curved guide vanes. This engine entered RAF service with the Harrier GR.1 in April 1969. The Pegasus 10 Mk 102 of 1968 was an

A production Pegasus 11 Mk 103 being lowered into a test cell at Patchway (Rolls-Royce Bristol). On top are the fuel control and oil tank, and into the space between them will fit the gas-turbine starter/ APU.

interim-standard engine rated at 20,500 lb, leading to the definitive Pegasus 11 Mk 103, first run in August 1969 and ever since serving as the standard engine of the Harrier GR.3 and T.4 and the US Marine Corps and Spanish navy AV–8A/TAV–8A/AV–8C. This engine is rated at 21,500 lb and has an increased mass flow fan (432 lb/s, with overall pr close to 15), revised fuel and water-injection systems, and improved turbine cooling. Weight, without nozzles which are part of the airframe, is 3,113 lb, giving the excellent T/W ratio for its day of 6.9. The US designation is F402–RR–402. Time between overhauls is 800 hours, with a hot-end rework at 400 h. The Sea Harrier is powered by the Mk 104 engine, designed to resist sea-water corrosion and with an increased-capacity gearbox for augmented electric and hydraulic power. This is now being replaced by the Mk 106, which is the ocean-going version of the Mk 105.

For the Harrier II (US Marine Corps and Spanish navy AV–8B and RAF Harrier GR.5) Rolls-Royce developed the Pegasus 11–21 (US F402–RR–406, British Pegasus Mk 105). This features improved turbine cooling, a new LP turbine with shrouded blades, a revised swan-neck intermediate casing leading to lengthened zero-scarf front nozzles, and other revisions to suit the airframe. Delivery of engines for the pilot-production AV–8Bs began in early 1983, full production Dash–406 engines following in June 1984. It had been intended that Pratt & Whitney should be a major participant, a licence having been signed in August 1975, but the US policy of funding a mere trickle of Marine Corps orders each year made this impossible, though the Connecticut giant does contribute a small proportion of each F402 engine.

Back in 1980 the MoD began modest funding of a FADEC (full-authority digital electronic control), also called a DECS (digital engine control system). The supplier was the new group DSIC, Dowty

and Smiths Industries Controls, and the Pegasus was one of the first engines in the world to have such a superior control system. Not only does a FADEC offer absolute precision in all the many facets of engine control but it also finds its own faults, needs no in-service adjustments (after changes to the engine or fuel, for example), and eliminates the need for prolonged high-power running both on the ground and in flight for trimming purposes. The FADEC was flown at Rolls-Royce Bristol in March 1982, and in an AV–8B in 1985. The Pegasus 105 had it from the start, the first engine being delivered in June 1986. The Marine Corps engine with FADEC is designated Dash–406A and was first delivered in October 1986, and all 406s are now being updated. Each installation comprises an FMU (fuel metering unit) and duplicated parallel DECUs (digital engine control units), which are fuel-cooled boxes mounted on the fan case. Suffice to say they have revolutionized what pilots and ground crews can do (and greatly reduce what they have to do) and now have an enviable record in very tough service.

For more than ten years development of the Pegasus was devoted almost entirely to extending life, improving reliability and reducing costs. This has resulted in the American Dash–406A and British Mk 105 for the RAF and Mk 106 for the Royal Navy, but all have roughly the same thrust as the Mk 103 of 1970, namely 95.64 kN, 21,500 lb. In fact this is now a guaranteed minimum rating, the average thrust being 22,000 lb. In 1983, however, Rolls-Royce and the MoD began jointly funding a programme to provide increased thrust to enhance the Harrier II's hot-day VL (Vertical Landing) capability, and to cater for planned future growth of the aircraft. There were many possibilities, but those selected comprised a new fan, with pr raised from 2.3 to 2.6, improved blading in the HP spool, an improved combustor delivering

A Pegasus Mk 105 for a Harrier GR.5 nearing completion. The large box is the digital engine control.

gas at a higher mean temperature, an HP turbine with a Waspalloy disc and single-crystal blades, an improved LP turbine, and generally improved cooling, and enhanced modularity, throughout. These features were built into a demonstrator, the XG–15, and from its first run on 22 October 1986 this has not only confirmed the new features planned for later production but has demonstrated a potential for further thrust growth beyond that planned.

The uprated engine is the Pegasus 11–61, and, as the RAF has been told it cannot have it, all initial deliveries will be for the US Marine Corps with designation F402–RR–408. Modification kits will be supplied to upgrade engines already in service. Thrust at temperate conditions is increased by 1,840 lb, and in tropical conditions by 3,000 lb. Much more than this, the Dash–408 doubles the hot-end life to the same

1,000-hour level as the main engine TBO. Perhaps most important of all, life-cycle costs will be reduced by a startling 40%. To the pilot, the Dash–408 means greater combat agility, higher speed over target and, best of all, the ability to recover with much greater fuel loads. A production 11–61 engine went on test in May 1988, and production deliveries are to begin in May 1990.

For the more distant future, work is once more being directed towards engines for STOVL aircraft with supersonic performance. This work actually began in 1959 when Hawker Aircraft—unable to propose any military aircraft to the RAF—saw an apparently huge market opening up in NATO for a jet-lift tactical aircraft with supersonic capability. By 1962 this had led to the project design of the P.1150 and P.1154, the latter powered by an impressive engine in the 33,000-lb class designated

The XG15 technology demonstrator quickly achieved thrusts higher than the 25,000 lb target of the Pegasus 11-61, which is envisaged as the next production engine. Amazingly, instead of being hustled forward as the only survivable combat engine in the West (because it frees the aircraft in which it is fitted from deadly airfields), the Pegasus story is one of procrastination and meagre funding.

BS.100. This was the first engine to feature PCB (plenum-chamber burning), which is essentially reheat in the pure airflow to the front nozzles.

PCB was a new technique, though it drew upon the technology of afterburners and ramjets. In 1962–65 a total of 325 hours' running was done on rigs, followed by exactly the same time on a Pegasus 2 and on actual BS.100 engines. The PCB engines were fitted with front nozzles pointing upward to avoid severe testbed impingement. PCB temperatures up to 1,177°C (2,150°F) were achieved. An important feature of the BS.100, not yet introduced to the Pegasus, was that the front nozzles had droop and trail. Located low down on each side, they improved exhaust thrust co-efficient by over 4% by reducing the total angle through which the flow has to be turned. The BS.100 was a major programme conducted at high pressure, prior to its abrupt cancellation by the incoming Labour government in February 1965. The day after cancellation the author wrote 'This is a decision we shall regret, because supersonic V/STOL is bound to come eventually and we have chosen merely to fritter away time, which is a commodity we can never recover. Moreover, when we pick up the threads again, when common sense returns, inflation will ensure that the work will cost much more'.

When all work was cancelled, a total of 650 hours of PCB had been logged, giving overall thrust boosts in the sea-level static regime up to 35%, including a flawless 25-hour run at 927°C. Many engineers at Bristol, led by Gordon M. Lewis (recently retired as RR Technical Director), regretted the hiatus, and in fact after ten years had been thrown away they resumed company-funded PCB studies in 1975. Later the Ministry began once more to fund this work, which by 1979 had led to the start of a protracted programme (the pace dictated by the meagre funding) for full-scale research on actual engines. Following rig testing to explore the design of the best PCB system—which is an unusual challenge in that the flow in which combustion takes place has to curve round into a nozzle which can itself rotate through some 100°—bench testing began on a PCB system mounted on an old Pegasus 2 at the Proof and Experimental Establishment at Shoeburyness. Subsequently, simulated altitude testing took place at the National Gas Turbine Establishment at Pyestock, followed by prolonged trials with the same Pegasus 2 mounted in an old Harrier airframe and suspended at various heights from a large gantry at Shoeburyness. This research was aimed at investigating the best way of minimizing reingestion of hot gas and the effect of jet blast on the ground (which may need to be covered by some protective sheet).

By 1985 in these and other ground-running rigs a great deal had been learned about PCB systems, nozzle geometry and integration with possible aircraft. Many, including the author, strongly favour the traditional vectored-thrust engine plus PCB as the powerplant for the eventual supersonic Advanced STOVL aircraft planned for the late 1990s, which of course will also have to be a totally 'stealth' design. The main argument not yet quite resolved is whether it should remain a 'four-poster' engine, as in the Harrier, or, as seems preferable, whether the core should discharge a single jet on the centreline. So far, bench testing has demonstrated thrust increase by PCB at the front nozzles of over 100%, equivalent to about 50% boost overall. A Pegasus 11 has now replaced the Pegasus 2 in the gantry, with fully modulated PCB giving a thrust of up to 28,000–32,000 lb, with very little increase in engine weight. As related in the final chapter, other schemes

PCB has at last moved on to use a representative Pegasus 11, with which thrusts exceed 30,000 lb. It looks impressive at night, but a daytime picture shows the nozzles better.

At one time seen as the progenitor of thousands of engines for military and civil aircraft of many kinds, the M45 petered away to nothing. Here M45H transport engines are in assembly at the former Armstrong Siddeley works in Coventry.

are also being investigated for future 'no airfields' warplanes, but the obvious mainline candidate seems to be the traditional vectored-thrust turbofan with PCB, though perhaps started again from a clean sheet of paper.

In 1964 Bristol Siddeley collaborated with SNECMA of France on an advanced augmented turbofan, the M45, to power the AFVG (Anglo-French Variable-Geometry) fighter. This aircraft was soon cancelled, but the M45 proliferated into various engine projects for fighters, business jets, trainers and transports. For the German VFW 614 transport the M45H–D was developed, the aircraft having two engines mounted in unique pods high above the inboard wings. The 45H–D was a neat two-spool turbofan of 2.8 bypass ratio, weighing 1,483 lb and rated at 7,760 lb thrust. It was soon type-tested, as the M45H Mk 501 rated at 7,600 lb, and entered service with

the German airliner in late 1975. A year later SNECMA requested that Rolls-Royce take over the whole programme, and RR agreed to do this even though by this time, though neither aircraft nor engines suffered from any technical shortcomings, it was apparent that there would be no sustained production. The VFW 614 was withdrawn from service except for three used by the Federal German Luftwaffe whose engines have been supported from Parkside works, Coventry.

Parkside collaborated with SNECMA and Dowty Rotol in the M45SD–02, an engine ahead of its time. Using the core of an M45H, this drove through a reduction gearbox of 2.38 ratio to a single-stage fan of greatly increased diameter with fourteen variable-pitch and reversing blades. Fan airflow was increased from 238 to 484 lb/s, bypass ratio rising to 8.73. Tested at Aston Down in April 1975, the SD–02 proved to be

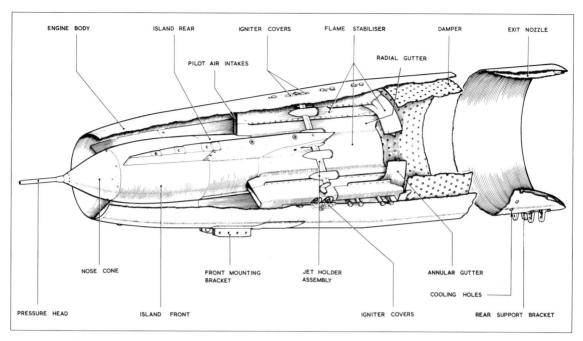

ENGINE BODY   ISLAND REAR   IGNITER COVERS   FLAME STABILISER   DAMPER   EXIT NOZZLE

PILOT AIR INTAKES   RADIAL GUTTER

NOSE CONE   FRONT MOUNTING BRACKET   JET HOLDER ASSEMBLY   ANNULAR GUTTER

COOLING HOLES

PRESSURE HEAD   ISLAND FRONT   IGNITER COVERS   REAR SUPPORT BRACKET

Prototype Bloodhound SAMs were powered by twin Thor BT.1 ramjets, as shown in this cutaway. This simple engine developed 100,000 hp at Mach 3, though it had a diameter of only 16 in. Its successors remain classified.

extremely quiet and economical, and it was planned to lead to a refined production engine, the RB.410–11, which was to weigh 2,885 lb and have a specific fuel consumption of 0.295 at the take-off rating of 14,370 lb. Like most things that are ahead of their time, the RB.410 was never built.

Though they have been used in missiles rather than aircraft, the forty years of work at Bristol on ramjets can hardly be ignored. From 1950 the king of this programme was South African Robin Jamison, who on the formation of BSEL became Assistant Chief Engineer in charge of the Advanced Propulsion Research Group. Following numerous launches of ramjet test vehicles, and a great deal of exciting tunnel testing, the Bristol Thor BT.2 went into production in 1956 for the Bloodhound Mk 1 SAM (surface-to-air missile), subsequently used in large numbers. More powerful BT.3 engines powered the Bloodhound 2, and despite their great age

these remain to this day as the only area-defence SAMs in Britain, deployed at a handful of sites near the coast of East Anglia and Lincolnshire. Rolls-Royce helps Nos 25 and 85 Squadrons keep the venerable missiles at instant readiness, and a modest refurbishment programme was recently funded. Money is at last being spent studying possible successors. A much later ramjet engine, the Odin, powers the Sea Dart SAM of the Royal and Argentine navies. No longer in production, this too is supported from the RR Bristol factories.

When Rolls-Royce bought BSEL in 1966, the RAF Strike Command still had Vulcan and Victor squadrons equipped with the large Blue Steel 'stand-off bomb'. This curious title actually referred to a cruise missile, 34 ft 9 in long, weighing over 15,000 lb and propelled at speeds up to more than Mach 2 (according to height) by a rocket engine named the Stentor. This had been

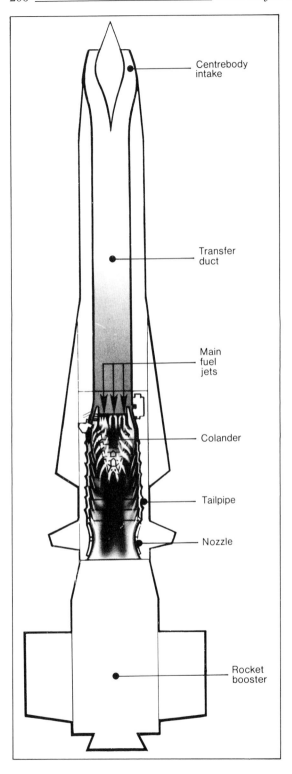

Centrebody
intake

Transfer
duct

Main
fuel
jets

Colander

Tailpipe

Nozzle

Rocket
booster

Left *This necessarily simpler cutaway shows the much newer Rolls-Royce Odin ramjet which powers the Sea Dart. It provides instant-starting, highly controllable, smoke-free propulsion over a wide range of Mach numbers and altitudes.*

designed by Armstrong Siddeley at Ansty, was produced by BSEL, and was supported in service by Rolls-Royce until withdrawal of the Blue Steels in 1975. The Stentor had one large thrust chamber for acceleration and one small chamber for cruise, both pump-fed with HTP and kerosene, purged after each test run with nitrogen, and then carefully dried with a flow of hot air prior to long periods of storage.

Below *The Gamma 201 rocket engine had four swivelling chambers giving 16,400 lb thrust (about 19,800 lb above the atmosphere) for the Black Knight rocket. Subsequently Britain opted out of building space launchers.*

Another ASM/BSEL/RR rocket engine for unmanned vehicles was the Gamma, the Gamma Types 2, 4 and 8 respectively having two, four or eight thrust chambers all pump-fed with HTP and kerosene. The Gamma 4 powered the Westland (previously Saro) Black Knight research rocket, and the Types 8 and 2 respectively powered the first and second stages of the Westland Black Arrow, the only satellite launch vehicle ever developed in Britain.

Third of the ASM/BSEL/RR rockets was the totally different BS.605, a small unit with either single or twin chambers for boosting the take-off of military aircraft.

The only application was the sixteen Buccaneer S.50 attack aircraft of the South African Air Force, in which the twin-chamber version imparted a sea-level thrust of 8,000 lb, for a total installed weight of 367 lb. The thrust chamber and turbopump were based on Gamma parts, the BS.605 having its own HTP tank but drawing kerosene from the aircraft's fuel system. Electrical controls governed operation of the twin chambers, including extension and retraction into the rear fuselage. The BS.605 remains in service, but Rolls-Royce is politically not permitted to provide support.

Chapter 17

THE NEW TURBOFANS

Today two of the most important and successful Rolls-Royce engines are the 535 and Tay, both of which are derivatives of earlier engines. Paradoxically, the company also designed and built two almost completely new turbofans which did not go into production. These, the Trent and RB.401, deserve a brief mention.

The RB.203 Trent was the first three-shaft engine actually built, the prototype running nine months ahead of the first RB.211 in December 1967. It had an inlet diameter of 38.7 in, compared with 32.4 in for the Spey. It looked roughly the same size, but was in fact a totally different engine. At the front was a single-stage fan which still looks modern today, with 21 wide-chord snubberless blades and no inlet guide vanes. Mass flow was 300 lb/s, 50 per cent greater than for the Spey, bpr at 3 being over three times higher. Next came a four-stage titanium IP (intermediate pressure) compressor, followed by a five-stage titanium HP spool (compared with twelve stages in the Spey), the overall pr of 16 being similar to the earlier engine. Both compressors were driven by single-stage turbines, the HP having cooled blades, and the fan required a two-stage LP turbine. Take-off rating was similar to early Speys at 9,980 lb, but weight was dramatically less at 1,776 lb. Obviously, noise and fuel consump-

tion would have been very significantly better. The Trent was seen as a Spey replacement, growing quickly in thrust to 12,000 lb, and being easily interchangeable in most civil installations. Fairchild, Fokker's US licensee, proposed to build an FH–228 based on the F28 Fellowship but powered by Trents, but in 1970 work on the engine was terminated for a variety of technical and political reasons, such as the need to pull design engineers off the Trent to concentrate on the sick RB.211.

In 1974 the company disclosed that what was then the Bristol Engine Division was developing as an internally-funded project a small turbofan in the 5,000-lb class designated RB.401. It was seen as a Viper replacement in business jets, light transports, military trainer and light attack aircraft, and RPVs. Obviously in the military markets it competed with the existing Adour (Chapter 19), but its advanced design suggested that it should find many customers attracted by the small number of parts and excellent brochure figures. An RB.401–06 demonstrator was run on 21 December 1975, achieving its design performance on the first test, followed by the definitive RB.401–07 in November 1977. The –07 engine had an advanced titanium fan based on the latest RB.211 technology, handling a mass flow of 182 lb/s, an eight-stage compressor with two rows of variable stators, an annular combustor with vaporizing burners, a single-stage HP turbine with cooled blades and a two-stage LP turbine. The bypass duct was full length, but there was no mixer for the hot and cold flows. Dry weight was 985 lb, and take-off rating 5,540 lb. Calculated specific fuel consumption was 0.449 at take-off and 0.707 in cruise. In the end, despite proposed collaboration with Pratt & Whitney Canada, the decision was taken in 1984 to terminate the project. There were several reasons for this, most of them unconnected with the design or performance of the engine, the latter being encouraging. Many people in aircraft companies told the author they regretted the decision, and today P & W Canada has the PW300/1 and General Electric and Garrett are collaborating on the CFE738 to scoop up precisely this market.

Chronologically, the next new turbofan to go ahead began life as an overt version of the RB.211, designated RB.211–535, but as the engine matured it became just the Rolls-Royce 535, and is now gradually forming its own sub-family of variants. As has all too often been the case, the 535 is a superb Rolls-Royce engine restricted by its lack of applications. On the other hand it dominates its single application and sales in early 1989 were well in excess of 500.

The advent of the giant wide-body airliners made it self-evident that their quiet, fuel-economical technology would have to percolate down to smaller airliners. Nevertheless, despite the staggering increase in the price of fuel in the years following 1973, the world's airlines showed seemingly unshakeable tenacity in buying hundreds—indeed thousands—of 'noisy, fuel-guzzling narrow-bodies' such as the 727, 737 and DC–9. In the year 1976, for example, over 400 such aircraft were sold, compared with a single example of the A300B, which was the only new-technology short-hauler. Despite this, the engine makers reasoned that

eventually the airlines must come to their senses, and they planned smaller high-bypass turbofans suitable for new short-haul transports. The daunting costs involved led initially to a lot of collaboration. General Electric teamed with SNECMA on the CFM56, while Pratt & Whitney collaborated with MTU and Fiat on the JT10D. Rolls-Royce came in on the JT10D programme in May 1975.

At first the JT10D was aimed at the same level of thrust as the CFM56, namely 22,000 lb, and the initial three collaborators had run a JT10D–1 at this level. Almost from the start this was recognized as inadequate, and the various potential customers kept asking for more and more. When the thrust required moved above the 30,000-lb level it became possible to start considering a derived version of the RB.211, which itself had started life at well under 40,000 lb. In late 1977 Boeing, busy with a revamped 727 which it called the 7N7 though actually its many variants were all versions of the Model 761, asked Rolls-Royce to offer a smaller version of the RB.211. Two key airlines, Eastern and British, expressed a clear preference for this derivative approach. Accordingly, in early 1978 Rolls-Royce withdrew from the JT10D programme and began to work intensively on the proposed 'smaller RB.211', which it called the RB.211–535. It was then picked as the launch engine for the new Boeing, which at the go-ahead in August 1978 was restyled the 757. This was originally launched with another engine option, GE's CF6–32, but despite partnership with Volvo the GE board decided not to go ahead.

Obviously, a derived design is a compromise, tending to weigh more than an all-new engine and also suffering a small penalty in sfc resulting from the reduced internal pressures and temperatures which depress the overall thermodynamic cycle efficiency. Against this, Rolls-Royce set the fact that the same factors of reduced temperatures and pressures were certain to result in longer life, extremely high reliability and lower spare-parts and maintenance costs. The solution finally agreed retains the HP section (04 module) or engine core of the RB.211–22B with hardly any change. The IP compressor has many parts common to the Dash–22B, but has six instead of seven stages. The biggest change is the fan, scaled down from the new fan of the RB.211–524 to a diameter 12 in less at 73.2 in. The fan duct and complete turbine section were new, but based closely on RB.211 technology.

Originally the 535 was the RB.211–85, designed to a thrust of 32,000 lb, at which it was calculated that the fan airflow would be 25% lower than that of the Dash–22B, and the core airflow 17% lower because of the reduced supercharging effect of the six-stage IP compressor. In fact the initial production engine, the 535C, has a full rating of 37,400 lb, at which the fan and core airflows are reduced by only 18 and 12% respectively. In service the 535C is operated to flexible ratings, and seldom needs to come near to its full power. The engine was certificated in March 1981, almost a year before the first flight of the 757, and entered service on 1 January 1983. As Rolls-Royce expected, it proved the most trouble-free engine in the company's history. During its first three years of service the total engine-attributable removal rate was 0.045 per 1,000 flight hours, 'many times better than the previously claimed industry best'. Moreover, as the higher efficiencies of the fan and LP turbine more than cancel out the slightly worse thermodynamic cycle, the 535C has a slightly better cruise sfc than the Dash–22B, namely (typical conditions at 35,000 ft) 0.612 compared with 0.618. Weight savings in both the engine and its nacelle resulted in the installed powerplant being 20% lighter than the Dash–22B, while the difference in thrust is only 10%.

From the outset it was planned that the 535 should be able to grow in power, and the initial proposal was a 535D rated at 39,410 lb. By July 1980, still two years from the 757's first flight and to meet the competition from the Pratt & Whitney PW2037, Rolls-Royce had announced the 535–C2A to incorporate a new wide-chord fan and integrated nozzle. By 1981 this had been refined into the 535E4, to be rated at 39,600 lb. In the event the E4 was certificated in November 1983 at 40,100 lb, with end-bend HP compressor blading and 3D HP turbine blades. At 7,264 lb its dry weight is actually 30 lb less than that of its predecessor, and its overall performance—reliability, low noise, fuel economy and low costs—have again set new industry standards.

The key feature of the E4 is the completely new fan, with 22 (instead of 33) blades. Each blade has roughly twice the chord of those in the 535C fan, and yet weight has been so dramatically reduced by making each blade from two thin titanium skins stabilized by a titanium honeycomb core that the blade is inherently aerodynamically stable, and snubbers are no longer needed to control the vibration modes. The fan alone increases thrust by handling a greater airflow (1,150 lb/s) without changing engine frontal area, while removing the snubbers reduces sfc by 2.5%. Other changes include the use of the advanced compressor and turbine blading, and an integrated nozzle and full-length pod cowl.

The new fan has a diameter increased from 73.2 in to 74.5 in. It is not mounted in a double-diaphragm disc, as in the 524L, but has a circular-arc curved dovetail root. The rotating spinner is lengthened and fabricated as a nosecone of composite material. The fan case of the 535C is of titanium, with a strong ring of wrapped continuous Kevlar aramid-fibre composite strip to contain any separated fan blade, but in the E4 the underlying case is of aluminium. The IP compressor has new Codib (controlled-

Above *From the start, the 535 has proved an outstandingly reliable and efficient engine, and this E4 version introduced considerable further improvements. Most significant advance is the wide-chord snubberless fan.*

Right *The hollow titanium fan blade used first in the E4 and later in the big RB.211-524G is one of the company's most significant 'firsts' of recent years. Note the curved dovetail root.*

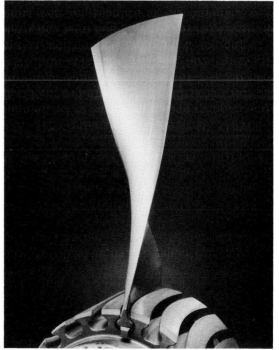

diffusion blades) on all stages, lightweight stator shrouds and reduced-weight split casings. The intermediate case downstream is redesigned with ten spokes and new IP and LP bearings with positive central-tube lubrication. The HP compressor, originally very like that of the –22B, now has advanced end-bend blading which, though it looks like the curved-down wingtips of some aircraft, is actually designed to give enhanced efficiency in the sluggish boundary layers along the inner and outer walls of the compressor. The HP rotors are made in a new titanium alloy which saves 95 lb in weight and can operate at higher temperatures.

The combustion chamber has burners without pintles (which were added in the 535C to reduce carbon formation), a flexible hairpin-mounted liner, lightweight outer casing, and two-piece OGV (outlet guide vane) casing to reduce cost. The HP turbine is probably the most advanced in commercial use anywhere, with directionally solidified blades with the most advanced internal cooling. In addition, thermal barrier coatings, which Rolls-Royce has used for years on combustion systems, are applied selectively to the HP nozzle guide vanes and other parts to reduce the cooling airflow required, while at the same time the combustion chamber offtake for cooling air has been redesigned. The IP and LP turbines have been rebladed for enhanced efficiency, with revised cooling, the IP disc being of Waspalloy instead of steel, and the IP casing is redesigned with twelve spokes.

A major change is the total redesign of the back end of the engine, with an integrated nozzle in which the hot core and cool fan flows are mixed. This has many advantages including greater fan efficiency at high power, 2% reduction in cruise sfc, elimination of supersonic scrubbing on the nacelle afterbody, and a 40% increase in reverse thrust by virtually eliminating residual core thrust. Whereas the 535C has reverser cascades of aluminium dip-brazed construction, those of the E4 are of stronger cast magnesium. The engine control system is an improved form of that on the 535C, with supervisory digital electronic control. The engine is installed in a pod generally similar to the 535C, but of course with a single integrated rear nozzle, with a Dyna-Rohr inner-barrel nose skin to reduce noise and carbon-fibre outer skins to reduce weight.

The E4 first flew on 17 August 1983 in the No 1 position on Boeing's in-house test 747, completing a stringent flight programme the following month (today engines can be tested so precisely in altitude cells on the ground that the flight programme is basically a demo to give the airframe builder confidence the thing can fly). The first E4-powered 757 flew ahead of schedule on 3 February 1984, and revenue service began the following October. As well as saving about 300,000 gallons per year per aircraft, compared with the 535C, the E4 achieved the almost unbelievable target of significantly bettering the unparalleled record of its predecessor in reliability and noise. It is unquestionably the most reliable large civil engine in the world, which probably means it is the most reliable aircraft engine in history. The 757 powered by it has been described as 'the quietest aircraft in the world with more than 100 seats'. Apart from the BAe 146 and Fokker 100 it is the only jet cleared for night operations from Washington National. In 1984–86 GE shared in manufacture and marketing, but this was terminated as explained in Chapter 11. In October 1987 Rolls-Royce and Allison signed an agreement covering use of the E4 in American military aircraft, with shared development, marketing and manufacturing. The immediate proposal was that the E4 should replace pairs of J57 turbojets in B–52G heavy bombers of the USAF; the competition here is of course the F117 (PW2000 series). The E4 is also competing with the F117 to power the fifth batch of C-17s.

Pratt & Whitney launched the PW2000 series, initially as the PW2037 and later as the PW2040, determined to beat the Rolls-Royce engine in the 757. The US company even promised Delta Airlines financial compensation if it failed to beat the 535 fuel burn by more than 7%. Delta was among the initial customers for the 757 who picked the P&W engine, but this was a clear case where striving for the last percentage point

Alone among modern high-bypass engines, the 535E4 is installed in a nacelle of perfect form with a single nozzle. Here it powers a 757 of Eastern.

in fuel burn has proved very costly. At least in its early years the reliability of the PW2037 was, in P&W's own admission, 'disappointing'. In contrast, the E4 has gone from strength to strength, its combination of economy, reliability, quietness and low overall cost proving demonstrably superior. Its marketing ascendancy is far greater than anyone would have dared to predict. By mid-1988 the 535 had been chosen by nineteen of the 24 customers for the 757, including every one of the twelve

Maintenance engineers at Royal Brunei don't have much work to do on their E4s, but they open them up occasionally to admire them.

most recent, who in May 1988 included American Airlines with an order for fifty aircraft plus fifty options.

Chronologically the next Rolls-Royce turbofan to appear was another derived engine, the Tay. It is based on the Spey (Chapter 9), and took a surprisingly long time to emerge, mainly because of a lack of applications. The Spey was designed just at the time that Rolls-Royce was recognizing that its choice of bpr was much too timid. To some degree the company's choice of class name for such engines—bypass turbojet—helped to focus attention on engines which were just basically turbojets which by-passed a small fraction of their inlet airflow. Incorrect estimations of pod drag also militated against ratios anything like the optimum, notwithstanding the demonstrated low specific fuel consumptions of such American engines as the JT3D and CJ805–23. But by the mid-1960s the writing was plainly on the wall, and a further mighty spur to higher bpr was legislation against aircraft noise. The author can readily tell a small One-Eleven from the procession of other higher-bpr aircraft passing over his

house along Amber One and Red One, by the crackling thunder of its Spey engines.

Rolls-Royce began studying refanned Speys before 1970. By 1972 the Spey 67 had reached the stage of detailed engineering design, based on the Spey 512 but with a new LP system comprising a large single-stage fan and two-stage IP compressor driven by a three-stage turbine. Bpr rose to 2.26, and minimum net thrust to 14,580 lb. By 1975 this had been refined into the Spey 605W, with water injection, and then into the Mk 606 with water injection removed. Whereas the –67 had a 44-in fan, the 606 had one enlarged to 47 in, though, as the core flow was increased, the bpr fell to 1.96. An extra (third) stage was added to the IP compressor, and thrust rating was 16,900 lb. The author, who handles the Engines section of *Jane's All the World's Aircraft*, was misguided enough to add to the 1975–76 edition of that annual 'The 606 is firmly committed to development, and production deliveries are expected to commence towards the end of 1978. The first application to be named is the One-Eleven 700. . .'

In the event, BAC became embroiled

The Spey 67C, or Mk 606, was one engine that never got started. As this comparison with the Spey Mk 512 shows, there were to be few changes in the HP spool, but the LP was completely new, and there was a single mixer nozzle.

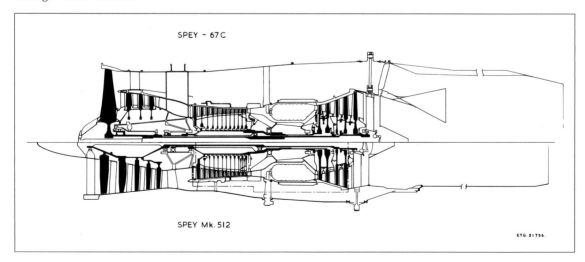

Today's engines have a lot of black parts, not because they are painted but because they are carbon (graphite) composite. This applies to the whole bypass duct of the Tay, a winner from the start and not too late to gain large global markets.

with nationalization and never launched the One-Eleven 700, and no market appeared for a refanned Spey until a further seven years had passed. Throughout this time there was pressure for such an engine from Gulfstream Aerospace and for re-engining existing One-Elevens, but the first definite market to materialize was at Fokker of Amsterdam. The F28 Fellowship, powered by RB.183 Mk 555 engines, had set an enviable record of reliability in some 4,000,000 engine hours, with an IFSD (inflight shutdown) rate consistently below 0.02 per 1,000 hours, but marketing the F28 was being adversely affected by noise and, to a lesser extent, high fuel burn. By 1982 Rolls-Royce was basing its refanned Spey on the Mk 555 engine, the lightest and most reliable of all Speys and with compressor bleeds matched to the F28 systems. It was found that a refanned Mk 555 would also closely match Gulfstream's requirements,

despite the executive jet's lighter weight and much higher cruising altitude. Indeed it was the US company that became launch customer for the new engine, ordering 200 in March 1983 worth some $300 million with spares. Fokker placed an order for 100 in November 1983. The new engine was called the RB.183–03 Tay, repeating the RB number of the Spey Mk 555 and the name of the turbojet of 1946.

The two big changes in the Tay, compared with previous refanned Speys, are that the fan uses the latest wide-chord snubberless type of blade—though solid titanium—and the core is based on that of the Mk 555 engine. Apart from giving at least a 2.5% improvement in sfc, the new fan blade ensures compliance with the most stringent (FAR 36 Stage 3) noise requirements. For the size of core, this demanded a bpr of 3. A fan pr of 1.75 was selected to provide the best altitude cruise performance. To capitalize on the efficiency of these blades, with adequate surge margin, a corrected tip speed of 1,520 ft/s was chosen, with hub/tip ratio of 0.3. The fan was based on the 535E4 fan, and studies were made of this scaled down to 40, 42 and 44 in. The 44-in size was chosen because it was the quietest, and the largest that could be installed on the new Gulfstream IV and still meet the demand for high-speed cruise thrust at up to 45,000 ft. Resulting take-off airflow is 390 lb/s, compared with 199 for the Mk 555 engine.

To provide the same flow conditions as before at the entry to the HP spool, a three-stage IP compressor rotates with the fan. To drive the LP shaft the turbine needs to extract 38% more power than before, and the result is a new three-stage LP turbine with efficiency 4% better than that of the Mk 555's two-stage turbine, and allowing for future growth in the Tay's thrust. The new turbine was also designed for minimum noise, along with every other part of the new engine including the inlet duct, bypass duct and mixing jetpipe downstream of the forced mixer with twelve deep lobes. A significant improvement to the core engine is that the combustion chamber is made from Transply material, a porous sandwich formed from chem-milled sheets brazed together to leave internal air passages, which reduces emissions such as unburnt fuel, and slashes cooling airflow from 12% to only 4%.

Rated thrusts for its initial applications are 12,420 lb flat-rated to 37°C for the Mk 610-8 engine for the GIV and 13,320 lb flat-rated to 28°C for the Mk 620-15 for the Fokker 100. Cruise sfc for both versions is around 0.7, compared with 0.8 for the Mk 555. The first Tay was run in August 1984, and from the start it was clear the new engine was a real winner. Like the 535C and E4 the Tay fairly romped through every test to which it was subjected. By June 1985 six engines had run an amazing 70% more test cycles than had been planned, and the Mk 610-8, flown on the first GIV on 19 September 1985 (using engines originally delivered for ground running only), was certificated on 26 June 1986. The engine entered service on the GIV in spring 1987. By this time orders for the Tay had exceeded 630. By 1987 the Mk 620-15 had been uprated to 13,850 lb to 30°C, but for reasons unconnected with the engine, and adding to Fokker's many worries, the Fokker 100 did not enter service until April

A Tay 610-8 in a Gulfstream IV. Not only the bypass duct but also the giant nacelle doors are of black carbon composite material. There is no longer any need for a noise-suppressing nozzle.

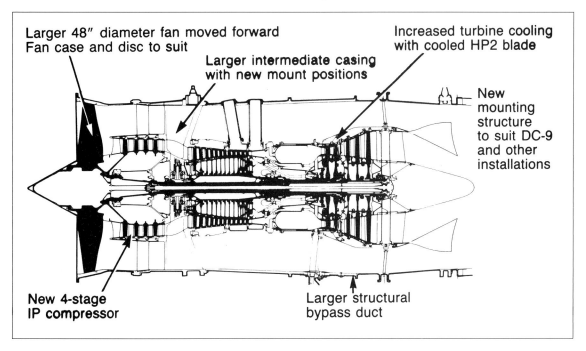

Larger 48″ diameter fan moved forward
Fan case and disc to suit

Larger intermediate casing
with new mount positions

Increased turbine cooling
with cooled HP2 blade

New mounting structure to suit DC-9 and other installations

New 4-stage IP compressor

Larger structural bypass duct

Likely to find enormous markets in replacing noisier and less fuel-efficient engines in existing 'narrow bodies', the Tay 670 will begin life at 18,000 lb. The differences shown are relative to the Mk 650.

1988. Cruise sfc at 30,000 ft of the 620–15 has improved to 0.69.

In July 1985 Rolls-Royce offered a more powerful Tay matched not only to a planned heavier Fokker 100 but also to re-engining programmes including the Dee Howard One-Eleven. This engine, the 650–14, has a fan enlarged by 0.8 in and a high-efficiency turbine. Rated at 15,100 lb to 30°C, it was certificated in June 1988.

From the start it has been increasingly evident that the Tay is a true RR engine, with enormous capacity for growth. Around the world there are over 3,000 jetliners powered by the JT8D which besides being relatively fuel-hungry will have great difficulty meeting Stage 3 noise legislation. The answer is a re-engining programme, but the CFM56 is too big, and so is the refanned JT8D–200. In contrast an upgraded Tay would be ideal, and on 7 September

1988 Rolls-Royce signed an agreement with ANACORP which launched the Tay 670 for retrofitting in DC-9s. ANACORP also expects to fit the Mk 670 into very large numbers of 727s and 737s. The Mk 670 was to begin rig testing in 1988 and run in 1989, for 1991 deliveries. It will have a 48-in fan, four-stage IP compressor, air-cooled second-stage HP turbine, new intermediate casing and larger bypass duct, new gearbox (twin boxes to meet 737 ground-clearance dimensions) and universal mountings to suit all applications. Initially rated at 18,000 lb, the 670 will also allow Fokker to go ahead with a long-planned stretched Fokker 100. Re-engining programmes will be managed by ANACORP and will also involve not only RR but also Gulfstream, Dee Howard (which has developed a nacelle and reverser for the Tay One-Eleven) and (as an equity-sharing partner in Dee Howard)

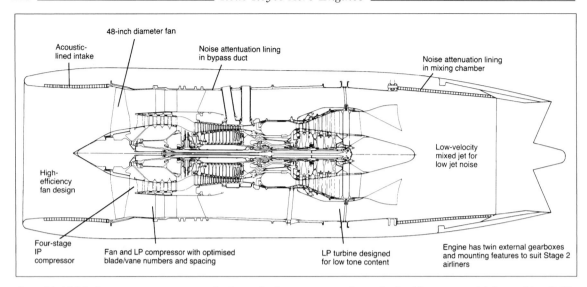

In mid-1988 the company was pondering whether or not to launch the Tay 670, which could sell like proverbial hot cakes in re-engining programmes. This longitudinal section shows the whole nacelle.

Aeritalia. Some idea of the potential market is given by RR's own estimate that over 1,700 aircraft are likely to benefit from the Tay 670. Indeed, almost 12,000 JT8Ds are at present in service.

These four marks of Tay are certain to be the first of others. There is not the slightest doubt that this engine will be built in large numbers for at least the next twenty years, and will gain additional applications in both new and existing airframes.

Last of the engines covered in this chapter is the V.2500, product of the world's most diverse and powerful engine manufacturing consortium. This engine has an equally long and convoluted history, starting in the 1970s as the RB.432 at Bristol. This project was the result of long study of the commercial jet market for narrow-body, or single-aisle, aircraft. The only new engine aimed at this market was the Franco-American CFM56, and this uses a core based on the GE9 (F101) originally designed in 1969 for a bomber. Rolls-Royce judged that there ought to be room for a competitor, and the RB.432 was planned mainly as a scaled

RB.401 with extra compressor stages to give a higher pr. The sheer cost of development and the absence of a customer kept the project on paper, but to increase the chance of a go-ahead Rolls-Royce opened discussions with possible foreign partners. In early 1980 Rolls-Royce & Japanese Aero Engines Ltd was formed with three major Japanese partners, IHI (Ishikawajima-Harima), KHI (Kawasaki) and MHI (Mitsubishi). They formed a joint engineering team to work at Bristol on a refined engine, the RJ.500. This had a 59-in fan, mass flow of 635 lb/s, cruise pr of 20, dry weight of 4,081 lb and thrust of 20,000 lb to ISA+15°C.

Prototypes of this engine were built, but in the author's opinion it would never have dislodged the CFM56 from its position of dominance in the 20,000–30,000-lb market. What was needed was an engine altogether more advanced in design, with a pr nearer to 35 than 20. Complicating factors were the emergence of various kinds of advanced propellers (propfans) and the unexpected decline in the price of fuel. All this increased the risks, while making the RJ.500

look less attractive. Other companies watching the situation were Pratt & Whitney, MTU of West Germany and Fiat of Italy. These three had collaborated on the JT10D in the 20,000-25,000-lb class in the 1970s, and continued to work together while this engine grew into the PW2037 in the 40,000-lb class. As these words are written, the PW2037 is being made at an uneconomically low rate because—apart from the USAF with the C-17—customers prefer the Rolls-Royce 535E4. This has left the three partners short of work, and in any case they have no engine in the 20,000–30,000-lb bracket. The upshot was an unprecedented meeting at Derby on 11 March 1983 at which five companies signed an agreement to develop an engine for 150-seat airliners. The signatories were Dennis Jackson for Rolls-Royce (30% of the equity and work-share), Robert E. Rosati of United Technologies Pratt & Whitney (30%), Yoshifumi Harayama for what had been renamed Japanese Aero Engines Corporation (23%), Martin Steinberger for MTU (11%) and Dr Ing Alessandro Martinotti for Fiat (6%).

Never before had such industrial might been applied to an aeronautical product. On 15 December 1983 the five partners registered IAE (International Aero Engines AG) in Zurich, Switzerland, announcing a thirty-year commitment to produce commercial turbofan engines in the range 18,000–30,000 lb thrust. The initial engine was designated the V.2500, V being the Roman numeral for the five partners and 2500 for some reason being chosen to indicate the baseline engine's target of 25,000 lb thrust. The basic work-split was announced as: RR, HP compressor; PW, combustor and HP turbine; JAEC, fan and LP compressor; MTU, LP turbine; and Fiat, accessory gearbox, turbine exhaust case (jetpipe) and various other parts. Design integration was assigned to the multinational IAE Engineering Group at Eastgate House on the east side of Derby, while V.2500 assembly and develop-

The RJ.500 was another of the non-starters—except on the testbed, where this RJ.500 is headed. RR Bristol, and their many foreign partners, put a lot of effort into this engine, but were certainly right to decide they were not aiming high enough.

ment test was assigned to Derby and East Hartford, Connecticut, home of P & W.

Detail design was launched formally in January 1984, and the first engine went on test in December 1985. It had a fan based on 535E4 technology but with a diameter of 63 in, compared with 74.5, handling an airflow of 789 lb/s with pr of 1.76 and with a bpr (climb) of 5.8. This rotated with a single LP core booster stage, the LP shaft being driven by a five-stage turbine. The HP compressor had ten stages of advanced end-bend blading with controlled-diffusion aerodynamics, the inlet guide vanes and first three stator rows being variable. Overall design pr was 36. The segmented annular combustor was remarkably compact, yet was designed to give an almost perfectly even temperature profile into the two-stage HP turbine. The latter had single-crystal blades in powder-metallurgy discs and, like the LP turbine, active clearance

Except for the fact it is appreciably smaller, with a 63-in fan compared with 74.5, the V.2500 could be mistaken for a 535E4. Its development was by 1988 coming out of the wood, with a new compression system. By April, 11 of the 12 development engines had been rebuilt to certification standard, with certification due in June.

control in which hot bleed air blown around the casing maintains an extremely small gap around the tips of the rotor blades and the inner ends of the stators.

As work went on in 1986 it was clear the HP spool was in considerable trouble, failing to deliver the promised performance. The author expressed the view to Frank Turner, director of the RR Civil Engine Group, that in an age of computer-aided design it ought to be possible to get everything right first time (knowing this to be a pious hope!). He replied that in the V.2500 HP compressor the engineers had aimed at a record pr and a record efficiency simultaneously, and that this was no small challenge. IAE agreed that Pratt & Whitney should adopt the role of technical coordinator, and by spring 1987 design had been completed of a V.2500 of significantly different configuration. The fan was moved forward and given recambered blades, and the LP core booster was redesigned with three stages to take the load off the troubled HP spool. With various minor changes this resulted in today's engine, which first ran in November 1987.

It has proved to be an engine of outstanding efficiency and toughness, and shows every sign of being a world-beater. Certification requirements get harder all the time, yet the V.2500 passed every test first time (no other modern civil engine is known to have done so). After the catastrophic test in which a fan blade is deliberately severed while the engine is running at redline speed a great deal of the engine was salvageable and built into a fresh engine, an unprecedented event. The flight programme was completed in only 35 hours in May/June 1988, using a Boeing 720 at St Hubert, Montreal. The engine was certificated in June 1988, and began flying A320s a month later. The problems of 1986 dented the V.2500's image, just as did the proposed SuperFan derivative described in the final chapter, and Lufthansa switched their A320 propulsion to the CFM56. This may have been a hasty judgement. Though the V.2500 has come out slightly heavy it is now demonstrating a cruise sfc advantage of about 4%, and this ought to rise to at least 5% at entry to service with Cyprus and India in spring 1989, mainly as a result of fitting NACA64 blading to the HP compressor, with revised inner and outer longitudinal profiles.

At certification in June 1988 the 12 V.2500 development engines had run over 4,400 hours. Of this, over 1,000 hours, all in arduous test cycles, had been logged by one engine. Here all its parts are laid out at Derby for inspection. Their condition could only be described as brilliant.

Once the V.2500 is in service it ought gradually to find not only more customers but also, what it needs just as much, additional applications. GE/SNECMA have sold over 5,000 CFM56s for many types of aircraft, and can afford to commit large sums to product improvement. One obvious such improvement is to upgrade the CFM56 to 31,200 lb for the A340, something IAE cannot yet afford. On the other hand IAE have no doubt they have a newer and superior basic engine. One of its strengths might be the LP turbine. MTU designed this conservatively, and gave it one stage more than most engineers might think necessary, but in the author's view it could extract a lot more power from the core flow than it does today, even after adding two extra core booster stages, and thus could drive a significantly larger fan, matched to thrusts suitable for the A340 and other aircraft. In the longer term, of course, we might see a V.2500 core driving an enormous UHB (ultra-high bypass) fan of the kind discussed in the final chapter.

At a totally different end of the size scale, Williams International in Michigan make their money mass-producing small turbofans for cruise missiles, but have also developed the FJ44 turbofan rated at 1,800 lb for executive transports and trainers. In October 1988 four companies announced that they were collaborating on the Swearingen SA-30 bizjet, powered by two FJ44s. Apart from the two already named the partners are Gulfstream (long a customer of RR) and Rolls-Royce, who are assisting with technical and product support and will make FJ44 parts.

Since this book went to press, Rolls-Royce has launched the RB.580, a turbofan in the 7,100-lb thrust class, growing to 10,000 lb later. The RB.580 will use the core of the Alison T406, mated with a Rolls-Royce fan, low-pressure turbine and bypass duct. This very efficient engine will weigh about 1,388 lb and is aimed at commercial aircraft from large business jets to 100-seaters.

Chapter 18

TODAY'S SHAFT ENGINES

This chapter deals mainly with turboshaft engines for helicopters, but it also briefly mentions the limited work that has been done on new turboprops. A further note on shaft-drive engines for projected propfans appears in the final chapter.

For twenty years the most important engine at Leavesden has been the Gem. This is despite the fact that more than 97% of the Gems so far delivered have been for versions of one helicopter, the Westland Lynx. This neat modular engine began life as the BS.360, the only one of more than thirty studies for small Bristol Siddeley turboshaft, turboprop and turbojet engines to reach main project status. In 1967 the 'BS' was changed to RS, at about the same time that its application stopped being the WG.13 and became the Lynx. In 1971 the RS.360–07 became the Gem, and this is interesting because, while 'Gem' has no affinity with any previous Rolls-Royce name, it recalls the fact that more than forty years ago the Metropolitan-Vickers turbojets were all named after gemstones!

In 1967 the British and French governments signed an agreement for collaboration on three types of helicopter. Two were established French helicopters, the Aérospatiale Gazelle, powered by the Turbomeca Astazou IIIN, and the Aérospatiale Puma, powered by twin Turbomeca Turmo IIIC4

engines. Under the terms of the agreement, Rolls-Royce Small Engine Division at Leavesden assembled and shared in the manufacture of both these French engines, including all examples bought for British use, and to this day it provides support for these engines in service with British operators. Small Engine Division also received a contract from what was then the Ministry of Technology for design study and rig evaluation for a completely new engine to power the third helicopter covered by the agreement, the British WG.13, soon named the Lynx. The first engine ran in mid-1969, and on the whole the subsequent programme has proved eminently satisfactory. By late 1987 about 1,200 Gems had been ordered, most having been delivered, Turbomeca sharing in manufacture.

There is nothing unusual about the basic configuration, because four axial compressor stages followed by a centrifugal stage might be considered today; but where the Gem is unusual is that the gas generator has two spools, claimed to eliminate the need (seldom apparent in such engines anyway) for variable-geometry features, and thus to simplify the control system. Obviously it helps to let the axial and centrifugal compressors run at their own best speed. Air is drawn in uniformly all round the final output gearbox, which is of the planetary type with double helical gears. The air then passes through the four-stage LP compressor and thence through the titanium centrifugal HP compressor, which has alternate inducer and radial vanes. Overall pr is about 12.15 in early versions and 14.1 in current production.

From the centrifugal impeller the air is slowed down and increased in pressure through radial and then axial diffusers which deliver it around the outside of the annular combustion chamber. As is usually the case with centrifugal turboshaft engines, this is of the reverse-flow type to bring the delivery of hot gas forward close behind the HP impeller, eliminating the need for a centre bearing, and at the correct small diameter for the HP turbine, which has uncooled blades. The gas continues through the LP turbine, with shrouded blades, and finally exits via the independent power turbine which has two stages of shrouded blades. The Gem can drive from either end, but existing Lynx versions take the drive to the front (inlet) end as described, the other end of the power shaft driving a bevel train in the exhaust cone connected to the free-turbine governor. Most Gems have very comprehensive accessory drives, and the Plessey hydromechanical control system incorporates fluidics circuits.

The Gem was one of the first turboshaft engines to be wholly modular, subdividing

A cutaway of a typical GEM, showing that today even small engines are quite complicated. On the left is the annular inlet, surrounding the double-helical reduction gear. Next comes the four-stage LP compressor, vertical bevel drive to the accessories, single centrifugal HP compressor, reverse (folded) flow combustion chamber, single-stage HP turbine (close-coupled to the HP compressor), single-stage LP turbine, and finally the two-stage free power turbine driving via a long central shaft to the reduction gear.

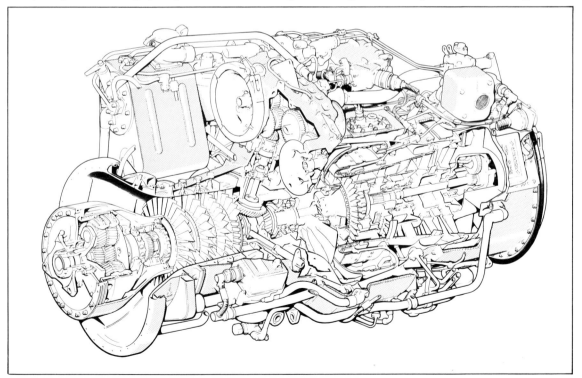

Left *Designated simply as the Rolls-Royce 1004, the production engine for the Agusta A129 Mangusta anti-tank helicopter is actually a direct-drive version of the Gem 2. Rated at 1,035 hp, it weighs 309 lb (140 kg).*

Right *Rolls-Royce and Turbomeca are using this Sikorsky S-70C to flight-test the RTM 322.*

into the reduction gearbox 01, power-turbine shaft 02, air-intake and LP compressor 03, accessory gearbox 04, HP spool and combustion module 05, LP turbine 06 and free power-turbine module 07. It is planned that, except for lifed rotating parts, all modules will be operated 'on condition'; most had attained this status by late 1987. The engine abounds in advanced features, such as the extensive use of friction welding between dissimilar metals and the incredible precision of EBW (electron-beam welding) needed to join pairs of fully machined helical gears so that they exactly share the tooth loading.

Leavesden used no fewer than fifty development engines and ran more than 40,000 hours in testing prior to 1980. This time included three intensive flight trials programmes, one at Bristol, one by a joint RN/RNethN unit at Yeovilton, and the third by the Army Air Corps at Middle Wallop. The early Lynxes consistently flew more than 100 hours per month, using the 900 shp Gem 2 Mk 100, weighing 330 lb,

with sfc of 0.65. The Agusta A.129 Mangusta anti-tank helicopter is powered by a version of the Gem 2 simply called the Rolls-Royce 1004, weighing 309 lb and with emergency power of 1,035 shp. This version has Hamilton Standard digital control. In 1978 the Gem 41 entered service, with a modified compressor system increasing mass flow from 7.0 to almost 8.0 lb/s, giving significantly higher powers to 1,120 shp for various Lynx and Westland 30 helicopters in numerous sub-versions. In 1983 the major growth engine, the Gem 60, entered service. This has a new LP compressor which increases airflow to about 9.5 lb/s, with a pr of 14 overall. Weighting 342 lb, various Gem 60s are in military and commercial service at conservative ratings of 1,203–1,260 shp. Beyond this the Gem has potential to go to at least 1,500 shp, mainly by running hotter and using cooled blades.

Obviously, there could be a lot more yet to come from the Gem, but like so many good aeronautical products the Gem is running into problems not of its own

making. Rolls-Royce has on the drawing board new engines in this class with higher performance yet with only two shafts and fewer compressor stages. Moreover, further increase in power brings the Gem into conflict with a newer engine, the RTM322.

Of all Rolls-Royce's smaller engines, the RTM322 appears likely to become by far the most important. Indeed the same basic core is hoped to go into production, with few changes, in turboshaft, turboprop and turbofan engines. All are expected to set record new levels of tough reliability, low weight, low fuel burn and low cost per shaft horsepower. The 322 is designed to make a head-on assault on the world market for shaft engines in the 1,800–3,000 hp class and for turbofans of 2,200–2,750 lb thrust. So far it could hardly have done better.

The programme began in 1979. At the Paris airshow in that year Rolls-Royce and Turbomeca of France both exhibited models of a proposed helicopter engine designated RTM321. This was said to incorporate all the experience gained by the two partners with such engines as the Gem and Makila to achieve simplicity, reliability, low costs and other good features. Its four modules included a three-stage axial followed by a centrifugal compressor, annular reverse-flow combustor, two-stage compressor and power turbines, and a drive to front or rear. Weight was put at 396 lb and contingency rating at 1,917 shp, to rise eventually to 2,500 shp.

A great deal of further effort refined the proposal into the RTM322, little changed on paper but actually a much more advanced engine, handling a greater airflow with the increased pr of 15. A fourth axial stage could be added later, to achieve a pr of 17.6–18, which is the optimum value for a future turboprop. Today's RTM322–01 engines actually weigh about 538 lb and have a contingency rating of 2,308 shp, with the outstanding cruise sfc of 0.48. Features include single-crystal HP turbine blades, the HP1 blades being cooled, a FADEC (Full-Authority Digital Electronic Control), choice of front or rear drive, air or electric starting systems, and the options of an inlet particle separator and (for military use) an infra-red suppressor.

It cannot be emphasized too strongly how great have been the advances in small gas turbines over the past twenty years, nor how important it is that Rolls-Royce, not only at Leavesden but at several RR locations in partnership, should be a world leader. In the United States the belief that the Army's LHX programme could lead to a run of at least 5,000 helicopters—now unlikely to be realized—has resulted in Allison/Garrett and Pratt and Whitney/ Textron Lycoming all concentrating on the 800-shp class, while for different markets General Electric is striving to wring a great

deal more power from the T700 designed in 1971. This has unexpectedly put the RTM322 in a very strong position, to the extent that Pratt & Whitney obtained an initial agreement in 1985 for licence rights for manufacture and marketing of the engine for US and Canadian government customers, and confirmed this in a definitive agreement in November 1986.

When the RTM322 was planned, the only visible market appeared to be the Anglo-Italian EH.101, at present flying with T700 engines. Next came the Sikorsky S–70 series, beginning with the UH–60A Black Hawk of the US Army and various S–70 export versions. In 1986 Rolls-Royce and Turbomeca acquired an S–70C, and on 14 June 1986

Major features of the RTM.322-01. As this book went to press this engine was battling with the GE T700 (CT7-6) to power production EH 101 helicopters. It would seem nonsense not to choose the newer and potentially much more powerful European engine, which has tremendous prospects as a T700 replacement in US helicopters.

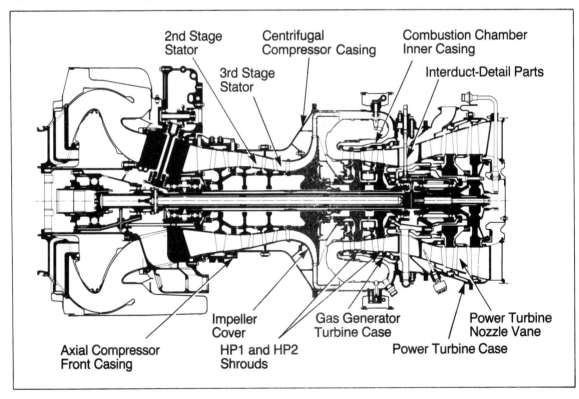

this flew with RTM322s, launching the engine's flight test programme. In October 1986 the first 150-hour type test was completed, by which time the engine in its original form had been run at 2,400 shp. By 1987 the S–70C, registered *G-RRTM* for the engine partners, was flying intensively at Bristol; pilots from an increasing range of companies and potential customers, including Sikorsky and the US Navy and Army, had commented favourably on the engine's overall behaviour and electronic control.

In February 1987 ground running began ahead of schedule in a US Navy SH–60B Seahawk at Sikorsky's test centre at West Palm Beach, flight development starting two months later. Throughout the summer this helicopter was flying at the Naval Air Test Center at Patuxent River, to evaluate the very large performance improvements possible, especially in hot/high conditions. The Navy is interested in the RTM322 for future SH–60B production, and also for the SH–60F Ocean Hawk (CV-HELO). The Army is studying the RTM322 not only for an uprated version of the UH–60A Black Hawk but also for the AH–64A Apache armed battlefield helicopter. Agusta of Italy has picked the engine for a planned single-engined version of the A129, named Tonal, and to this end Piaggio SpA signed an agreement in September 1986 for a 10% share in the engine programme, which could be increased in the event of an Italian order. The RTM322 is also by far the favoured engine for the potentially very large European NH90 (NATO helicopter 1990) programme.

Broadly, Rolls-Royce is responsible for the combustion chamber and turbines, and for an inlet particle separator if fitted, while Turbomeca handles the compressor, output shaft and torqumeter, and accessory gearbox. The control system and dressings are shared, a major supplier item being the FADEC which is by Lucas (UK) and ELECMA (France). Qualification to US MIL specification was due in 1988, with European military and civil certification following.

While development of the 322 continued to go splendidly in 1988, at the political level things could hardly have been more discouraging. Predictably the US Department of Defense, acting for all user services, placed a massive order for a further five years of production of the rival (and basically older and less powerful) T700. And without offering any explanation the British MoD announced in August that it would put off for at least six months deciding which engine would power the British versions of EH.101 Merlin. In the world of aerospace having a demonstrably superior product is often not enough.

As for derived versions, the immediate market would seem to be for a turboprop. The author was for many years surprised at the way in which Rolls-Royce appeared voluntarily to abandon the large market it had gained with the Dart. He once went so far as to write to the company expressing the view that, because the Dart had been around a long time and the price of each engine was peanuts compared with the RB.211, the management at Derby appeared to have adopted a *laissez faire* attitude which in the longer term would be seen to be gravely mistaken. He does not regret a word of this letter, but unfortunately nothing was done and the entire market so laboriously won by the Dart has been thrown away. Now, in the late 1980s, Rolls-Royce would like to climb back, and the only way to do so appears to be to mate the RTM322 with an axially centred reduction gear based on the latest Dart practice. In 1986 the company issued a brochure on the RB.550–02, which followed this formula but had an increased mass flow to give 3,200 shp to 20°C for a total weight of 1,300 lb, cruise sfc being 0.41. At the same time, a direct turboprop version of the RTM322 is also being studied, rated at 1,600–2,000 shp

Predictably the US Department of Defense decided in 1988 to stick with the all-American T700 rather than switch to the European RTM322, despite the latter's greater potential. Here an RTM322 was being readied for test at Leavesden in summer 1988.

with growth to 2,800 shp. In June 1987 Managing Director Sir Ralph Robins said 'There is a surprising lack of agreement about just what the airlines and manufacturers want. It may be that we shall simply have to take a decision ourselves'. As this book goes to press, Rolls-Royce has still done nothing publicly to recover its once global Dart market, but the position does not look wholly irretrievable. At a guess about one-quarter might be recovered.

In a much lower power category Rolls-Royce studied engines in the 600-shp class in the late 1960s, and from 1971 collaborated with Alfa Romeo of Italy and MTU of West Germany on projects designated the EPU 600 and ESU 600, the P and S meaning 'propeller' and 'shaft'. From 1977 this narrowed down to the RB.318, a 600-hp turboprop developed in partnership with the Italian company only, and test-flown by Alfa Romeo with complete success in a Beech King Air A90. In 1980, in accord with

a prior agreement, the programme was transferred entirely to Alfa Romeo, the engine being redesignated AR.318. By late 1987 over fourteen engines had run more than 5,000 hours, and RAI (Italian) certification had been achieved, but no applications had been announced.

In 1978 France and Germany appeared to be trying to reinvent the wheel, launching the MTU/Turbomeca MTM385 with a specification closely resembling the Gem. This engine was considered to be needed to power the Eurocopter family of battlefield helicopters. The first gas generator, or core engine, ran in 1979, but over the following eight years the concept was changed into the MTR390, Rolls-Royce joining as a third risk-sharing partner. The MTR390 is a straightforward single-shaft engine, with two tandem centrifugal stages, reverse-annular combustor, single-stage air-cooled core turbine, and two-stage free power turbine, to be rated at about 1,200 shp. In

RR (Bristol and Leavesden), Westland, Sikorsky and various potential customers have all been encouraged by the excellent performance improvement and reliability of twin RTM322-01 engines flying in this S-70C Black Hawk.

April 1985 Rolls-Royce joined with Turbomeca and MTU in the European Small Engines Co-operation Agreement aimed at preserving a strong European capability in engines for military helicopters and related markets. The agreement included the RTM-322 at the top end of the power range, the MTM385 and the small TM333. It is the MTM385 which has been refined into the MTR390, which is still intended to power the Eurocopters.

Rolls-Royce has also assumed responsibility for supporting the 1,119-shp Garrett TPE331–12B turboprop which powers the RAF Shorts Tucano T.1 basic trainer. Rolls-Royce also produces up to 30% by value of each of these engines for RAF service.

Chapter 19

TODAY'S MILITARY JETS

Virtually all modern combat aircraft are powered by turbofans of low bpr, engines for supersonic aircraft being fitted with what Americans call afterburning, the British call reheat, and which strictly (for a turbofan in which extra fuel is burned in both the core jet and bypass air) is better called augmentation. One of the first engines in this category was the Spey 202/203, described in Chapter 9, designed in 1965. At just the same time Rolls-Royce (Derby) and the French Société Turbomeca were beginning to work together on a smaller engine to power the Anglo-French Jaguar.

This aircraft was planned as a light strike fighter and advanced trainer. Rolls-Royce had studied a design designated RB.172, while Turbomeca had drawn the T260. It was found that these could be merged into a joint proposal which was later named Adour, thus preserving the RR tradition of the names of rivers but choosing one which flows near the Turbomeca plant at Tarnos in extreme south-western France. No attempt was made to design to the limits of what was attainable, but instead to create a simple, robust augmented turbofan that would give long and reliable service, with good FOD (foreign-object damage) resistance, easy maintenance and low costs, despite the arduous nature of the low-level attack and military training roles. Rolls-

Royce Turbomeca Ltd was formed in 1966 to manage the programme, and today it also manages the RTM322 described in the preceding chapter.

The Adour first ran at Derby on 9 May 1967. Turbomeca has responsibility for the two-stage fan (LP compressor), five-stage HP compressor, intermediate casing, external gearbox and pipework. Rolls-Royce is responsible for the combustion chamber, turbines and jetpipe, though where an afterburner is fitted this is subcontracted to SNECMA to preserve the 50/50 Anglo-French parity in manufacturing.

The bpr was fixed at only 0.8 to hold the inlet diameter to only 22 in, mass flow being 95 lb/s, and overall pr is modest at 11. There are no inlet guide vanes or variable stators, and the HP bleed valve is open only during starting. The drive shafts have curvic couplings which enable complete compressor or turbine modules to be removed and replaced without the need for rebalancing. The annular combustion chamber has eighteen airspray burners and gives smokeless burning. The simple hydro-mechanical fuel control is based on that of the Dart turboprop. Both turbines have single stages, the HP rotor blades being air-cooled. Originally the afterburner, which has four vapour gutter rings and twin platinum/rhodium catalytic igniters, was fully variable only over a boost range from 30 to 50% of maximum dry thrust. The sudden jump from 100 to 130% thrust on selecting reheat proved undesirable—for example during single-engined approach— and soon the original Adour Mk 102 for the Jaguar was modified to give smooth modulation of thrust over the entire range. This feature, at first called PTR (part-throttle reheat) and now known as PTA (part-throttle afterburning), enables the afterburner to remain lit while the engine is throttled back to only about 30% power.

Partly because the engine and airframe were developed in parallel, and also because the HATF (High Altitude Test Facility) at Derby had then been completed, it was decided not to fly the Adour in a testbed aircraft. The first flight was thus also the first flight of a Jaguar (E.01) on 8 September 1968. The original fluted (multi-lobe) mixer

was replaced by a plain annular mixer, and a lot of work was needed to perfect the afterburner, but ten Mk 101 production engines were delivered in 1971, followed by the main run of Mk 102 Adours for production Jaguars. These weighed 1,556 lb and were rated at 5,115 lb dry and 7,305 lb with maximum afterburner, which compares well with the design objectives of 'over 4,400 lb' and 'over 6,600 lb' respectively. From 1972 IHI in Japan has been producing an almost identical engine, the Adour 801A, with US-style Japanese designation of TF40–IHI–801A. This powers the Mitsubishi T–2 and F–1, 430 being delivered.

In 1976 the Mk 804 was qualified to power export Jaguar International aircraft, with take-off thrust increased over the Mk 102 by 10% to 8,040 lb, and thrust at Mach 0.9 at low level increased by 28%. The RAF engines have been modified to the almost identical

Adour flight time is approaching 3 million hours, most of it logged in the severe environment of Jaguar low-level attack aircraft. This afterburning Mk 804 is installed in a Jaguar of No 8 Squadron, Sultan of Oman's air force. At 117 inches, it is probably the shortest afterburning engine in squadron service in history.

Latest of the Adours, the Mk 861-49 is also known as the F405-RR-400. It powers the T-45A Goshawk, future pilot trainer of the US Navy, which predicts fuel savings of 60 per cent.

Mk 104 standard. In 1981 the Mk 811 engine was qualified for Indian Jaguars, subsequently being assembled by Hindustan Aeronautics with an increasing local content. This version has a new fan and improved combustor, turbine and afterburner, to give dry and afterburning ratings of 5,520 and 8,400 lb.

In 1975 production began of the non-afterburning Mk 151 for the BAe Hawk. This engine weighs 1,220 lb and is rated at 5,200 lb, being almost identical to the Mk 102 except for the jetpipe, apart from minor rematching and the provision of dual control amplifiers and a drive for a second hydraulic pump. Export Hawks have the almost identical Adour 851, those for Finland being assembled by Valmet in 1981–85. From 1981 export Hawks have had the option of the Mk 861, based on the uprated Mk 811

and with a thrust of 5,700 lb. Most powerful of the Hawk engines is the Mk 871, fitted to the Hawk 100 and 200 combat variants and rated at 5,845 lb. The US Navy's T–45A Goshawk is powered by the F405–RR–400 (Adour 861–49), derated to 5,450 lb, a derivative of the 861 modified for long-life, low-cost operation from aircraft carriers. At the time of writing, over 2,200 Adour engines worldwide had flown about 2.7 million hours.

As this book was written, the Advanced Military Engines team at Bristol, under Chief Engineer Alaster Duncan, was studying the pros and cons of building a demonstrator for a next-generation Adour. This engine, the ADX, would support the development of a family of RB.543 engines with thrusts from 5,000 to 12,000 lb. They are being discussed with Turbomeca. With a vigorous component-improvement programme for existing Adours in full swing, it was appropriate in 1988 to decide on the Adour's long-term future.

The biggest programme for a combat aircraft engine in Western Europe is that for the RB.199, which powers all versions of the Tornado as well as the single BAe EAP demonstrator. The choice of engine for the Tornado was narrowed in summer 1969 to the Pratt & Whitney JTF16 and the RB.199 designed by Rolls-Royce Bristol. The European engine was picked on 4 September 1969, and a month later a company called Turbo-Union Ltd was formed to manage the engine programme. Shares are held by Rolls-Royce (40%), MTU (40%) and Fiat (20%). Work went ahead under high pressure, and the first RB.199 ran in September 1971. Very extensive ground testing involved no fewer than four altitude cells, among other facilities, while a Vulcan carrying a replica of the right side of a Tornado fuselage, complete with 27-mm gun, opened the flight programme in April 1973. The first Tornado flew with early RB.199–01 engines on 14 August 1974.

Cycling the reverser of a prototype RB.199 in 1972. The stripes on the afterburner skin are temperature-sensitive paint.

The RB.199 was required to meet an exceptional set of requirements. Tornado aircraft have to undertake almost every kind of tactical task at all levels and in all weathers, as well as long-distance air interception and training. The engine obviously had to be an augmented turbofan of modular design, cleared to 60,000 ft and at least Mach 2.2 but (in most Tornado versions) likely to spend most of its life at very low altitudes at the unprecedented indicated airspeed of up to 800 kt (902 mph). The design chosen has three shafts and an extraordinarily compact combined augmentor (afterburner) and reverser, resulting in an engine with tremendous FOD (birdstrike) resistance, an exceptionally wide operating envelope, no variable blading, outstanding cruise sfc, and an augmentation boost of almost 90%. In comparison with its most immediate rival, the GE F404, the basic Mk 103 engine has higher airflow (160 against

142 lb/s), lighter weight (2,040 lb without reverser against 2,180 lb), slightly greater maximum thrust (16,100 against 16,000 lb) and shorter length (128 against 158.8 in despite incorporating a reverser).

The LP compressor has three stages of robust titanium blades in welded discs overhung ahead of the front bearing, with a bpr of about unity. The IP compressor also has three stages, and rotates in the same direction as the LP but naturally faster. The HP spool rotates in the opposite direction (anti-clockwise, seen from the rear) and has six stages with the discs held by ten through-bolts. Overall pr exceeds 23. The combustion chamber is annular, and has thirteen double-headed T-shaped vaporizers giving smokeless burning. Entry temperature to the single-stage air-cooled HP turbine exceeds 1,327°C, the cooling air passing out through holes in the leading and trailing edges and the tip of each blade. The IP tur-

Left *Rolls-Royce and its partners in Turbo-Union had delivered roughly 2,000 RB.199 engines as this book went to press, most of them similar to this Mk 103. Its compactness (including reverser) is obvious; less evident is its unrivalled fuel economy.*

Right *An RB.199 Mk 105 on flight development in Germany. The much-used development Tornado has a sooty fin from numerous reversed thrust landings.*

bine also has a single stage of cooled blades, while the LP turbine has two stages of solid blades.

The augmentor is coupled directly behind the core, with no mixing section. In the core flow are two gutter rings fed by upstream atomizers, while the bypass duct contains a reverse colander with large radial extensions each housing a primary vaporizing burner and with pairs of additional jets in the gaps between them. The convergent nozzle has fourteen master and fourteen secondary petals, precision-cast in cobalt alloy and positioned by a translating shroud driven by a bleed-air motor. Numerous detailed studies have confirmed the decision not to have a variable divergent section. The reverser is of the twin-bucket target type, which in the stowed position forms the top and bottom of the rear fuselage. Rocking the pilot's throttle levers to the left selects reverser operation at any setting up to maximum dry thrust, cycling taking one second. The engine control system is an optimized mix of electronics, pneumatics and hydromechanics, the central full-authority box being the MECU (main electronic control unit).

Initial flying was done with RB.199–01

engines rated at about 7,000 lb dry and 14,000 lb maximum. By the time of the FQT (Formal Qualification Test) in November 1978 the Tornado prototypes were flying with the –02 engine, with increased annulus area in the IP and LP turbines to give increased thrust at reduced temperatures. The initial production engine was the Mk 101, superseded in 1983 by the Mk 103, the production engine installed in most Tornados, which offers a small improvement in sea level performance to dry and maximum ratings of 9,100 and 16,100 lb respectively, together with a significant extension of life. The RAF's Tornado F.3 interceptor has Mk 104 engines with a jetpipe lengthened by 14 in, to give a thrust increase of 8% coupled with a useful reduction in sfc. This engine, which also powers export interceptor versions, is the first in the world to have a FADEC (full-authority digital electronic control) without a mechanical back-up. Mk 104 engines without reversers or APU/secondary-power drives are fitted to the EAP aircraft. The Luftwaffe Tornado ECR is to enter service in 1989, powered by the Mk 105 engine. This incorporates the Type 62B fan of greater pr, as well as single-crystal HP turbine

blades. As well as providing major life-cycle cost improvements, the Mk 105 is capable of thrust increase of up to 10%, to well over 17,000 lb at sea level. This represents a major step towards full clearance of the RB.199B with a thrust increase of at least 20%.

For many years Rolls-Royce has been working on studies for new fighter engines, in the ACME (advanced-core military engine) programme. In 1982 Ministry of Defence support was forthcoming for an advanced-technology demonstrator, the XG.40. Following rig testing, a complete XG.40 went on test in December 1986, and on its first full-reheat run exceeded 20,000 lb thrust. By this time the governments of

Britain, West Germany, Italy and Spain had agreed a common Air Staff Requirement for an EFA (European Fighter Aircraft). In August 1986 the engine companies of the four nations—Rolls-Royce, MTU, Fiat and SENER—formed a company similar in structure to Turbo-Union to manage the EFA engine programme. Respective share-holdings are 33%, 33%, 21% and 13%. The company is called EUROJET Turbo GmbH, and is registered in Munich. The engine is known as the EJ200, and it is similar in configuration to the XG.40.

In general the EJ200 is of fractionally smaller size and weight than the RB.199, though the thermodynamic cycle is matched

The XG.40 was built to test and demonstrate new technologies for future fighter engines.

to the different flight envelope of an air-combat fighter and the overall design reflects today's great emphasis on minimizing life-cycle costs. The EJ200 is thus the simplest new fighter engine in the Western world; it has only 1,800 fixed and moving aerofoils, compared with 2,845 for the RB.199, and the total parts-count is much less than half that of earlier or competitor engines.

Predictably, the EJ200 is a two-spool augmented turbofan, with the very low bpr of about 0.4. The three-stage fan has blades which, compared with those of the RB.199, seem enormous. Forged in advanced titanium alloy, they have a thin

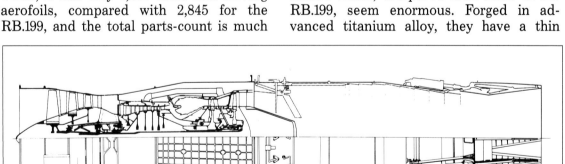

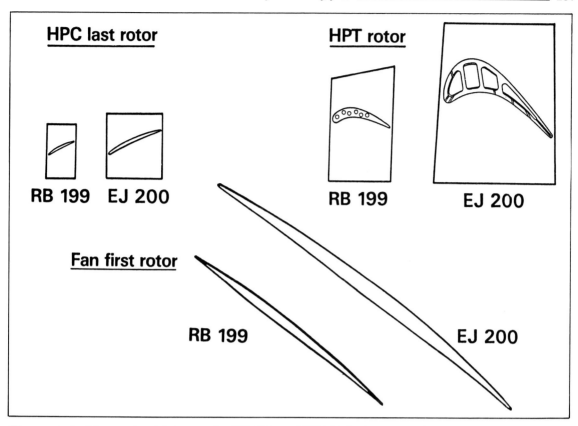

HPC last rotor

RB 199   EJ 200

HPT rotor

RB 199   EJ 200

Fan first rotor

RB 199   EJ 200

The most startling contrast between the RB.199 and EJ.200 is the comparison of blade size. Here are typical cross sections of the first fan stage (which must resist bird strikes), final HP compressor stage and the high-pressure turbine rotor (which also shows the EJ.200's more sophisticated air cooling). Work per stage is roughly doubled in tomorrow's engine.

lenticular section, the outer half being transonic. FOD resistance should be exceptional. The third stage is a blisk, blades and disc being integral. A single row of variable stators leads to the five-stage HP compressor, with blisks welded into one unit and active clearance control. Overall pr exceeds 25—not bad from eight stages! The annular combustor has vaporizing burners pointing downstream and advanced cooling and protection. The HP turbine has low-density single-crystal air-cooled blades, and the LP turbine also has single-crystal blades, both turbines having a single stage with a powder-metallurgy disc. A short duct leads to the high-efficiency augmentor of

the burn-then-mix type, and the nozzle is of the convergent/divergent type for peak supersonic performance. The EJ200 will have brush seals, a central gearbox driven via the interstage support, a FADEC control system, integrated health monitoring, and a rapidly spinning oil tank to give the lubrication system artificial positive gravity at all times.

EUROJET's Managing Director is Colin Green, from RR Bristol. In early 1987 the company submitted to NEFMA (NATO EFA Management Agency) a fully costed technical proposal for the EJ200, and then had to wait until 16 May 1988 to get a decision to start full development. (Even then, as this was written, Spain had failed to ratify the EFA Memo, and said the chief problem was SENER's apparent inability to handle its part in the EJ200 programme!) Though the engine's overall dimensions are rather smaller than the RB.199, the mass flow is greater and the initial thrust rating will be in the 20,000-lb class. In combat the thrust would be '23% greater than that of the RB.199'. The proposed worksplit is: RR, combustion system, HP turbine and intermediate casing; MTU, fan and HP compressor; Fiat, LP turbine and shaft, interstage support, augmentation (reheat) system, gearbox and oil system; and SENER, bypass duct, exhaust diffuser, jetpipe and nozzle. Each partner would assemble complete engines, and would also support engines of its national air force.

The first DVE (design verification engine) was to run before the end of 1988, and entry into service is predicted for 1995.

With a T/W ratio of 10, EJ200 will be a competitive engine. The ACME technology can lead to a T/W of 12, and Duncan has launched ACME II aiming at a T/W of 20 by 2005. This, he concedes, 'may be overly ambitious. For one thing, we have a new element in the equation in the customer demand for nine years of tough combat duty with minimal maintenance and cost. The author ought not to inject his own opinions, but cannot help commenting that any combat aircraft designed today ought to be a total 'stealth' design able to operate without needing conventional airfields. Astovl is the obvious way to go, surely?

Chapter 20

THE FUTURE

With the EJ200 and RTM322 Rolls-Royce can see a probable future extending into the next century, and a turboprop derivative of the 322 also appears likely to have a long life ahead. But in the matter of small jet engines for trainers, business jets and similar markets, the company has failed to produce a successor to the Viper and will now find such an engine difficult to launch. Likewise it has no turbofan in the 5,000–10,000-lb thrust class, nor a turboprop in the 1,000-hp class, and it must be galling to see all the British Aerospace civil aircraft—Jetstream, BAe 125, ATP, BAe 146 and the entire Airbus range—powered exclusively by foreign engines.

In the matter of combat aircraft, the need to survive in war must eventually force air forces to give up operating from airbases of known location, and to use instead low-observable 'stealth' aircraft with both STOVL and supersonic performance. To the author this indicates widespread use of vectored-thrust engines with a very large airflow for quietness and low IR signature. At present, following five years of conferences, planning meetings and in 1985 a three-phase review, work is at last going ahead in Britain and the USA under the terms of a five-year MoU (Memorandum of Understanding) signed in January 1986.

The first tier of management comprises four officials from the Department of Defense, NASA and the Ministry of Defense, with a second tier of eleven from the MoD, NASA, USAF and USN. Current work is

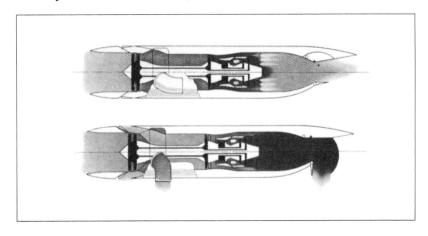

One of the more attractive schemes for a future Astovl engine is the hybrid fan, on which Rolls-Royce has worked with Vought, the US Navy and others. It resembles a 'three-poster' version of the Pegasus, but with hinged and translating doors to separate the fan and core airflows in jet-borne flight.

aimed at picking a configuration for an Astovl (said as a word, but meaning Advanced STOVL) with all technology proven and demonstrated, by 1995. This is matched to an in-service date between 2005 and 2010 (so nobody had better start a war for the next twenty years). Four configurations are being examined. Rolls-Royce and Lockheed are looking at tandem-fan or hybrid-fan arrangements. McDonnell Douglas and Pratt & Whitney are concentrating on the traditional vectored turbofan. Grumman and GE are studying the RALS (remote augmented lift system). General Dynamics and GE are collaborating on ejector-lift arrangements. British Aerospace and Rolls-Royce are keeping an eye on the whole lot. There is exchange of information 'on a balanced basis' between the partners. Just who might share in eventual production has yet to be determined, but in January 1986 Rolls-Royce signed an agreement with Pratt & Whitney for collaboration within

the terms of the MoU, and it can probably be taken as certain that both companies will be involved in whatever Astovl is finally selected.

The author cannot comprehend how aircraft parked on airfields could survive in a future war, but at present conventional fighters continue to absorb massive amounts of funding. For their propulsion, augmented turbofans designed almost perfectly by computer, and 'got right first time', will use higher work-per-stage fans and compressors to achieve a pr well beyond 20 with fewer and fewer stages, while ever-greater turbine gas temperatures will enable more power to be wrung from smaller engines. The results are already dramatic. The diagram comparing the engine of the RAF Phantoms with successive later generations of Rolls-Royce fighter engines makes one wonder how far the process of miniaturization can continue. Already we have achieved in long-life supersonic fighter engines the thrust/

Engines for supersonic fighters are getting smaller, hotter and simpler. Four generations of Rolls-Royce fighter jets are shown here, without afterburners, all scaled to the same dry thrust at Mach 0.75 at sea level. T/W ratio is shown at the right. The simplicity is to some degree superficial, because such items as flame tubes and turbine blades get ever more 'hi-tech'.

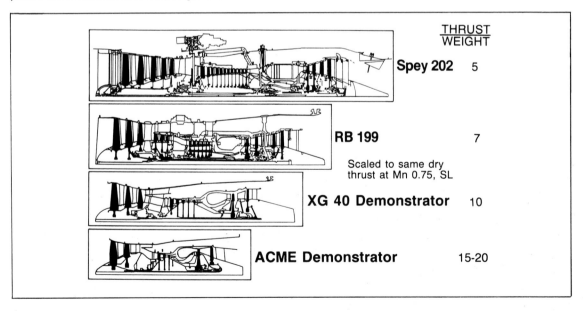

	THRUST / WEIGHT
Spey 202	5
RB 199	7
Scaled to same dry thrust at Mn 0.75, SL	
XG 40 Demonstrator	10
ACME Demonstrator	15-20

weight ratio that 25 years ago was thought amazing for a short-life specialized lift jet. Equally important is the fact that fewer parts means lower total cost of ownership, and probably higher reliability. Certainly, Rolls-Royce means to stay in the forefront with military engines.

This leaves to be discussed one of the biggest and most fascinating markets, the propulsion of commercial transports, or, as they are called in Britain, airliners. Here there are many conflicting factors, and even conflicting requirements. Obviously future engines must retain the almost perfect reliability of today's large turbofans, as well as having the lowest possible total cost of ownership. But the decisions taken by the engine manufacturer are complicated by such factors as the large and capricious rises and falls in the price of fuel, the extremely long timescale of a new engine programme, the rapid and often unpredictable advance in technologies, and the enormous financial risk of the major choices. This is not the place to analyse the problem, but clearly in any breakdown of operating costs the price of fuel, and engine-related costs generally, are relatively unimportant in small short-haul and commuter aircraft, but dominant in long-range aircraft. Over a sector of 3,500 miles, for example, fuel alone accounts for some 40% of the total operating cost. A further important factor is that, even if fuel were to cost nothing, an engine offering improved efficiency would enable an airliner to carry more or fly further (for the same size) or be made significantly smaller and cheaper (for the same range and payload).

The giant question which has been intensively studied for years by everyone interested in air transport is how far propfans and turbofans of very high (say, over 15) bpr will supersede today's engines, and in what timescale. The only new (post-1985) large jetliners now being built in the West are the A320, A330/340, 747–300/400,

and MD-11, and all have conventional turbofan engines. To the embarrassment of Airbus Industrie, IAE discussed a Super-Fan derivative of the V.2500 to power the A340 and then, after one customer had picked this aircraft/engine combination, concluded the feasibility study. The media got the idea that IAE had somehow 'cancelled' the SuperFan. Nothing could be further from the truth; Rolls-Royce, Pratt & Whitney and their partners in IAE have no doubt whatever that engines of this type, with a ducted fan of bpr 10 to 15, will be built, and hope that a lot of them will use a core derived from the V.2500. The trouble with the A340 was that the aircraft manufacturer wanted a guaranteed certificated engine ready for delivery to airline customers from May 1992, and IAE considered that they were unable to make such a promise. From the public relations viewpoint they could hardly have played things worse!

Not least of the problems with future high-bpr engines is that they can be arranged in many different ways. The most obvious is to adhere to today's turbofan formula, with a tractor fan on the front, but with the fan relatively larger and driven via a reduction gear. A second arrangement, pioneered by General Electric, is to add extra intermeshing contra-rotating turbines in the gas flow downstream of the core engine and mount the propfan blades around the outside of these. This has many advantages, and about the same number of disadvantages. Another arrangement, pioneered jointly by Allison and Pratt & Whitney, assisted by propfan pioneer Hamilton Standard, is to put the gearbox behind the core and drive pusher contra-rotating propfans.

GE's UDF (unducted fan) had flown in two successive versions by late 1987, and the PW/Allison 578DX pusher was about to fly. This gives the impression that Rolls-Royce is an also-ran in what could be the universal form of propulsion for all major airliners, but the author takes a more encouraging view. In major advances in technology it sometimes pays to sit on the fence for a while, whilst continuing to fund research at the greatest rate that can be afforded. This is just what Rolls-Royce has done, and indeed continues to do. As this was written, in late 1988, the company had proposed three quite dissimilar types of advanced civil engine. All are apparently superior to engines already flying in the USA, and picked for the Boeing 7J7 which in 1987 was put on ice. The crunch, of course, is that at some time at least one of these new RR engines will probably have to be committed to full development. This costs much more than mere research, and there is no room for mistakes.

Models of the three configurations were exhibited at the 1987 Paris airshow. All have RB numbers, but as these are liable to change some will be omitted. The most con-

ventional engine is thus the GFDF (geared front ducted fan). Matched to the propulsion of fast (up to Mach 0.9) long-range transports, this would be installed in a wing-mounted pod looking not very different from that for an RB.211, though the diameter would be greater. The single-stage fan would have a diameter of perhaps 120 in, the bpr being about 15. Take-off rating might be a little over 70,000 lb.

An alternative much favoured by the company is the Contrafan, originally the RB.529. This comprises a high-efficiency core mounted as a gas generator in front of tandem sets of free power turbines each directly driving a single-stage fan, the two units rotating in opposite directions and the whole assembly being enclosed in an efficient duct. This has a great deal in common with the Griffith CR.1 of 1940. In some ways this also resembles a ducted version of GE's UDF, but it offers several significant advan-

Today the notion that the optimum bypass ratio for an airline turbofan could be less than unity is totally discredited. Indeed, parametric studies are throwing up answers in double figures, but to match the contrasting speeds of the LP turbine and fan demands a gearbox. This shows a typical engine study, but nobody is enamoured at the idea of developing a gearbox for an engine in the RB.211 class.

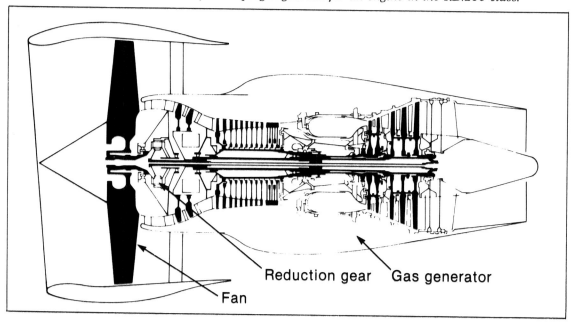

Reduction gear   Gas generator

Fan

Above *Rolls-Royce is spending quite substantial sums trying to make certain what the various possible future civil-transport engine concepts have to offer. Rather surprisingly, it devoted some of the money to this impressive full-scale model of the RB.529 Contrafan in one example.*

Below *October 1985 artwork showing how an A340-style aircraft might look with Contrafans. The pylon strut comes round the top of the fan case and down to carry the forward-projecting core.*

tages. One is the duct, which reduces noise, increases efficiency and contains shed blades. In late 1986 David Marshall, who heads new civil projects, wrote 'The Contra-fan will be tested at model size to measure aerodynamic and noise performance, and the requirement for a lightweight low-drag nacelle will be supported by a structural and aerodynamic programme. This . . . will be a two- to three-year effort. It will probably lead to a full-scale demonstration including flight test, so that the decision to launch a production programme could be taken on the basis of a full-scale evaluation in the early 1990s.'

The third concept is, of course, the geared open fan or propfan. Rolls-Royce has done extensive work on such engines, and incidentally is flying the last airworthy Gannet AEW.3 at Hucknall to obtain useful data on noise from contra-rotating propellers.

After careful study the company has come to the conclusion that the preferred configuration is the contra-rotating geared pusher, broadly similar to the PW/Allison 578DX but very greatly improved. The American engine has its core, gearbox and fan arranged in series, one behind the other. It also has a long rear cone, and the hot gas from the core flows past the roots of the propfan blades. By integrating a different type of gearbox into the propfan hub, Rolls-Royce found that the powerplant could be made 32 in shorter and 800 lb lighter.

Further work led to today's RB.509 propfan concept, which retains the integrated gearbox but has an annular core exhaust to give a 'clean and cool' propfan environment and a short rear cone. Compared with the 578DX, this 13,000-hp engine would be a remarkable 92 in shorter

The unshrouded propfan is applicable in low and medium power levels (say, below 20,000 shp) to medium-range aircraft cruising at between Mn 0.7 and 0.8. Use of a speed-reducing gearbox allows speeds of the three-stage power turbine and the propellers to be optimized. This engine could readily be an aft-mounted pusher or a wing-mounted tractor.

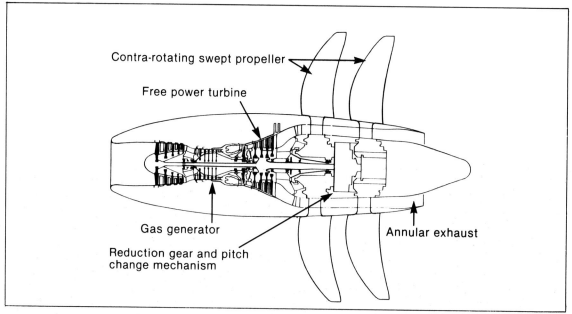

A model of the RB.509 in which the core drives contra-rotating open prop-fans via a very neat gearbox integrated into the hubs. This has significant advantages over today's PW-Allison 578DX, but on the other hand the US engine exists and is flying.

and 1,500 lb lighter! This engine would also require only a modest core pr and turbine entry temperature. It would have a single rear power turbine, the drive from which is translated into two contra-rotating outputs inside the hub, both including the mechanism to vary the pitch of the blades. The biggest single new item of test plant so far built to underpin the new civil engines is a 15,000-hp gearbox test facility. In another research programme the 535E4 hollow fan blade technology is being investigated in trial manufacturing of propfan blades.

Thus, while not the first to fly new propfan engines, Rolls-Royce intends to remain fully competitive in the propulsion

The most costly single research tool built by Rolls-Royce for research into future airline engines is this rig for testing 15,000-horsepower gearboxes. Strange: 30 years ago gearboxes were things the most advanced airlines no longer had!

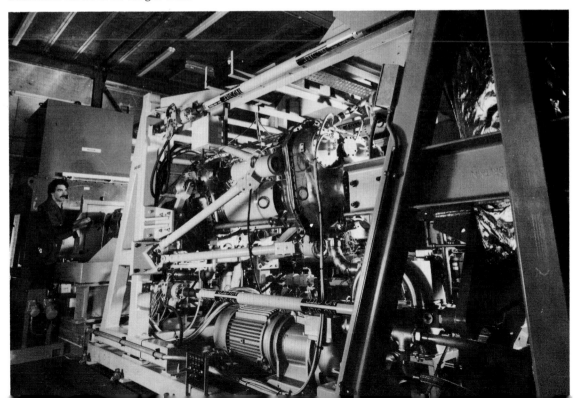

of future airliners. It is a field where even the biggest customer airlines are technically extended in trying to understand the alternatives, and acquire an ability to weigh up what they are told by the makers of engines and aircraft. Never before have the airlines been able to hear such a clashing cacophony of contrasting views. Nobody's opinions carry more weight than those of Rolls-Royce. I am grateful to the then Technical Director D. J. Pickerell for the following:

'The propfan, as pioneered by Hamilton Standard and NASA, is undoubtedly the most innovative attempt to improve fuel consumption since the advent of the high-bpr turbofans twenty years ago. Compared with a JT8D, improvements of about 50% in cruise fuel consumption have been demonstrated during flight tests, although it should be noted that, against the best conventional turbofan that will be available in the same timescale as the propfan, the improvement is more like 20%.

'There is virtually unanimous agreement from everyone working on propfans that, due to noise and installation considerations, the preferred configuration is a contra-rotating pusher mounted as a twin at the rear of the fuselage. This, plus the fact that the optimum propfan cruise speed is probably somewhat below Mach 0.8 rather than above it, means that the propfan is most applicable to short/medium-haul twins of small/medium size, such as the Boeing 7J7, MD–91X and –92X. For this type of operation, first cost has a more powerful impact on direct operating cost than fuel burn (at currently foreseeable fuel prices). Thus, it has not been apparent that the modest improvement in direct operating cost from the improved fuel burn of the propfan, compared with the best conventional turbofan to be available, is sufficient to justify the large non-recurring investment required. In addition, although the noise characteristics of the propfan are sufficiently well understood to predict compliance with FAR Part

36 St.3 with confidence, it is not yet clear that the technology exists to achieve the more stringent local airport noise levels which are now essential for any new short/medium-haul aircraft.

'Thus, rather than embarking on premature demonstrator engine programmes, Rolls-Royce has preferred to concentrate on technology acquisition aimed at refining some of the technical issues and at designing a powerplant optimized for lowest direct operating cost rather than lowest fuel burn. The RB.509–11 proposal with contra-rotating propeller blades driven by an integral gearbox and annular exhaust was derived in 1986, and is identical to the configuration that Pratt & Whitney/Allison have now [1988] concluded is the optimum.

'For medium/long-haul operation, where fuel burn does have a more powerful impact on direct operating cost, the propfan seems less applicable. Notwithstanding the expansion of EROPS*, some operators will wish to have more than two engines for long overwater routes, which calls for cowled engines which can be installed underwing. In addition the trend to higher cruise speeds for long-haul operation (M 0.85) militates against the open rotor.

'Thus for this type of operation, Rolls-Royce has been studying cowled ultra-high-bpr fan engines. With a bpr of 12–15, the disparity between the low rotational speed of the fan and the high rotational speed of the LP turbine can be resolved by the use of a reduction gearbox of about 3:1 ratio. For a 30,000-lb static-thrust engine this gearbox would have to transmit up to about 20,000 shp. Whilst this is three times higher than any aero reduction gearbox in service in the Western world, the low reduction ratio means that the output torque—the limiting design criterion—is of the same order as for the Tyne turboprop. Such a

_____

*Extended-range (overwater) operations with twin-engined aircraft.

geared front-fan engine with a slimline cowl to minimise cowl drag could use an existing core (as was proposed with SuperFan).

'For much larger high-bpr cowled engines of over 60,000 lb static thrust the use of such a front-fan geared configuration would require a reduction gearbox of up to 50,000 shp. It is not apparent that lightweight reliable gearboxes of this size are viable, and it is for this size of engine that Rolls-Royce has been pursuing the Contrafan configuration.'

From Chapter 7 onwards it has been emphasized how inexorable is the pressure for engines to be run at ever increasing temperature. Rolls-Royce is a world leader in the search for improved refractory materials, and this search inevitably involves moving away from metals—even the latest so-called 'superalloys'—and into the field of ceramics and metal-matrix composites. As far back as 1959 the author had on his desk a test specimen of Rolls-Royce composite consisting of an aluminium matrix containing hair-like fibres of silicon carbide, but of course this had little to do with high temperatures. Today the company is testing a wealth of advanced materials, such as (in ascending order of thermal capability) silicon nitride, silicon carbide, chromium oxide, alumina, calcium oxide, yttrium oxide, zirconium oxide, boron nitride, zirconium boride, titanium boride, hafnium boride, thorium oxide and carbon/carbon. Among a host of problems are inherent brittleness and the difficulty of avoiding flaws in the sub-microscopic bulk structure which can lead to sudden catastrophic failure. Conversely, the good news is that the company can see no thermal barrier, even in the far distance.

For an even more distant future Rolls-

As this book went to press the RB.545 Hotol engine was still classified, but this greatly simplified block diagram shows the basic principle. From take-off up to Mach 5 at 85,000 ft the engine works as a turbo-jet, taking in air at the left. The air is cooled and made denser by passing through a clever heat exchanger cooled by the liquid hydrogen fuel. The latter drives the turbine connected to the air compressor. Above Mach 5 the turbomachinery is throttled down and valved off, and the onboard liquid oxygen starts to be used, turning the engine into a space rocket.

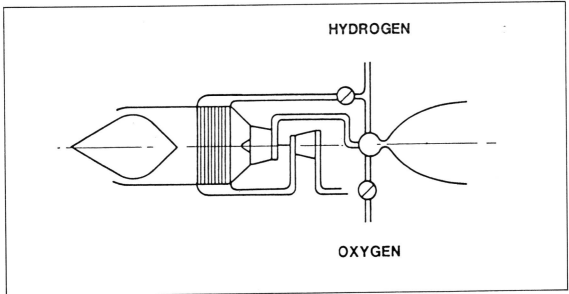

HYDROGEN

OXYGEN

It is tragically shortsighted that France is gathering international partners to try to reinvent the Space Shuttle, because Hotol could do the same job for a fraction of the initial cost and an even smaller fraction of the cost per launch. It is considerably smaller, and nothing has to be thrown away on each mission. But when nationalistic issues are involved, few people are big enough to consider the facts.

Royce has a small team working on the RB.545, the exciting propulsion concept for the British Aerospace Hotol (HOrizontal Take-Off and Landing). Why Hotol is exciting is because, after taking off like any conventional aeroplane, it goes on to fly into orbit or out into space, thereafter returning to make a normal landing. It thus promises enormous advantages in cost and convenience over traditional rocket-launched vehicles such as the American Shuttle Orbiter and the French-sponsored Hermès. Most unfortunately, the British government has chosen to adopt an extremely narrow and shortsighted attitude to spaceflight, saying 'If it's so promising, industry and the banks can finance it'. One might have thought that an objective assessment of Hotol, which takes off and flies for the first nine minutes on atmospheric oxygen, thereafter using on-board lox supplies, might serve to convince even the British Treasury that in the longer term this was another Whittle—something potentially so important that it needs men with strategic vision to see the possibilities. Probably this is yet another British invention that we will appreciate only when the technology has been taken over by others. Rolls-Royce hope for the miracle to happen, putting us in a competitive position in the 21st century.

Appendix 1

PISTON ENGINES

PISTON ENGINES	Config- uration	Cool- ing	Bore × stroke (mm)	Capacity (litres)	Take-off rating	High-altitude rating	Dry weight (kg)
Eagle I	V12	W	114.3 × 165	20.32	225 hp at 1,800 rpm	-	372
Eagle VIII	V12	W	114.3 × 165	20.32	375 hp at 2,000 rpm	-	384
Hawk	L 6	W	101.6 × 152.4	7.414	100 hp at 1,500 rpm	-	184
Falcon I	V12	W	101.6 × 146	14.2	228 hp at 1,800 rpm	-	295
Falcon III	V12	W	101.6 × 146	14.2	270 hp at 2,000 rpm	-	299
Condor I	V12	W	139.7 × 190.5	35.04	600 hp at 1,900 rpm	-	728
Condor III	V12	W	139.7 × 190.5	35.04	705 hp at 1,900 rpm	-	599
Eagle XVI	X16	W	114.3 × 120.7	19.82	500 hp at 2,500 rpm	-	c.400
F.10 (Kestrel)	V12	W	127 × 139.7	21.24	490 hp at 2,350 rpm	-	345
Kestrel XVI	V12	W	127 × 139.7	21.24	690 hp at 2,600 rpm	745 hp at 4420 m at 3,000 rpm	442
Buzzard	V12	W	152.4 × 167.6	36.69	825 hp at 2,000 rpm	-	699
R 1929	V12	W	152.4 × 167.6	36.69	1,900 hp at 2,900 rpm	-	694
R 1931	V12	W	152.4 × 167.6	36.69	2,530 hp at 3,200 rpm	-	739
Goshawk I	V12	S	127 × 139.7	21.24	650 hp at 2,600 rpm	600 hp at 3658 m	443
Peregrine	V12	L	127 × 139.7	21.24	765 hp at 3,000 rpm	885 hp at 4572 m ‡	517
Merlin I	V12	L	138 × 152.4	26.99	890 hp at 3,000 rpm	1,030 hp at 4953 m	628
Merlin X	V12	L	138 × 152.4	26.99	1,280 hp at 3,000 rpm	1,010 hp at 5410 m	658
Merlin XX	V12	L	138 × 152.4	26.99	1,390 hp at 3,000 rpm	1,435 hp at 3353 m	658
Merlin 32	V12	L	138 × 152.4	26.99	1,620 hp at 3,000 rpm	1,640 hp at 610 m	649
Merlin 45	V12	L	138 × 152.4	26.99	1,185 hp at 3,000 rpm	1,470 hp at 2820 m	628
Merlin 61	V12	L	138 × 152.4	26.99	1,280 hp at 3,000 rpm	1,370 hp at 7315 m	744
Merlin 66, 266	V12	L	138 × 152.4	26.99	1,315 hp at 3,000 rpm	1,580 hp at 4877 m	746
Merlin 113, 114	V12	L	138 × 152.4	26.99	1,535 hp at 3,000 rpm	1,435 hp at 8306 m	753
Merlin 130	V12	L	138 × 152.4	26.99	1,670 hp at 3,000 rpm	1,890 hp at 4191 m	755
Merlin 140	V12	L	138 × 152.4	26.99	1,725 hp at 3,000 rpm	1,890 hp at 4496 m	753
Merlin 620, 626	V12	L	138 × 152.4	26.99	1,760 hp at 3,000 rpm	1,650 hp at 5105 m	792
Griffon II	V12	L	152.4 × 167.6	36.69	1,720 hp at 2,750 rpm	1,495 hp at 4420 m	816
Griffon 57	V12	L	152.4 × 167.6	36.69	2,450 hp at 2,750 rpm	1,540 hp at 3825 m	916
Griffon 67	V12	L	152.4 × 167.6	36.69	1,540 hp at 2,750 rpm	2,145 hp at 4724 m	948
Griffon 101	V12	L	152.4 × 167.6	36.69	1,540 hp at 2,750 rpm	2,020 hp at 6250 m	959
Vulture II	X24	L	127 × 139.7	42.48	2,010 hp at 3,000 rpm	1,710 hp at 4572 m	1,111
Exe	X24 †	A	106.7 × 101.6	22.09	1,200 hp at 3,800 rpm	950 hp at 4572 m	555
Crecy	V12* †	L	129.5 × 165.1	26.1	2,000 hp at 2,600 rpm	?	749
Pennine	X24 †	A	137.2 × 137.2	45.73	2,750 hp at 3,500 rpm	2,520 hp at 4267 m	1,294
Eagle 22	I24 †	L	138 × 130.2	46.01	3,415 hp at 3,500 rpm	3,020 hp at 4648 m	1,769

* 2-stroke, † sleeve valves, ‡ 100 octane (all 100 oct from Merlin XX on), W, water; S, steam; L, liquid (Glycol or mix); A, air.

Appendix 2

SHAFT ENGINES

SHAFT ENGINES	Config-uration	Com-pressor(s)	Turbine(s)	Mass flow (kg/s)	Pressure ratio	Gear ratio	Takeoff rating (kW; sh)	Dry weight (kg)
RB.50 Trent	P1	C	1	17.4	3.6	0.11	560; 750	600
Clyde	P2	9 + 1C	1(C)+1(A+P)	19.6	6.23	0.467	3,133; 4,200*	1,150
Dart 505 (RDa.3)	P1	2C	2	9.1	5.5	0.106	1,044; 1,400	468
Dart 21 (RDa.7)	P1	2C	3	9.75	5.4		1,425; 1,910	575
Dart 536 (RDa.7)	P1	2C	3	10.66	5.75	0.093	1,700; 2,280	560
Dart 542(RDa.10)	P1	2C	3	12.25	6.2	0.0775	2,256; 3,025	628
Dart 201(RDa.12)	P1	2C	3	12.02	6.1	0.0775	2,420; 3,245*	675
Tyne 512	P2	6 + 9	1H + 3L/P	21.09	13.85	0.064	4,101; 5,500	1,032
Tyne 21	P2	6 + 9	1H + 3L/P	21.09	13.97	0.064	4,549; 6,100	1,000
Nimbus 105	S2	2 + 1C	2 + 1S	4.76	6.5	-	529.5; 710 to 30C/2134m	177
Gnome H.1200	S2	10	2 + 1S	5.67	8.12	-	1,007; 1,350	142
Gnome H.1400–1	S2	10	2 + 1S	6.26	8.5	-	1,238; 1,660	148
Gem 2	S3	4 + 1C	1 + 1 + 2S	3.2	11.8	0.22	671; 900	150
Gem 42	S3	4 + 1C	1 + 1 + 2S	3.41	12.0	0.22	835; 1,120	156
Gem 60	S3	4 + 1C	1 + 1 + 2S	4.13	14.1	0.22	897; 1,203	155
RTM 322	S2	3 + 1C	2 + 2S	5.7	14.5	-	1,721; 2308	240

* With water/methanol injection, A axial, C centrifugal, H high-pressure, L low-pressure,
  P propeller, S shaft.

Appendix 3

JET ENGINES

JET ENGINES	Configuration	Compressor(s)	Turbine(s)	Mass flow (kg/s)	Pressure ratio	Bypass ratio	Takeoff rating (kN; lb)	Dry weight (kg)
WR.1	J	1C	1	20.9	2.68	-	8.9; 2,000 (design)	499
Welland 1	J	1C	1	14.7	3.78	-	7.56; 1,700	386
Derwent 1	J	1C	1	17.5	3.9	-	8.9; 2,000	443
Derwent 8	J	1C	1	29.7	4.19	-	16.0; 3,600	580
Nene RN.2	J	1C	1	39.3	4.45	-	22.68; 5,100	735
Nene 103 (RN.6)	J	1C	1	41	4.54	-	24.0; 5,400	731
Tay	J	1C	1	52	4.0	-	27.93; 6,280	895
Avon RA.2	J	12	1	43.5	6.3	-	26.69; 6,000	1,135
Avon 101 (RA.3)	J	12	2	54.5	6.5	-	28.9; 6,500	1,016
Avon 114 (RA.7R)	JA	12	2	54	6.5	-	42.0; 9,450‡	1,343
Avon 115 (RA.21)	J	12	2	56	6.5	-	35.8; 8,050	1,143
Avon 203 (RA.28)	J	15	2	68.95	7.45	-	44.26; 9,950	1,301
Avon 210 (RA.24R)	JA	15	2	68.6	7.5	-	64.18; 14,430‡	1,402
Avon 302C (RB.146)	JA	16	2	77.1	8.43	-	69.75; 15,680‡	1,360
Avon 533R (RA.29/6)	J	17	3	83.92	10.33	-	56.05; 12,600	1,578
Conway 201 (RCo.17)	FL	(4+3) + 9	1 + 2	130.5	14	0.6	91.63; 20,600	2,099
Conway 301 (RCo.43)	FL	(4+4) + 9	1 + 2	170.1	15	0.42	100; 22,500	2,335
Soar	J	7	1	13.47	4.9	-	8.05; 1,810	121
RB.108	JV	8	1	17.3	5.28	-	10.4; 2,340	122
RB.141 Medway	FL	5 + 11	2 + 2	116.1	18.5	0.75	61.34; 13,790	1,499
RB.145	J	9	2	19.1	6.02	-	12.2; 2,750	207
RB.153	FLA	4 + 12	2 + 2	55	18	0.7	51.8; 11,645‡	777
RB.162–31	JV	6	1	38	4.25	-	19.57; 4,400	140
RB.162–86	J	6	1	39.01	4.4	-	23.35; 5,250	236
Spey 101	FL	4 + 12	2 + 2	91.63	16.5	0.96	49.06; 11,030	1,121
Spey 512–14DW	FL	5 + 12	2 + 2	94.35	21	0.71	55.8; 12,550*	1,168
Spey 202/203	FLA	5 + 12	2 + 2	92.53	20	0.62	91.25; 20,515‡	1,857
Spey 555–15P	FL	4 + 12	2 + 2	90.27	15.4	1.0	44.0; 9,900 to 29.7C	1,024
XJ99	JV	2 + 4	1 + 1	46.2	8.3	-	40; 9,000 class	205
RB.193	FR	(3+2) + 6	1 + 3	92	16.2	1.12	45.2; 10,163	790
Adour 102	FLA	2 + 5	1 + 1	43.09	11	0.8	32.49; 7,305‡	704
Adour 811	FLA	2 + 5	1 + 1	43.09	11.3	0.75	37.4; 8,400‡	738
Adour 871	FL	2 + 5	1 + 1	44.0	11.3	0.8	26.0; 5,845	603
RB.203 Trent	FH	1 + 4 + 5	1 + 1 + 2	136	16	3.1	44.35; 9,980	806
RB.211–22B	FH	1 + 7 + 6	1 + 1 + 3	626	25	5	187; 42,000 to 28.9C	4,171
RB.211–524B	FH	1 + 7 + 6	1 + 1 + 3	671.3	29	4.4	222; 50,000 to 28.9C	4,452
RB.211–524G	FH	1 + 7 + 6	1 + 1 + 3	728.0	33	4.3	258; 58,000 to 28.9C	4,479
RB.211–524L	FH	1 + 8 + 6	1 + 1 + 4	869.1	34	5.1	up to 333.5; 75.000	4,470
M45H	FH	(1+5) + 7	1 + 3	106.59	16	3	33.81; 7,600	708
Olympus 593/610	JA	7 + 7	1 + 1	186	15.5	-	169.03; 38,000‡	3,386†
Viper 100 (ASV.3)	J	7	1	14.06	3.8	-	7.29; 1,640	186
Viper 535	J	8	1	23.9	5.5	-	14.95; 3,360	340
Viper 633	JA	8	2	26.5	5.8	-	22.3; 5,000‡	421
Pegasus 103	FR	3 + 8	2 + 2	196	14	1.38	95.64; 21,500*	1,412

JET ENGINES	Config-uration	Com-pressor(s)	Turbine(s)	Mass flow (kg/s)	Pressure ratio	Bypass ratio	Takeoff rating (kN; lb)	Dry weight (kg)
Pegasus 105	FR	3 + 8	2 + 2	196	14	1.4	96.75; 21,750	1,470
Pegasus 11–61	FR	3 + 8	2 + 2	208	15.9	1.2	105.9; 23,800	1,570
535C	FH	1 + 6 + 6	1 + 1 + 3	518	21.2	4.4	166.4; 37,400	3,309
535E4	FH	1 + 6 + 6	1 + 1 + 3	522	28.5	4.1	178.4; 40,100	3,295
Tay 610-8	FH	(1+3) +12	2 + 3	176	14.6	3.18	55.24; 12,420 to 37C	1,406
Tay 650-14/15	FH	(1+3) +12	2 + 3	193	16.4	3.10	67.17; 15,100 to 30C	1,515
RB.199 Mk 103	FLA	3 + 3 + 6	1 + 1 + 2	70	23+	1	71.2; 16,000 ‡	900
RB.199 Mk 105	FLA	3 + 3 + 6	1 + 1 + 2	75.3	23+	0.97	74.7; 16,800 ‡	980
EJ200	FLA	3 + 5	1 + 1	na	25+	0.4	90; 20,000 class ‡	c.1,000

A afterburner or augmented, F turbofan, H high bypass ratio, J turbojet, L low bypass ratio, R rotating (vectored) nozzles, V vertical (lift), * with water injection, † with complete exhaust system and reverser, ‡ augmented

INDEX